Shakespearean Rhetoric

Arden Performance Companions

Series Editors: Michael Dobson, Abigail Rokison-Woodall and
Simon Russell Beale

Published titles
Shakespeare and Meisner by Aileen Gonsalves and Tracy Irish
'You' and 'Thou' in Shakespeare by Penelope Freedman

Further titles in preparation
Shakespeare and Laban by Jacquelyn Bessell and Laura Weston

Arden Performance Editions

Series Editors: Michael Dobson, Abigail Rokison-Woodall and
Simon Russell Beale

Published titles
A Midsummer Night's Dream edited by Abigail Rokison-Woodall
Hamlet edited by Abigail Rokison-Woodall
Macbeth edited by Katherine Brokaw
Much Ado About Nothing edited by Anna Kamaralli
Othello edited by Paul Prescott
Romeo and Juliet edited by Abigail Rokison-Woodall
Twelfth Night edited by Gretchen Minton

Further titles in preparation
As You Like It edited by Nora Williams
The Tempest edited by Miranda Fay Thomas

Shakespearean Rhetoric

A Practical Guide for Actors, Directors, Students and Teachers

Benet Brandreth

THE ARDEN SHAKESPEARE

LONDON • NEW YORK • OXFORD • NEW DELHI • SYDNEY

THE ARDEN SHAKESPEARE
Bloomsbury Publishing Plc
50 Bedford Square, London, WC1B 3DP, UK
1385 Broadway, New York, NY 10018, USA
29 Earlsfort Terrace, Dublin 2, Ireland

BLOOMSBURY, THE ARDEN SHAKESPEARE and the Arden Shakespeare logo
are trademarks of Bloomsbury Publishing Plc

First published in Great Britain 2021

For legal purposes the Acknowledgements on pp. xii–xiii constitute an extension
of this copyright page.

Series design by Charlotte Daniels
Cover image © Melinda Podor / Getty Images

A catalogue record for this book is available from the British Library.

A catalog record for this book is available from the Library of Congress.

ISBN: HB: 978-1-3500-8797-2
       PB: 978-1-3500-8796-5
       ePDF: 978-1-3500-8798-9
       eBook: 978-1-3500-8800-9

Series: Arden Performance Companions

Typeset by RefineCatch Limited, Bungay, Suffolk
Printed and bound in Great Britain

To find out more about our authors and books visit www.bloomsbury.com
and sign up for our newsletters.

To Kosha Engler
Not only the finest actor I know
but also the woman I love

CONTENTS

SERIES PREFACE

The Arden Performance Companions offer practice-focussed introductions to different aspects of staging Shakespeare's plays: whether accounts of how Shakespearean drama may respond to particular systems of rehearsal and preparation, guides to how today's actors can understand and use different facets of Shakespeare's verbal style, or explorations of how particular modern practitioners have used Shakespeare's scripts as starting points for their own embodied thinking about the social and aesthetic possibilities of popular theatre.

The premise of this series is that the interpretation of Shakespeare is not confined to the literary analysis of his scripts, but also includes their rehearsal and performance. With this in mind, the Arden list of editions of Shakespeare expanded in 2017 to include not only heavily-annotated scholarly texts of each play, designed primarily for use in colleges and universities, but a new series, the Arden Performance Editions of Shakespeare, designed primarily for use in rehearsal rooms and at drama schools. Just as academic editions of Shakespeare may be supplemented by books introducing students to different modes of academic criticism, so these Arden Performance Companions seek to supplement the Arden Performance Editions, offering a rich variety of practical guidance on how Shakespeare's plays can be brought to life in contemporary performance.

FOREWORD

Josie Rourke

There is probably a Latin word for *taking pride in one's friends*, and if I needed to find that out, Benet would be the friend I phoned.

I've asked Benet to work with several casts over the years, and – without fail – they've found him to be practical, fascinating and seriously impressive.

Impressing a rehearsal room of actors is no mean feat. Most casts are unmoved by smooth, lawyerly tones (if they went to drama school, they were made to study phonics). The whiff of expensive education is more likely to build suspicion than confidence but Benet is an exceptional person. I have seen him wow multiple rehearsal rooms with this work.

He's wowed mine. Fifteen years ago. I had a problem in rehearsals at the Royal Shakespeare Company. I was working on an obscure classical play, with a courtroom scene at its centre. The actors were great at charging the scene with pace and passion but the language wasn't muscular. Who do I know, I thought to myself, who loves winning arguments . . .?

Benet hit Stratford-upon-Avon like a planet (to borrow from *Coriolanus*). Within an hour, he had the actors trained up in basic rhetoric, and by the end of the session, we were debating each other like pros. The work was so successful, I had an inkling that might develop into a new and deep understanding of these plays.

And here it is: the realisation of what first began in that rehearsal room fifteen years ago, when I was failing to direct a scene, and phoned my argumentative friend. It is your explanation of how this thing – rhetoric – works.

As Benet writes in the Appendix to this book, Shakespeare did not go to university. In my experience, this is the case with the majority of actors, who either went for a conservatoire training or entered the profession directly after school. Although actors may have studied a range of acting methods, it's unlikely that they will have encountered the kind of book that teaches them how to break down an argument.

Arguably, that's because such a book didn't exist until now. From my own background, I didn't go to the kind of school that held debating competitions (on the plus side, I do come from an intensely fighty family). But what a huge amount of one-up-personship at the Rourke kitchen table couldn't give me, was the knowledge of how to break down the techniques of persuasion that Shakespeare's characters were deploying. Above all, this book provides a clear and new way of breaking down Shakespeare's speeches and scenes and, through that, a fresh encounter with his plays.

The point I tend to make when introducing Benet to a rehearsal room, is that rhetoric is something Shakespeare and his contemporaries really knew about. They used it to help them write lines and construct scenes. Not to acknowledge the presence of rhetoric in Shakespeare's writing is like denying Jed Mercurio's detailed use of police procedure in *Line of Duty* or suggesting that Peter Morgan could write *The Crown* without a team of Royal researchers. It is just a reality of their day-to-day writing routine.

As an actor or director living now, you don't have to become expert in rhetoric (Benet has done that for you) but as with all acting, I advise you to try the note. To test an idea – even briefly – is to award yourself the right to either own it or reject it. At the very least, it will bring you closer to the author of those plays, and who doesn't want to be closer to Shakespeare?

May 2020

ACKNOWLEDGEMENTS

I am hugely grateful to Line Scholdjen, Rob Ferguson, and my parents who read through the early drafts and gave invaluable pointers towards readability, to Eileen Atkins who gave me hours of her time and decades of insight, to Edward Bennett and Joseph Kloska, who gave me the opportunity to work with outstanding actors, Avita Jay, Jonnie Broadbent, Andrew French, Alice Blundell and Dyfrig Morris, testing my ideas and how they might work in the rehearsal room. The experience reassured me that theory translated effectively into practice. The book would have been considerably worse without their input. Any errors that remain are mine alone.

There wouldn't be a book at all if Josie Rourke hadn't invited me to come and speak to her company of actors at the RSC in 2005. Her play featured a trial scene and I was brought in for my experience as a lawyer. It transpired there wasn't much connection between twenty-first-century English court procedure and a trial set in first-century Rome. What proved much more interesting and valuable, both for the actors and for me, was to ask why the characters were advancing the argument they did and in the way that they did. From this discussion came an abiding interest in rhetoric. It's already a matter of public record that Josie is one of the cleverest people out there but I add thanks here for her equally incredible generosity.

Fortunately for me, the then head of voice, Lyn Darnley, encouraged me to keep coming back to the RSC. Through the opportunity Josie, Lyn and the RSC created and sustained I have been able to learn by working in some amazing theatres with amazing actors and had the most wonderful time doing it.

I am also grateful to Lloyd Trott, who invited me to give workshops at RADA, by virtue of which I was in the right place at the right time to pester Abigail Rokison-Woodall into letting me pitch the idea of this book to her without the whole premise appearing completely incredible. I am grateful to her and to Margaret Bartley and to all the series editors for trusting me to produce a book worth reading, and then hanging on while I took twice as long as promised to deliver it.

I am particularly grateful to my parents, whose love of words and of Shakespeare's words in particular, has been an extraordinary legacy. Through them I have also had the good fortune to meet and speak to actors with an outstanding mastery of Shakespeare such as Simon Russell Beale and Eileen Atkins who have given me tremendous insights drawn from their long experience.

This book took far longer to write than it should have done. For their patience during that process I must thank both Ivan Mulcahy and Ashley Carr – respectively my literary and legal agents. (I think Ashley prefers the term 'Senior Clerk' but he's a stickler for tradition.) I promise there will be no more passion projects until such time as I have made you both some money.

Finally, the most important acknowledgement is to my children and wife. Once again they endured a distracted father and husband as he juggled numerous jobs. In thanks and praise for your love and support I can find no adequate words, which is an irony . . .

NOTES ON TEXT

Where possible I have used the Arden Performance Editions to give Act and Scene references from Shakespeare's plays. Where there is not yet an Arden Performance Edition of the play, then I have used the Arden Third Series edition.

I have drawn on a number of classical texts on the theory of rhetoric but four are chief among them:

Aristotle's *Art of Rhetoric*, a collection of notes from the teachings of Aristotle on rhetoric. Many of the theoretical aspects of rhetoric are first codified in this book.

Quintilian's *Institutes of Oratory*, circa 95 CE, a comprehensive manual for rhetors on the education of an orator.

Along with Quintilian's manual another work, the *Rhetorica Ad Herrenium*, circa 85 BCE, provided a practical guide to rhetorical technique. Long attributed to Cicero, by the sixteenth century it was understood that this was a false connection, but the book remained a popular and widely referenced guide to classical rhetorical theory and technique in Elizabethan times. It provides practical insights on the purpose of many facets of rhetoric.

Finally, Cicero's writings on aspects of rhetoric, from *Brutus* in which he provides a history of rhetoric, to his works *The Orator* and *On Invention*, which delve into specific aspects of rhetorical theory also provide insight into what rhetoric aimed to achieve.

In each case my schoolboy Latin is not adequate to the task of translation and so I have started from various out-of-copyright English translations of the works in question making such adjustments to the language as I thought appropriate to make the point clear to a modern audience. In each case references are given as (book.chapter).

I have also drawn heavily on Thomas Wilson's *Arte of Rhetorique* (1560). This was among the first Elizabethan rhetorical textbooks in English (as opposed to Latin) and, for the reasons given later in this book, almost certainly a work to which Shakespeare had reference. This I have not had to translate, however, I have freely paraphrased for readability. Undoubtedly something is lost by the paraphrase but I hope more is gained because the wisdom and insight of Wilson are retained without the reader being put off by having to cut through the thicket of Elizabethan archaisms. For completeness, the original is retained as a footnote.

ABBREVIATIONS

AC	*Antony and Cleopatra*	MM	*Measure for Measure*
AW	*All's Well That Ends Well*	MND	*A Midsummer Night's Dream*
AYL	*As You Like It*	MV	*The Merchant of Venice*
Cor	*Coriolanus*		
Cym	*Cymbeline*	Oth	*Othello*
Ham	*Hamlet*	R2	*King Richard II*
2H4	*King Henry IV, Part 2*	R3	*King Richard III*
		RJ	*Romeo and Juliet*
H5	*King Henry V*	Son	*Sonnets*
JC	*Julius Caesar*	TA	*Titus Andronicus*
KJ	*King John*	TC	*Troilus and Cressida*
KL	*King Lear*	Tem	*The Tempest*
LLL	*Love's Labour's Lost*	TN	*Twelfth Night*
MA	*Much Ado about Nothing*	TS	*The Taming of the Shrew*
Mac	*Macbeth*	WT	*The Winter's Tale*

1

Why this book?

And shall I lose my life for want of language?
AW 4.1

This is a book about a particular understanding of language and how it works on the mind and emotions. That understanding will give anyone engaging with Shakespeare's plays a powerful tool for bringing them alive in performance. That tool is classical rhetoric.

What is rhetoric?

Rhetoric is the study of how language and ideas influence other people. It seeks to provide an organised way of thinking about how to persuade most effectively in any situation. As such, rhetoric encompasses within it psychology, poetry and philosophy but is unique in trying to explain how these three interact in the minds of others. That unique combination gives rhetoric tremendous power to reveal the meaning of a text, to unpick the thinking behind an argument.

Consider President Obama speaking in 2004:

That is the true genius of America, a faith, a faith in simple dreams, an insistence on small miracles.

And Constance in *King John* 3.1:

Gone to be married? Gone to swear a peace?
False blood to false blood join'd. Gone to be friends?

Why does President Obama repeat 'a faith'? What did he hope to
convey to his audience by the repetition? Is it connected to the
missing 'and' between 'simple dreams' and 'small miracles'? Is the
repetition of 'gone' by Constance to the same effect? If not, how
can we recognise the difference? What of the repetition of 'false
blood'? What do these repetitions tell us about the character of
Constance in that moment? What do they convey about her mental
and emotional state?

Rhetoric gives us the answers to all these questions and more.[1]

What is rhetoric not?

Rhetoric is not simply public speaking, oratory. Although it was the
need to speak well and effectively in the ancient law courts and
political forums that historically prompted the study of rhetoric its
scope is, and was from the start, much broader. Its insights apply
whenever we communicate, whether by speech, in writing, or even
by gesture.

Nor is rhetoric only applicable to politics or philosophy or the
law. Its first application may have been in the ancient law courts or
political forums but it applies to any subject. We can use it whenever
we seek to move others – whether to urge them to go to war, to find
our client innocent, or to spare our brother the penalty of death
(Isabella), convince our lover to kill his best friend to avenge a
young girl's honour (Beatrice), that our new wife is not mad to love
us (Sebastian), or that the king is mad (Paulina).

Finally, rhetoric is not simply about style, that is to say, how to
make our words sound beautiful or memorable. Style is an important
aspect of rhetoric but only one part of it. After all, as we shall see,
you can only decide *how* to say something after you have worked
out *what* it is that you want to say.

There are good historical reasons for all these mistaken beliefs
about the scope and focus of rhetoric. However, their existence is
a sadness because it has led to rhetoric having a diminished status
and appreciation. Rhetoric is much more than just oratory, or
beautiful expression, or the tool of politicians. It offers huge insights
for performers, particularly when it comes to understanding a play's
text. That is not just theory speaking – in fifteen years of giving
workshops on rhetoric at the RSC, the Donmar Warehouse, the

Sheffield Crucible, RADA and elsewhere I have been struck both by how unfamiliar many actors, directors and writers are with rhetoric and also with how readily the insights it offers are absorbed and put to good use. It is with the aim of making those insights more widely available that this book is written.

Why aren't we more familiar with classical rhetoric?

As this book unfolds you will realise that you are already familiar with many of the ideas of classical rhetoric. It would be surprising if you weren't. After all rhetoric is about communication, which we all do, all the time. What rhetoric seeks to do is to analyse communication so that we can think about it systematically and spot rules for communicating persuasively. Rhetoric simply identifies and gives a name to many of these already familiar ideas.

Despite their continued use the ideas and insights of rhetoric have become obscure to many in the twenty-first century. It is no longer any part of most people's education; let alone at its heart. It has come to be seen as an academic subject of study rather than appreciated as a powerful, practical tool for approaching language. Shrouded in academic jargon and confined to academic journals, the simplicity and profundity of its key insights have been hidden. Yet, once jargon is stripped away, the concepts of rhetoric are easily grasped.

The aim of this book is not to present new ideas. Its aim is simply to make a two-and-a-half-thousand-year-old subject more widely accessible, modern, and relevant to contemporary productions.

What does rhetoric have to do with Shakespeare?

William Shakespeare's writing is grounded in rhetoric. It was the sum and substance of Shakespeare's education at the grammar school in Stratford. It was the lens through which every educated Elizabethan viewed literature, poetry, history, politics, morality.

Unsurprising then that Shakespeare's plays are shot through with references to rhetoric and rhetorical education. This book will help you recognise those references.[2]

More than that, the use of language in the plays is based on rhetorical theory about how words work to convey meaning or emotion or argument. Understanding the theory of rhetoric therefore tells us how Shakespeare thought language worked. It tells us what effect Shakespeare intended to create when using particular words in a particular order.

And what does Shakespeare have to do with rhetoric?

Shakespeare's understanding of drama is closely linked to rhetoric. Three arguments illustrate the point:

First, the argument that Shakespeare represents a significant advance in dramatic form because he takes the oration and makes it integral to plot and character developments where before it stood apart as display (see Kennedy 1942). If that argument is correct, it reinforces how carefully a production must view Shakespeare's moments of oratory – looking in them for either a significant moment of dramatic change or character revelation.

Second, the argument that there is a period in Shakespeare's career where his works not only make use of rhetoric but are also heavily influenced by the theories of rhetoric and, in particular, the kind of rhetoric encountered in judicial[3] deliberation (see Skinner 2014 and McDonald 2017). During this period plays like *Hamlet*, *Othello* and *Measure for Measure* are consciously creating debates that are left unresolved, for the audience to answer as they think right. If correct, this argument emphasises the intended ambiguity of the resolution of the debates within these plays. Answers are deliberately left for the audience to find.

Third, the argument that throughout his career Shakespeare shows a particular interest in the central question of rhetoric: what is the power of language to affect change in the world? The context in which Shakespeare asks that question is the creation of art. If correct, this argument reinforces the central importance of Shakespeare's choice of language, image and argument for the characters. Shakespeare is exploring the difference that language can make and his characters do so too.

These are all reasons why understanding rhetoric help us understand Shakespeare in performance, but it cuts both ways: Shakespeare, because he is a master of it, is the perfect subject-matter from which to learn rhetoric.

Understanding rhetoric is valuable in itself because it provides a framework for analysing language, ideas and arguments that can be applied to the text of any play, including but not limited to Shakespeare's. Learning about rhetoric in the context of Shakespeare in performance, one becomes equipped with a powerful framework for thinking and for understanding language in general, for analysing questions of identity, of power, of manipulation, and for communicating persuasively. All of which has application beyond Shakespeare, beyond acting – to life in general.[4]

What does rhetoric have to do with drama?

Drama is, much simplified, about conflict, about the desires of a character and the obstacles to the achievement of that desire. Often the obstacle they wish to overcome is the conflicting desire of another character. Sometimes the obstacle is ignorance of the desires of another character. Sometimes the conflicting desires are internal. Rhetoric asks questions that go to the heart of these dramas – understanding motives, conflict, action and reaction, intention and obstacle. That is because rhetoric, again much simplified, is about persuasion. When we consider how best to persuade we are inherently concerned with the persuader's understanding of the relationship between persuader and the audience they seek to persuade.

Characters alive in the moment

Rhetoric provides an easy and structured way of framing those questions of the text that generate insights for performers. In particular, identifying the arguments, the patterns of language, results in an approach to the text that is granular. That is particularly helpful in addressing one of the challenges of approaching Shakespeare in the twenty-first century: Shakespeare's plays are to us now so familiar as to seem over-familiar. A play like *Hamlet* may now seem almost a tapestry of clichés. Rhetorical analysis can make the language appear alive and fresh again. In their introduction to the Arden Third Edition of the play, the editors Ann Thompson and Neil Taylor make this very point:

> Another problematic legacy of the formidable 'Hamlet tradition' is the sheer (over-) familiarity of the play's language: it can seem a mere tissue of quotations, causing actors difficulty in making the lines sound fresh. We have lost the rhetorical training of Shakespeare's time and the technical vocabulary of linguistic effects which went with it: we are often impatient with studies of style, rhetoric and metre, preferring to move straight to 'the meaning of the play', that is, to larger patterns relating to themes, characters, historical and religious contexts.

A consequence of that loss of intricate understanding is that too often we see performances in which the actor simply plays an attitude: Hamlet is melancholy and thus his speech is delivered with that over-arching emotion infusing it, leaving the speech itself inadequately differentiated. The greatest performances always convey the sense that the actor is discovering each word, each sentence, each thought in the moment – thinking it, hearing it, for the first time. It is in this way that the words become alive again. Understanding the rhetorical techniques underlying the words encourages and makes easier performances of this kind. Facilitating that understanding is a key objective of this book.

An intellectual exercise?

As an actor you are looking for character. Who is this person that I am to play? The clues are in the text. Rhetoric is a tool for unpicking that text. Some actors think, mistakenly, that this means treating the text as separate to living the part, being the character. It isn't. Rhetoric simply allows the actor to appreciate the full message of the text. In particular it brings out how much of the message of language arises from things other than the simple meanings of the words: It is also to be found in the way those words are ordered, where and how the stress is created and placed and in the choice to use some words rather than others. Ultimately, a rhetorical analysis of the text is simply a scaffold that allows the construction of a full understanding of character. Once the edifice is built the intellectual scaffolding is no longer needed. Yet, without it, the building is never as high or as beautiful as it might have been.

What of instinct?

Many actors consider that they act on instinct. That thought should be unpicked: Often what we call instinct is simply the benefit of experience. Rare is the eight-year-old who instinctively reads verse beautifully at first sight. Yet, through familiarity and through education, an eighteen-year-old may sight-read a sonnet well. What happens though when that 'instinct' encounters something new or unfamiliar or struggles to reconcile different interpretations both of which seem instinctively right? Does it not help to have a tool to turn to that guides one through the thicket? For the instinctual appreciation of language and its effects does not mean that it is impossible to identify rules, or to analyse how language works. Nor does it mean that one cannot take that knowledge and apply it to a text with which one is struggling to see if it helps. Nor does it mean that, having done so on a number of occasions, what was at the start done *with* thought cannot become later something done *without* formal analysis.

Rhetoric in performance focuses on the language as a way of unpicking the character but character is not only expressed through language. Once the character is understood it must also be expressed in action. Rhetorical analysis is part of the process of embodying the character but is not the whole of that process.

Will we not just play the form?

Although it is anchored in the text, rhetoric helps us to avoid simply resting on the lyricism of the language. It guides us to making the characters real and the way they speak alive whether they do so in prose or verse, rhyming couplets or not. Understanding the form simply helps us on the journey to find the reality; it is not the end in itself.

Peter Hall in his book, *Shakespeare's Advice to the Players*, argues that Shakespeare's form needs to be the first point of study in a text and that (emphasis in the original), 'the first question that the actor must ask about a speech is not who he is playing or what the character wants; first he must ask *what* the character says and *how* he says it.' I would qualify that statement by saying that it is through asking what the character says and how she says it that one understands, fully and deeply, who the character is and what she wants. It is the point Shakespeare's contemporary Ben Jonson (1641) makes:

Language most shows a man: Speak, that I may see thee.

Rhetoric is only a tool; in the context of a Shakespearean text, a particularly useful one because it is the same tool that Shakespeare used and understood. It need not be applied prescriptively but an awareness of it brings benefits even to the most spontaneous and unfussy of actors.

An anecdote

An anecdote illustrates all these points: Dame Eileen Atkins, who has a deep understanding of Shakespearean verse born of long experience, worked with Peter Hall in 1988 on a production of *The Winter's Tale* at the National Theatre, in which she played Paulina, a role for which she won the Olivier Award for best supporting performance. In the course of the rehearsals Peter Hall was insistent on the rigour of the requirements of the verse.[5] The technical instruction was new to Dame Eileen even though she was, by this point, a hugely experienced Shakespearean actor. Dame Eileen speaks of what that instruction added to her experience and instinct: In Paulina's great succession of speeches in the trial scene one begins on a shared line,[6] that is to say it is a continuation of the line before it:

FIRST LORD
    Say no more:
    Howe'er the business goes, you have made fault
    I' the boldness of your speech.

PAULINA   I am sorry for't:
  All faults I make, when I shall come to know them,
  I do repent.

(WT 3.3)

In many productions this speech of Paulina's carries on at a more moderate tone, as if the First Lord has managed to bring to Paulina an awareness of the aggression with which first she was speaking. The indication from Peter Hall that the demands of the verse line required Paulina to carry on the First Lord's line led Dame Eileen to a different delivery: 'I felt as if I was in Shakespeare's head and it was all because of [Peter Hall] telling me about the iambic pentameter and having to finish somebody else's line. Because, of course, when you are that furious somebody coming in and saying, "excuse me, you've gone too far", well you say, "I'M SORRY FOR'T", and its fury still.'[7] The knowledge of technique gave, as it should, an insight to the character in that moment. That is the purpose of the rhetorical analysis. Just as important to note is Peter Hall's reported response at the end of rehearsals, 'Eileen, you've absorbed my note to such a degree that now I'd like to say to you, "just forget it".'

Summary

1   Rhetoric is about how words can influence others and sits where psychology and poetry and philosophy meet.

2   Rhetoric is concerned with human relations, as is Drama.

3   Rhetoric provides a structured way of thinking about relationships between people, about the kinds of arguments that are appropriate for particular relationships, and about how words influence and generate emotional and mental states. As a result, it provides a structured approach to the analysis of text that is particularly helpful to performers.

4   The level of analysis is sufficiently granular that it assists the performer to generate a nuanced and active performance without becoming overwhelming. The kind of analysis it promotes engages with the inner life of the character. As a result, it creates active, engaging characterisation.

2

How to read this book

Teaching all that read to know

AYL 3.2

Who is this book for?

It is hoped that all those engaged in Shakespeare in performance, directors and actors, will benefit from a practical rather than academic book on rhetoric, focused on Shakespeare. Even if you are a student or a teacher of Shakespeare, and your immediate objective is not performance of one of the plays but rather literary criticism, you will find it an accessible introduction and guide to a fascinating and powerful tool of analysis.

Directors

If you are a director, rhetoric gives you an insight into the text that can shape the argument of your production. It also gives you a way of explaining your vision for the play to your cast that is rooted in the text and which, therefore, commands objective respect.

Actors

If you are an actor, rhetoric solves questions of meaning and intent, it creates a structure for performance and for creating light and shade in delivery. Its insights are not arbitrary or guided simply by an overarching objective and obstacle but follow the argument and move with it. The rhetorical lens empowers the actor to see, and thus to hear and to speak, the words afresh.

How can rhetoric help with performance?

When one approaches the text of a play, the questions that rhetoric asks, of the arguments made and of the language used to express those arguments, prove to be an ideal way of approaching characterisation. To foreshadow but one part of the discussion to come: when we ask of Hamlet, why did you use a logical appeal to Ophelia in this moment? that is both the sort of question that rhetoric wants us to ask but also the sort of question that, answered, guides the performance of the play in that moment.

Further, rhetoric's understanding of language, how words work, reveals clues in Shakespeare's writing as to his intentions. Again, to foreshadow, we begin to recognise that certain patterns of words are used to convey mental disorder, or anger, and thus recognition of the pattern of the words can prove a starting point for the actor's performance.

To illustrate both points, take a line from a passage in the opening of Othello's speech to the Senate of Venice when charged with having seduced Desdemona:

> Yet, by your gracious patience,
> I will a round unvarnished tale deliver
> Of my whole course of love, what drugs, what charms,
> What conjurations and what mighty magic –
> For such proceeding I am charg'd withal –
> I won his daughter.
>
> (*Oth* 1.3)

Rhetoric asks us to consider that verb 'won'. Out of all the words that Othello might have used to describe how he and Desdemona came to be married why 'won'? Why not simply 'married' or 'seduced', 'bewitched', 'wooed' or any of the myriad options available to him? What is it in Othello the man that makes him see matters – present matters to the Senate – in these terms? As we shall see when we come to look at this speech in greater detail later in the book the way that Othello shapes the argument and the language he chooses to express those arguments reveals volumes about him.

But we must ask the questions first and if we do, even actors from the RSC experienced in working with Shakespeare have said that they prove, 'so helpful for revealing character and relationships and gave life and electricity to the text . . .'; that rhetorical analysis helps to 'explain so clearly what is already there if you know what you are looking for, and then allows the instinct of the actor to be built on that understanding . . .'[1]

Teachers and students

If you are a teacher or a student of Shakespeare, then rhetoric provides an ideal framework for analysis, aligned with Shakespeare's own understanding, supported by centuries of critical reading, and directly connected to the text.

How should I read this book?

This book is intended to be a practical tool. It attempts to avoid jargon and present the ideas in a straightforward way illustrated by examples from Shakespeare's plays. While it is perfectly possible to read it straight through, perhaps nestled in a leather wing-back with a cup of tea by your side pausing to reflect every so often on the wisdom of the ages, that is not how the author anticipates that it will be most useful. Rather, it is designed to be taken in chunks and to offer the information at various levels of detail depending on your need. It also includes direct, practical suggestions for how to apply the theory in rehearsal and performance.

An overview

The book begins with a short summary of the main ideas of classical rhetoric in Chapter 3. This is supposed to act as a framework document, establishing a scaffold onto which the more complex and detailed information in later chapters can be built. It is easier to grasp specifics if one has an idea of the whole already in mind. The chapter also provides a useful introduction to rhetoric and functions as an aide-memoire. Directors, for example, may wish to provide their actors with this brief introduction as a way of quickly laying groundwork for rhetoric work in rehearsal without intimidating a company with the need to absorb detailed information that may not be necessary for rehearsal purposes.

The core lessons

Thereafter, the book turns to a detailed consideration of classical rhetoric and how it applies to performance. In structure it adopts the historic division of rhetoric into five canons, or areas, of study. It does so, in part, because that division would have been used in Shakespeare's time. In the case of the three most useful of the areas of study – Invention, Disposition and Style – the book provides a detailed explanation of the rhetorical theory followed by a chapter that shows how that theory applies to performance using worked examples to illustrate the connection. There is then a chapter that offers suggestions for practical exercises to bring the theoretical understanding into the rehearsal and performance process.

Style, a potentially vast topic, is dealt with by setting out the most important concepts for performance first. Thereafter, further chapters explore particular rhetorical techniques in detail for those.

Help along the way

There is a comprehensive glossary at the end of the book for quick reference at any point. There are also suggestions for further reading that will direct those taken by rhetoric's magic deeper into the study.

Endnotes

The book contains many endnotes. Anticipating that the book will not be read through cover to cover, sometimes these provide a quick clarification, reminder of a term that is being discussed, or cross-reference to another part of the book where the topic is dealt with in more detail. In others the endnote simply serves to provide further information that may be of interest. In no case is the information in the endnote necessary to the understanding or appreciation of the text.

What is the quick way in?

Start with the overview of the theory given in Chapter 3. Thereafter, I suggest you read Chapters 11 and 12, which show how the concepts in Invention and Disposition apply to performance with worked examples from *The Winter's Tale*, *All's Well That Ends Well* and *Henry V*. Those three chapters will introduce you to the basics and give you a good feel for how they work in performance. Equipped with the information in these chapters, and the enthusiasm they will generate for the study of rhetoric, the rest of your reading will suggest itself according to your interests and needs.

3

What is rhetoric?

Sweet smoke of rhetoric!
LLL 3.1

A definition

As you become more familiar with rhetoric you will notice common themes among those that talk about it, themes perhaps unsurprising among those who are studying how to argue: a love of giving definitions for things, a desire to divide things into categories and a tendency to explain why the definitions and categories given by others must be wrong. The subtleties of these debates are not important for the purpose of this book.

As an example of those themes and the irrelevance of the disputes behind them to this book consider the question, what is rhetoric? There is a traditional definition given by the Greek philosopher Aristotle (*Art of Rhetoric*: Bk 1.2): rhetoric is the faculty of discerning in any given case the available means of persuasion. It is my preferred definition because it highlights both the idea that rhetoric is concerned not just with knowing *what* sorts of things persuade but also with understanding *why* those things are persuasive and the idea that rhetoric is concerned with particular situations, 'the given case', and its answers will vary, case by case. Aristotle's definition was a response to the Greek philosopher Plato who had given a different definition, dismissing rhetoric as mere flattery, calling it, 'that golden art of enchanting the soul'.[1] Still others have defined rhetoric not as the study of how to persuade but as simply the art of persuasion itself. There are important distinctions wrapped up in these three definitions and the debates that underlie them. But what is important for our purpose is not these debates but an appreciation that, whatever its precise scope, these definitions have in common that rhetoric involves the study of language and people, and how those two interact. It is concerned with how words work upon the mind.

The specifics

A general definition does not take us far. We need to break down the study of rhetoric into its constituent parts in order to get at the details that bring its benefits for performance. Traditionally rhetoric divides itself into five 'canons' or areas of instruction, each of which focuses on a different aspect of rhetoric. The five areas of study are called Invention, Disposition, Memory, Style and Delivery. The basic idea of these five canons is shortly stated by Quintilian (*Institutes of Oratory*: 8.1), the first-century CE rhetoric tutor to the Emperor Domitian's children:

> All speech consists of ideas and words. As to the ideas we study Invention, as to the words, Style, and as to the arrangement of both, Disposition. All of which the Memory must guard and Delivery recommend.

In the following chapters we will look in much greater detail at three of these canons, Invention, Disposition and Style, because these three give the most value for performance. Before looking at the detail it is useful to have an overview of all five so that we can understand how they relate to each other.

Invention

Words without thoughts never to heaven go.

(*Ham* 3.3)

Invention is the identification and generation of arguments, ideas and images that will serve to persuade a target audience. It is the part where we work out what we want to say and, for that reason, the starting point. Invention seeks to guide us by thinking about what kinds of arguments work and in what situations. It then provides ways to generate good arguments – to help overcome the tyranny of the blank page and find responses to challenging arguments. Invention was considered the most difficult but also the most important part of rhetorical study by classical authors.

As I noted at the outset, the rhetorical manuals are fond of division and classification. There is a reason for that. Their purpose is to help us to think in a manageable way about what would be otherwise potentially infinite – the scope of human thought. Many of the divisions that follow come from Aristotle's great work, *Art of Rhetoric*. There he begins by asking us to think about the kinds of occasions when we speak so that we can think about what our purpose is in speaking on those occasions and thus what kinds of arguments will work and which will fall flat. Aristotle identifies three kinds of speech: *Demonstrative* – where we speak in praise or condemnation of some person, thing or deed. *Deliberative* – where we speak to advise on a particular cause of action. *Judicial* – where we speak to some charge – either to prosecute it or to defend against it. It is this last category, the debate over the rightness or wrongness of action, that seems to have fascinated Shakespeare most.

The next division we need to know about is concerned with proofs, by which we mean simply 'things we might refer to in support of our position'. Aristotle divides proofs into two kinds: natural and invented. By natural he means, essentially, evidence including witness testimony. By invented, he means the proofs that are derived from the imagination of the speaker; these are things like logical arguments, appropriate images, examples and so forth.

Both kinds of proof fall within a further, famous division, Aristotle's Modes of Persuasion. This divides the types of persuasive arguments into three groups:

- *Ethos* – the argument from authority, why the speaker should be heard.
- *Logos* – the argument from reason, why the speaker is right.
- *Pathos* – the argument from emotion, why it matters that the speaker is right.

We will look at the Modes of Persuasion in considerable detail later. It is an incredibly powerful tool for thinking about argument. As Aristotle (2.1) explains:

> Since rhetoric exists to influence decisions the speaker must not only try to make the argument of his speech worthy of belief [*logos*] but he must also make his own character look right [*ethos*] and put those who are to decide into the right frame of mind [*pathos*].

The questions that the Modes of Persuasion bring out, namely what motivates people to act, fascinate Shakespeare and run through his plays, from Paulina striving to win round Leontes and his court, to Hamlet struggling to decide what to do after meeting the ghost, to Coriolanus acceding to his mother's plea when all other argument fails, and onwards. Why we do what we do is, after all, the answer to the question of who we are, what our character consists in; that is Shakespeare's obsession and his exploration of it, his genius.

Disposition

But, orderly to end where I begun,

(*Ham* 3.2)

Disposition is the arrangement of the ideas in the most effective format to be understood and to persuade. Generally, it was agreed that one should divide the argument into five parts. First, the opening,[2] in which the speaker seeks to gain the attention of the judge, sets out their authority to speak on the issue and summarises their argument and its focus. Second, the narration,[3] where the speaker lays out the facts of the case. Third, the proof,[4] where the points that the speaker relies on are set out, beginning with the strongest argument and ending with the second strongest. Fourth, the rebuttal,[5] where the speaker sets out why any counterarguments are wrong. Fifth, the conclusion,[6] where the speaker sums up, pithily and with emotional force.

Essentially, Disposition follows the order *ethos, logos, pathos* – First, tell them why they should listen to you, *ethos*. Once they are listening – tell them why you are right and everyone else wrong, *logos*. Finish by telling them why it matters that you are right, *pathos*. Generally speaking, therefore, the opening of a character's argument is where we should look for their perception of their authority to speak. The closing of the character's argument is where we look to find why they think the argument matters.

Style

Madam, I swear I use no art at all.

(*Ham* 2.2)

Style[7] is the most important of the five canons after Invention. It is the study of how to dress your ideas in the most suitable words. What makes them suitable? Above all else one should speak clearly and intelligibly. With that guiding principle in mind, it then becomes a question of how words might be used to convey ideas forcefully and memorably and how certain combinations of words help to convey meaning and emotion, not just by the meaning of the words used, but also by the way that these words are combined and arranged. To a certain extent Style is about the beauty of language, but it is beauty with a purpose. Rhetorical Style is not simply the gilding of the lily but the enhancement of the ideas. As Quintilian (9.4) puts it, speaking of a particular rhetorical technique, 'it is a fault when it burdens the words with useless addition but a beauty when it adds strength to plain thought.' Note that distinction – in rhetoric Style is not supposed to be 'useless', there for its own sake. Style has a purpose, a use to which it is being put: to give the illusion of logic, to generate an emotion in the listener or convey that the speaker is in that emotional state, to make clear the structure of the speech. That Style has purpose is a lesson Shakespeare has learned well. We explore what that means in the chapters on Style.

Rhetoric's deep, near obsessional, love of division and classification is never more clearly demonstrated than in respect of rhetorical techniques. This can be a distraction. One does not need to know the Latin name for a technique to recognise it or to understand how it works. As Quintilian (9.4) says, 'the great judge of composition is the ear . . . Thus, while the learned understand the art of composition, the unlearned enjoy pleasure from it.'[8] Indeed, the techniques would be valueless if they only worked once known and understood. Many, if not all of them, should be familiar already, even if they cannot be named. As Quintilian (8.1) explains, 'the various topics I speak about should not be understood as having been invented by teachers of rhetoric so much as to have been noticed by them.' The purpose of the study of Style is to make us aware of the existence of these patterns of words so that we can recognise them and deploy them consciously. More than that, once aware of their intended purpose, noting their use suggests a particular intention on the part of the author for that passage of text. This is the power of Style to aid those engaged in performance.

Memory

And these few precepts in thy memory
See thou character.

(Ham 1.3)

Memory[9] covers two matters: First, the simple act of memorising a speech that one has to deliver. For this purpose there is discussion in the classical rhetoric manuals of various memory techniques including the famous 'memory palaces' that saw different parts of a speech 'stored' in a visualisation of a place that was well-known to the speaker. Quintilian is dismissive of these techniques and considers that practice is, in truth, what makes for a good memory. But there is a second aspect of Memory that is more interesting: it is the encouragement to memorise stories, facts, fables, images and wise sayings so that one has a stock to draw on in argument. A large part of rhetorical education revolved around building such stores, drawn from the great writers of the classical period.

Delivery

Speak the speech, I pray you, as I pronounced it to
you, trippingly on the tongue:

(Ham 3.2)

The last canon of rhetoric is Delivery.[10] This is the art of the actor in matching the manner of the speaking to the matter that is to be spoken about. The advice given in the manuals will be familiar even after two thousand years. Quintilian (1.11) advises:

> The teacher will be careful to ensure that concluding syllables are not lost ... and that whenever [the orator] raises his voice the effort is that of the lungs and not of the head and that his gesture may be suited to his voice and his looks to his gesture.[11]

What voice coach has not, two thousand years after Quintilian, had cause to give the same advice? How many voice coaches realise their profession is 2,500 years old?

Summary

1   Rhetoric is concerned with how language works on the minds of others.

2   It can be divided into five areas of study: Invention, Disposition, Style, Memory and Delivery.

- *Invention* – what arguments matter and how to come up with ones that will work to persuade.
- *Disposition* – how to arrange our arguments most effectively.
- *Style* – how to express our arguments most effectively. In particular, how particular patterns of words can create or convey emotional or mental states.
- *Memory* – how to remember what we want to say and how to build up a stock of knowledge to use in our arguments.
- *Delivery* – how to get our argument across in speech and movement.

3   The five canons work together to create a cohesive whole, we come up with the argument, order it, craft the words for it, memorise it, and then deliver it.

4

Memory and Delivery

I deal first and briefly with Memory and Delivery. The chief interest in these two topics is not their direct applicability to performance but the awareness they create of issues for productions of plays now 400 years old.

Memory

Fast holding both of matter and words couched together.

THOMAS WILSON, *Arte of Rhetorique*[1]

Under Memory we give consideration to two things. The first is the art and technique of memorisation. A carefully prepared speech must be memorised so it can be delivered in all its parts. On top of which the orator must recall what her opponent has said, so that she can respond to the arguments. Finally, as Quintilian explains, a sharp memory allows the speaker to multi-task: at once to speak and also to think about what to say next. Doing so calls for a good memory because the speaker must remember what she wished to say in that moment even as her mind is ranging over what she will want to say in the next moment.

The classical texts devote a little time to teaching techniques for swiftly and accurately learning a long speech. Quintilian (11.2) sets out the famous technique, which he attributes to Simonides, of using places as stores for information: memory palaces. Simonides was a famous poet in Ancient Greece. He lived a life full of story, one of these is that he went to dinner and, having just left, the roof fell in, crushing all within. So badly were the bodies broken that those wishing to bury them could not tell who was who. Simonides was able to identify each body by where they had sat at dinner. Certainly, a memorable image for the origin of this technique. However, Quintilian is largely unimpressed by this method of memorising, which he thinks is useful enough when you want to remember a specific set of things. He considers it too limited for a speech with multiple parts and multiple images within it.

Ultimately, there is no replacement for practice and repetition. Quintilian suggests breaking a long speech into parts, so as not to be overwhelmed by it, but not making the chunks too small so that they prove a distraction to recall. He thinks it helps to learn from a written text, because the image of that text may come back to the mind. One should speak out loud when memorising, both to fill the silence that might distract and to support memory by both reading and hearing. Finally, once a passage has been reviewed a couple of times, one should immediately try to recall that passage.

It is interesting to note that the modern understanding of memory[2] supports Quintilian in his methods: first in that the brain is associative when forming memories, so connecting sounds and sights ('dual coding') to the material that is to be learned is the best way to build those associations. Second in that attempts to recall the material are more effective for making it go in than simply reading and re-reading that which you would remember.

This first aspect of Memory is interesting and, perhaps, gives some comfort to actors anticipating learning their parts both in its specific advice and in the realisation that theirs is a struggle as old as civilisation. It is the second aspect of Memory, however, that is more challenging and yet more fundamental to rhetorical practice. For developing one's memory is also about building up a stock of knowledge of facts, sayings, examples, images, allegories, that one can draw on to persuade. Thomas Wilson (1560: 132, 220), explaining the rhetorical technique of amplification (which much simplified is where we take a base idea and enrich it for effect and which Wilson considers the most important of all the rhetorical techniques), says:

> We must always be well stored with such good proverbs, sayings and adages as are often used in life, which being improved through artistry, help much to persuade.[3]

In a similar vein, Cicero explains that richness of language depends, in part, on the possession of a wide vocabulary to draw upon in amplifying and adorning one's words.

Absence

The Elizabethan schoolboy was expected to start building up their own store of knowledge of this kind. They would record fine passages in their commonplace books, which were notes of useful sayings, examples, images, culled from the great classical authors. From the perspective of performance this creates an interesting difficulty. If Shakespeare anticipated that there would be this common stock of knowledge and drew on it in his plays, what is to be done when that common stock of knowledge is absent?

Quentin Skinner (2014) points out that an audience familiar with rhetorical principles will hear silences when those principles are followed only up to a certain point. He gives an example from Hamlet's scene with the ghost, where we would anticipate the ghost should finish by praising the person he seeks to persuade, that is Hamlet. That praise never comes. It is noticeable, to those anticipating it, by its absence.

There are examples of this kind throughout the plays. The final trial scene in *Measure for Measure* sees Isabella following rhetorical precepts: first she gets the attention of the judge and then she begins her speech but is cut off before she has the opportunity to present her arguments in proof. This denial of the chance to argue her case by the Duke, in his role as judge, is significant to the question of whether the Duke truly cares for justice. Yet that significance is only apparent if you are aware of the absence. A production may choose to bring this to the audience's attention, perhaps by having Isabella attempt to thrust papers at him that he ignores. Or they might acknowledge it by having the idea in mind when considering the characterisation of the Duke even though the particular point is not itself made apparent by something outwardly visible to the audience. Lastly, they might decide to ignore it altogether. All choices are acceptable. The only sin is to be unaware of the need for a choice at all.

Delivery

Framing of the voice, countenance, and gesture after a comely manner.

THOMAS WILSON, *Arte of Rhetorique*

There appears to have been a convention among rhetors (those who teach rhetoric) of acknowledging that, in practice, skilful Delivery was the most important attribute of the great orator. The great Athenian orator, Demosthenes, is often cited on this point. Demosthenes is said to have been asked to identify the most important aspect of oratory, and in answer to have given gold, silver and bronze medals to 'delivery' (Quintilian 11.3.6).

Yet, though the crown is usually given to Delivery, surprisingly, it is rarely discussed in any depth in the manuals. Part of this disdain appears to derive from the fact that actors were acknowledged to be consummate masters, and teachers, of Delivery. Quintilian, for example, tells us that Demosthenes held Delivery in such high regard that he studied it under Andronicus the actor. Actors in classical times, as in Elizabethan, occupied a strange status – admired for their skill and for the way they could make you feel, they were nonetheless, not respectable figures.

Quintilian says that Cicero also maintained that Delivery had 'supreme power' in oratory. Maybe so, but Cicero demonstrates the tension between acknowledging the power and importance of Delivery and the senatorial Roman's disdain for the actor. In *The Orator*, Cicero states that great orators require

the voice of the tragedian, as well as the gestures of the consummate actor.

Yet later Cicero (5.18) can be heard to say:

I need hardly add, I presume, any remarks on mere delivery. This must be combined with appropriate movement of the body, gestures, looks and modulation and variety of tone.

One cannot help but hear those words echoed by Hamlet (3.2) when he calls upon the actors to be neither too loud so as 'to split the ears of the groundlings' nor too tame in their speech and to 'suit the action to the word, the word to the action'. Hamlet's patronising of the players reflects Cicero's own attitude, for he goes on in *The Orator* (5.18) to say of Delivery:

> How important this is in itself may be seen from the insignificant art of the actor and the procedure of the stage; for though all actors pay great attention to the due management of their features, voice and gestures it is a matter of common notoriety how few there are, or have been, whom we can watch without discomfort.

Cicero's point, stripped of insulting language, is that performance is nothing on its own. The key words in the quote are when he damns Delivery 'in itself'. What is said derives its merit from the subject matter that it delivers. Actors can offer only part of the merit of the orator because they have only part of what the orator is. The full quote thus places the art of the tragedian and the comic actor in the context of a wider skill set needed by the orator:

> [The Orator requires] . . . the subtlety of the logician, the thoughts of the philosopher, the language almost of the poet, the memory of the lawyer, the voice of the tragedian, [and] the gestures of the consummate actor.

Practical wisdom

The actual advice contained in the rhetorical manuals is surprising by its familiarity. Quintilian's advice includes an admonishment to the speaker not to bite off the ends of her words and, when seeking to be heard, to let the voice come from the diaphragm and not from the head. I say surprising but it shouldn't be; it may be thousands of years later but it is still about a human trying to be heard and understood by other humans.

Most intriguing is the advice Quintilian (6.27) offers on the evocation of emotions. The purpose of good Delivery is not simply to ensure that the speaker can be seen, heard and understood. The good orator also wants the audience to be moved by her argument. To achieve that the speaker needs to convey that the emotion she wants to see in others is found in her too. By so doing, the speaker makes vivid the matter she is discussing and thus helps to convey it to her audience.

> Above all else, to move the emotions of others, we most show ourselves to be moved . . . In delivering our speech, therefore, let us appear to have the same emotions as one truly affected and let our words come from the same emotional place that we wish to bring the judges.

How then is one to do this? For, as Quintilian acknowledges, the orator may be far from that emotional state themselves. His answer is to suggest that the speaker picture the scene they describe themselves:

> So our feelings are moved as much as if we had actually been there at the moment that we now talk about. . . . We must imagine ourselves to be the people for whom we now plead as having suffered terrible and piteous treatment. We must not plead as if we spoke for another but rather, for that moment, endeavour to feel as if we ourselves had endured them: I have often seen actors, when they laid aside their mask after a sorrowful scene, leave the theatre weeping. If saying the words of others can give such force of feeling, what effect ought we to produce when we seek to express and move on behalf of our clients?

Thus we find that 2,000 years ago Quintilian was teaching the Stanislavski method.[4]

5

Invention

The finding out of apt matter.
THOMAS WILSON, *ARTE OF RHETORIQUE*

Invention is the identification and generation of good arguments. It was considered the most important part of the study of rhetoric by the classical authors. Quentin Skinner (2014) suggests that Shakespeare, like the classical authors, treated Invention as the most important aspect of rhetoric, never in the plays speaking of Style but only of Invention:

> O for a Muse of fire, that would ascend
> The brightest heaven of invention

(H5 1.1)

The discussion of Invention in the classical manuals is distinguished by the numerous divisions and categorisations, beloved of teachers of rhetoric from Aristotle onwards, that are presented to the student. These divisions are introduced in order to allow the authors to set out a series of general rules for generating arguments. Many of them were first set down in Aristotle's *Art of Rhetoric*.

Occasions for speaking

The first division is of the occasions for speaking, of which there are said to be three: First, the *demonstrative* (sometimes called the epideictic), second, the *deliberative* and, third, the *judicial* (sometimes called the forensic). This three-fold division is presented because it allows us to think, in general terms, about what is in issue on each of these occasions. It, therefore, guides us towards various ideas, 'topics of invention' appropriate to the occasion of speaking. These are discussed further below.

A demonstrative speech is one in praise or condemnation of some person, thing or deed. An obvious occasion for such a speech is the eulogy at a funeral.

A deliberative speech is one that seeks to advise on any issue. We are to think of a politician urging a course of action in the forum. The *Rhetorica ad Herrenium* gives the example, 'Does it seem better to destroy Carthage, or to leave her standing?'

Finally, a judicial speech is one that, in Thomas Wilson's (1560: 96) words, is 'an earnest debating in open assembly of some weighty matter before a judge, where the complainant commences the action and the defendant answers at his peril to all such things as are laid to his charge.'

Honest, vile, doubtful, trifling

The next division is concerned with another aspect of the kinds of occasion on which one may speak. It is concerned not with the nature of the problem (what should we do versus defence from a charge), but with the significance and moral value of what we discuss. Thomas Wilson (1560: 9) suggests that there are only four different 'matters' or 'causes' of this kind: honest, vile, doubtful and trifling. Again, the significance of identifying which kind of matter we are dealing with is that by making that identification we point towards particular types of argument as most appropriate.

- Honest matter is the kind where we support something that is generally agreed to be good or attack something that is generally agreed to be bad. Brutus considers that he speaks in support of an honest matter when he defends his assassination in *Julius Caesar* by reference to the freedom of the citizens of Rome.

- A filthy or vile matter is one where we must speak against our own conscience or against an upright truth. Isabella

finds herself in this situation in *Measure for Measure*
when she must speak in defence of her brother, when he is
charged with violating that which she herself considers most
dear – chastity.

- A doubtful cause is one that is half honest, half filthy.
  Mark Antony finds himself in this situation when he
  comes to speak of his friend Caesar, who, at that point,
  the mob of Rome considers to have been dangerously
  ambitious.

- Last is the trifling matter, one where the cause matters
  not. Wilson gives us an example – is the goose the best
  animal?

Once we know what the nature of our cause is, we can identify
appropriate tactics. For example, as discussed when looking at the
worked example from *Julius Caesar* in the section on insinuation in
Chapter 10 on 'Disposition', those who speak to an honest cause
may be well advised to engage in what is called an 'open' or 'plain'
beginning to their argument, and those who speak in a doubtful
cause to adopt 'insinuation' or the 'closed' opening. The difference
between an open and a closed beginning is examined in detail in the
section on Disposition but briefly, an open beginning comes straight
to the point and doesn't linger over the argument whereas a closed
beginning takes its time to come to the point and first suggests
agreement with the opponent.

Equally, Wilson suggests that identifying the nature of the cause
may indicate the strength of your opponent's arguments: If you
speak in support of a vile cause, you may anticipate that your
opponent's arguments will be strong and so your tactic should be to
draw attention away from them. If, however, you speak in an honest
cause your opponent may have only weak counterarguments and so
you are better off concentrating on their weaknesses than on your
own positive arguments, which may themselves be weak. Wilson
also suggests that if we are clearly in the wrong on some issue then
it is better either to ignore that point or to 'brag of it' as if it were
nothing, thus to draw some of its power by appearing unbothered
by it. In terms of tactics the chief advice is to be brief and to the
point: more than trying to win, Wilson (1560: 11) tells us, we
should try not to harm our cause and for that reason, speak no
more than is necessary.

Evidence and argument

Next we have the divisions of proof. Here there are two kinds: inartificial and artificial. Inartificial proofs are what we would think of as evidential proof, witness testimony, documentary evidence and the like (including that produced under torture which Aristotle (1:15) tells us is: 'a kind of evidence, which appears trustworthy, because a sort of compulsion is attached to it.') Artificial proofs are those that are derived from the cunning of the orator and are of various kinds: On the one hand we have the kinds of proof that might be thought of as aspects of logical reasoning. On the other hand, we have the kinds of proof that consist more of appeals to the status and experience of the speaker or the imagery and stories that the speaker can conjure.

The Modes of Persuasion

All these proofs may be divided into three kinds, these being the most important of the divisions of Invention: Aristotle's Modes of Persuasion. There are three:

- *Ethos*: the arguments *from authority*, the character of the speaker;
- *Pathos*: the arguments *from emotion*, the passions that the speaker is able to stir in the audience; and
- *Logos*: the arguments *from reason*, the logical steps, the facts, the probabilities that the speaker draws out.

This division is a hugely helpful lens for considering the nature of arguments. For that reason, and because it has particular pertinence to the use of rhetoric in performance, we delve into in greater detail in the next chapters.

The topics of Invention

After consideration of the proofs we turn to consideration of the topics. The topics may be thought of as prompts to possible arguments. Cicero calls them in his *Treatise on the Topics*, 'a system for the discovery of arguments'. They differ according to the occasion of speaking: deliberative, demonstrative and judicial.

The *Rhetorica ad Herrenium* (Bk 3), for example, suggests, that every deliberative speech boils down to identifying how to deliver one of two things – security or honour. It then suggests (3.16 to 3.23) a number of ways in which these might be found in the particular circumstances of the case:

> To discuss security is to offer some plan for avoiding a present danger. Sub-topics under security are military might and cunning, which may be thought of individually or in combination. . . . Honour may be sub-divided into questions of what is right and what is creditable. Things are right that are done in accord with virtue and duty and we may talk of the sub-topics of wisdom, justice, courage, and moderation. . . .

As this quotation indicates, the rhetorical manuals offer common starting points for the speaker to consider. Through the prompts offered by the topics of Invention, the tyranny of the blank piece of paper is overcome and we begin to prepare possible arguments.

Similarly, the *Rhetorica ad Herrenium* (3.30) presents topics for demonstrative speeches:

> When we speak of others we may praise the following: their situation, their physical qualities, their character. To the question of their situations belongs discussion of what chance or good fortune brought to them: lineage, education, wealth, power, fame, citizenship, friends – but also their opposites. We can also speak of their physical qualities: agility, strength, beauty, health – and again of their opposites. Questions of character rest upon judgement and thought: wisdom, justice, courage, moderation, and, again, their opposites.

Unsurprisingly, given that most of the authors of rhetorical manuals had been lawyers, such as Quintilian and Cicero, or judges, such as Wilson, the focus is on the topics as they arise in judicial speeches. Cicero identifies sixteen topics of Invention for judicial rhetoric: Definition, Division, Name, Conjugates, Genus, Species, Similarity, Difference, Contraries, Adjuncts, Consequents, Antecedents, Things incompatible with each other, Causes, Effects, Comparison with things greater or lesser or equal. (To that sixteen Cicero adds testimony as a topic though other authors treat that separately as natural proof.) It suffices to take just five of these sixteen to illustrate how they might prompt us to arguments – *Definition*, *Comparison*, *Genus*, *Causes and Effects*.

Definition asks the orator to consider how to define the issue to be debated. Control over how the issue is defined, where its borders lie and what forms the proper basis for discussion, gives tremendous power to the person whose definition prevails.

> Define, define, well-educated infant.
>
> (*LLL* 1.2)

Comparison suggests to the speaker consideration of what appropriate analogies there are and how they might serve to illustrate the issue being debated in a way that serves our purposes in argument.

> That same Diomed's a false-hearted rogue, a most unjust knave.
> I will no more trust him when he leers than I will a serpent
> when he hisses.
>
> (*TC* 5.1)

Genus prompts the speaker to think in terms of the *kind* or *family* of thing being discussed, to see if there are arguments that apply to the kind in general or to say that the particular subject of discussion is but an instance of something general that is already dealt with in a time accustomed manner.

> Think we King Harry strong;
> . . .
> Witness our too much memorable shame
> When Cressey battle fatally was struck.
>
> (*H5* 2.4)

Causes and Effects ask us to think of speaking of what will follow if a particular course of action is followed or why we find ourselves in a particular dilemma to begin with.

> Therefore, you men of Harfleur,
> Take pity of your town and of your people,
> Whiles yet my soldiers are in my command,
> . . .
> If not – why, in a moment look to see
> The blind and bloody soldier with foul hand
> Defile the locks of your shrill-shrieking daughters

> (*H5* 3.3)

Accepted wisdom

Lastly, we have *commonplaces*. As conceived by Aristotle these were originally topics that applied across multiple subjects and occasions of speaking – as, for example, the suggestion always to consider greater and lesser examples of the thing discussed. (For example, where one asks, if this was true for this individual what would it look like if it applied to everyone?) Commonplaces became, over the course of time, distant from this Aristotelian conception and more akin to commonly accepted wisdom and consequently lost their force as they became clichés. We see an example of that diminution in Justice Shallow's observations about the inevitability of death, which goes from the sublime to the mundane:

> Certain, 'tis certain; very sure, very sure: death,
> as the Psalmist saith, is certain to all; all shall
> die. How a good yoke of bullocks at Stamford fair?

> (*2H4* 3.2)

The teaching of Invention

As can be seen, the teaching of Invention (and Disposition) is both general and straightforward. As Quintilian (8.1.5) explains the rhetorical teacher has greater difficulty working out what to teach than actually teaching it:

> [As regards] Invention and Disposition, there are but very few general rules, and if the pupil is diligent in studying them, everything else follows.

Invention's chief concerns are to establish the circumstances of speaking and then to offer mental prompts to effective arguments that are relevant to that circumstance of speaking. Above all else Invention is concerned with the question of what matters to the person who is to be persuaded. Almost all the general advice concerns that question. Approaching it is best done – both from a rhetorical and performative perspective – within the framework of Aristotle's Modes of Persuasion. To this I now turn.

Summary

1 Invention is concerned with developing arguments and ideas.

2 To assist in that development it identifies categories of speaking and their characteristics:

- Deliberative, Demonstrative and Judicial.
- Honest, Vile, Doubtful and Trivial

3 Invention considers the shape of certain arguments and what they have in common. In particular it looks at the Modes of Persuasion: Ethos, Pathos and Logos.

4 Invention gives prompts to the creation of arguments. These prompts are called the 'Topics' of Invention. They encourage the speaker to think about certain patterns of argument and how they might apply to the particular subject matter under discussion.

6

The Modes of Persuasion

I swear I will not die today for any man's persuasion

MM 4.3

The importance of the three Modes of Persuasion, *ethos*, *pathos* and *logos*, is explained by Aristotle (2.1):

> Since rhetoric exists to influence decisions the speaker must not only try to make the argument of his speech worthy of belief [*logos*] but he must also make his own character look right [*ethos*] and put those who are to decide into the right frame of mind [*pathos*].

The basic idea is that all persuasive proof divides into three kinds: proofs that rely on some quality to do with the speaker, *ethos*, on appeals to the emotional needs or concerns of the audience, *pathos*, or on some question of logic or of fact, *logos*. Like any simplification, something is lost in the process, some nuance; not least because, in practice, most arguments that persuade rely on a combination of the three or are mixtures of the three. However, something is also gained – it makes thinking about the nature of the argument easier. Just as a map is not the terrain that it represents but makes it easier to navigate that terrain by removing unnecessary detail, so thinking of arguments as being of one of these three kinds becomes a powerful tool for breaking apart a piece of text and thinking about its message.

Horses for courses

One way in which thinking in terms of the Modes of Persuasion illuminate matters is by asking which of the three kinds one would emphasise in particular scenarios.

Consider the lawyer who must persuade a judge, which of the three Modes of Persuasion will be her focus? The answer is surely *logos*, arguments from reason and from evidence. Why? Ultimately the judge must produce written reasons for her decision and when doing so she cannot rely on admiration for the lawyer or liking for the client. That is because the judge is constrained by her situation, and by her oath to do justice according to the law, without fear or favour. Similarly, if one is confronted by an angry mob, their heightened emotional state makes leading with *logos* fruitless. Some form of appeal either to the status of the speaker or to the emotions of the mob will take the fore. Why? The mob is too hot to think clearly or logically. Emotion drives them and either an emotional appeal or something equally direct, such as the authority of the speaker, must countervail. The choice of the Mode of Persuasion is dictated by the circumstances of persuasion and, specifically, the circumstances of the tribunal that must be persuaded.

This is a crucial point – the argument that a speaker chooses to emphasise reflects her understanding of those circumstances and, in particular, her understanding of the person spoken to and what they care about. From the perspective of performance those questions are central to the dynamic of the drama. Within a text it does not matter if the character answers those questions accurately or not, whether they persuade or not. What matters is that the rhetorical lens is focusing us on, is getting us to think about, precisely the issues that are central to the dramatic tension of the piece.

Repeatedly in the rhetorical manuals there are explanations of the importance of understanding the minds of others and what motivates them. In Angel Day's *The English Secretary*,[1] a late-sixteenth-century guide to persuasive writing, the author exhorts the reader to consider the person to whom he writes:

> To apply now this praise in exhorting or counselling any one, it behoveth we first conceive what disposition, habiliments or other matter of value are in him whom we have to deal with, furthering

or convenient to such a purpose, whereunto we would exhort or persuade him and the likelihood of the same greatly to put forth or commend.[2]

This echoes the advice given by Erasmus in one of the most common Elizabethan grammar school textbooks, *De conscribendis epistolis*:

The letter writer should first consider their subject matter, then the person to whom they write: his nature, his character, his feelings, and what status they have with him, what merit, what favour.

This is why psychology is such a central part of rhetoric. Where one places the emphasis in the argument, whether on character, reason or emotion, usually reflects some aspect of the understanding of the relationship between the speaker and the spoken to. How a character argues is telling us something about how they see themselves (do they think they have authority with the person they try to persuade or not), and how they see the other person (do they think this person is assessing matters coolly and rationally, emphasis on *logos*, or do they need to be spurred to action, emphasis on *pathos*). Analyse the arguments a character uses and one learns much about a character.

7

Logos

What is *logos*? It is the process of reasoning towards the truth. It covers any attempt to discern the truth whether by considering evidence, posing tests or applying formal deductive logic. It is, in itself, dry, in the sense of dispassionate, although those attempting to apply such reasoning may be in a high emotional state or have passion as their motive for reasoning.

It is worth considering the different types of reasoning in a little detail because each has its own nature.

Logic

It comes as no surprise to discover that the bulk of Aristotle's *Art of Rhetoric* is devoted to consideration of the third of the Modes of Persuasion, *logos*, which takes up much of the first of the three parts of the work. In considering *logos* Aristotle's focus is on dialectic, logic, formal reasoning. Logic is what supplies rhetoric with its route to the truth.

Aristotle's rhetoric employs a particular form of logical syllogism. Syllogisms are a form of deductive reasoning in which necessary conclusions are derived from two or more premises, e.g. (A) All men are mortal, (B) Socrates is a man, therefore (C) Socrates is mortal. By 'necessary' we mean that the truth of the conclusion is guaranteed by the truth of the premises. Although formal logic can be applied in a speech, it is difficult to do so in an engaging and comprehensible way. Accordingly, rhetoric employs an equivalent of the syllogism called the 'enthymeme'. The enthymeme is distinguished from the syllogism in two ways that reflect rhetoric's nature as a practical art concerned with achieving the goals of persuasion in a particular context: First, they have one or more premises that are not made explicit. Second, they often use premises that are probable rather than certain and lead to particular rather than universal conclusions.

Shakespeare's understanding of logic and reasoning

Shakespeare would not have had much, if any, formal training in dialectic but would have had access to books that addressed it. Certainly, he is familiar with aspects of it. At various points in the plays Shakespeare uses the form and even the vocabulary of formal logic but it is often mockingly done, left to fools:

OLIVIA
Go to, you're a dry fool, I'll no more of
you. Besides, you grow dishonest.

FESTE
Two faults, madonna, that drink and good
counsel will amend: for give the dry fool drink,
then is the fool not dry: bid the dishonest man
mend himself – if he mend, he is no longer
dishonest, if he cannot, let the botcher mend
him. Anything that's mended is but patched:
virtue that transgresses is but patched with sin,
and sin that amends is but patched with virtue.
If that this simple syllogism will serve, so;
if it will not, what remedy? As there is no true cuckold
but calamity, so beauty's a flower. –
The lady bade take away the fool, therefore I
say again, take her away.

(*TN* 1.5)

At other times Shakespeare has the characters discover plot by a process of reasoning as in *Twelfth Night* when Sebastian, having been swept up by Olivia (who believes him to be Cesario) to be married, tries to discern if Olivia is mad by proposing a test – mad people cannot organise their own wits let alone a household – and then examining Olivia against that standard. Since he observes Olivia organises her household with smooth, discreet and stable bearing he concludes she is not mad:

> [Antonio's] counsel now might do me golden service,
> For though my soul disputes well with my sense
> That this may be some error but no madness,
> Yet doth this accident and flood of fortune
> So far exceed all instance, all discourse,
> That I am ready to distrust mine eyes
> And wrangle with my reason that persuades me
> To any other trust but that I am mad,
> Or else the lady's mad. Yet if 'twere so
> She could not sway her house, command her followers,
> Take and give back affairs and their dispatch
> With such a smooth, discreet and stable bearing
> As I perceive she does. There's something in't
> That is deceivable.

(*TN* 4.3)

When confronted by the unusual or the unexpected, Shakespeare will often have a character try to reason out his or her position, to ensure they are not mad. Viola does so in *Twelfth Night* when Malvolio presents her with the ring she is supposed to have given Olivia. Hamlet does so when confronted with the ghost. Leontes does so when uncertain if Hermione is cuckolding him. This process of reasoning is prompted by a deep uncertainty in the character. The articulation of their reasoning allows Shakespeare to make audible their concerns, their values and their hopes and desires.

Maxims and commonplaces

When considering *logos* Aristotle also considers the use of maxims. These are general statements whose truth is either self-evident or generally recognised. (*Commonplaces*, discussed in Chapter 5, can be considered an extended form of maxim. Not just simple statements that are generally true, but whole arguments.) Aristotle considers that maxims resemble a logical argument's conclusion without stating the premises.[1]

It is interesting to note, given how Shakespeare often mocks characters such as Polonius or Touchstone by having them speak in portentous maxims, that Aristotle's (2.21) advice is that maxims should be used only by those who have, by experience or age, earned the right to deploy them:

> The use of maxims is suitable for one who is advanced in years, and in regard to things in which one has experience; since the use of maxims before such an age is unseemly, as also is story-telling; and to speak about things of which one has no experience shows foolishness and lack of education. A sufficient proof of this is that rustics especially are fond of coining maxims and ready to make display of them.

When Shakespeare puts a maxim into someone's mouth we might ask, does he do so to highlight the lack of self-awareness of the character? Or does he do it to show how wise and experienced that character is?

The maxim as moral compass

A further point to note is that maxims were considered to reveal the speaker's moral preferences, to reveal his *ethos*:

> This is the effect of all maxims, because he who employs them in a general manner declares his moral preferences; if then the maxims are good, they show the speaker also to be a man of good character.

Certainly, that seems so for the Dauphin in *Henry V* who advises his father to war with England with the self-serving maxim:

> Self-love, my liege, is not so vile a sin
> As self-neglecting

> (*H5* 2.4)

And arguably so of Hamlet, whose predilection for maxims is manifest. Consider his telling answer to Rosencrantz when challenged on his claim that Denmark is a prison:

> Why, then 'tis none to you; for there is nothing either good
> or bad but thinking makes it so. To me it is a prison.
>
> (*Ham* 2.2)

The use of maxims in the plays may be suggestive of character. Consider, as an example, Orlando's reference in the final act of *As You Like It* and what it may say about Orlando the man, and the lover:

> O, how bitter a thing it is to look into
> happiness through another man's eyes!
>
> (*AYL* 5.2)

The power of example

Along with dialectic and maxims, *logos* also concerns the use of examples drawn from history and fable. They persuade by resembling induction, having the form: 'so it was on this occasion in the past and so it must be now'. The continuing devotion of rhetoric to division and categorisation leads Aristotle to identify two kinds of examples, those drawn from history, and those invented, such as the fables of Aesop. As Aristotle (2.20) explains:

> Fables are suitable for public speaking, and they have this advantage that, while it is difficult to find similar things that have really happened in the past, it is easier to invent fables. Thus, while the lessons conveyed by fables are easier to provide, those derived from facts are more useful for deliberative oratory, because as a rule the future resembles the past.

Plutarch's biography of Coriolanus includes Aesop's fable of The Belly and the Members, which tells of grumbling by the feet at the stomach getting all the nourishment and in various versions either coming to their senses when they realise they are weakening themselves or the body dying when its parts cease to work together. Shakespeare took this fable from Plutarch and dramatized it in *Coriolanus* 1.1.

Where these fables are found in Shakespeare the question that they prompt is why the character thinks the fable is applicable or persuasive. In this example from Coriolanus, why does Shakespeare adopt the example from Plutarch? What does Menenius think of the citizens of Rome that he seeks to persuade them by images of their body and its base needs?

In performance

When it comes to performance, the first question *logos* raises is the quality of the reasoning. Does it show a calm and ordered mind or one wrestling to find rational support for an irrational feeling? The significance of the evidence that has been offered in support lies in what it may tell us about the character's belief as to what matters. Often that evidence is dressed in particular imagery and the symbolism is telling – is it personal, or remote? Does it exaggerate or downplay the matter? Looking at a character's reasons allows us to look at the character's thinking.

Summary

1   *Logos* seeks to persuade by reason and has, as its basic premise, the belief that the truth compels.

2   *Logos* draws on many forms of reasoning from formal logic, to evidence, to experimental proof, to comparative example and so on.

3   For performance, the use of *logos* by a character prompts the questions: Why do they think reason, as opposed to emotion or authority, will prevail here? What kind of reasoning have they applied? What images have they selected?

8

Ethos

The most effective means of persuasion

Although *logos* receives the most pages in the *Art of Rhetoric*, it was *ethos* Aristotle considered to be the most effective means of proof. For it was by convincing the hearers that the speaker was a person of trust and goodwill that the argument found its most receptive home. There are many reasons for this but the principal one is that thinking is hard. If we as the listener – hearing the speaker say they have looked at the problem with care, weighed the arguments and believe that they have the right answer – feel we can trust them then we can off-load the hard work of thinking for ourselves onto the speaker and simply agree with them. This is why nebulous ideas such as credibility, sincerity, honest belief, are counted so highly in our appreciation of a speaker. That is so even though not a one of them is relevant to the truth or rightness of that speaker's argument. A speaker can credibly argue to an unreliable conclusion. The sincerity with which Hitler held his anti-Semitic views did not provide any validity to them.[1]

Good people

Authority was something that, for Aristotle, the speaker needed to establish within the speech itself rather than relying on any public image or reputation. The principal measure of a speaker's ethos in the classical texts was his own status as person of good character. To that end consideration is given to the question of how to set out the speaker's achievements while at the same time not appearing arrogant so as to provoke the hearer's jealousy. Yet there is more to a speaker's *ethos* than simply questions of achievement. Personality, whether the speaker is likeable or loveable for example, matters when trying to keep the attention of the listener.

Entertaining

The ability of the speaker to entertain is also pointed to as a means of gaining and keeping the audience's attention. In the *Arte of Rhetorique* Thomas Wilson (1560: 154) gives some advice on the use of comedy that explains the presence and the timing of the appearance of the Porter in *Macbeth* or the Gravediggers in *Hamlet*:

> Men are dull and need to be made attentive . . . Therefore, the learned . . . devise much variety . . . sometimes in telling a weighty matter, they bring a heavy tale and when the audience have been moved to be sad but then are wearied . . . by the heaviness of the report . . . some pleasant matter is invented to make them attentive again and to keep them from being sated.[2]

As to the comedy itself, Wilson (1560: 154) thinks it a gift rather than a learnable skill. He does, however, suggest that what causes laughter are the failings of other men:

> The fondness, filthiest, deformity and all such evil behaviour as we see in each other.[3]

The popularity of Falstaff speaks to the accuracy of Wilson's observation.

Wilson's view is that comedy should be used with care. The skill of persuasion lies in knowing when to stop speaking as much as in what it is one should say. Moreover, he considers that the measure of an oration is in the listener's response not the speaker's appreciation of his own wit. To that end Wilson suggests that great orators have often used their wit to win over the audience and show that audience their cleverness. In doing so, says Wilson, the orator should not go too far. He gives the example of teasing or taunting people who are regarded as generally liked. Stick to the middle course is Wilson's advice.

Experience

Last, but far from least, the experience of the speaker is important to establishing her *ethos*. Whether they are able to advise on an issue by virtue of their own direct knowledge of events or of the person in question, matters a great deal to the trustworthiness of the speaker.

Choice of language

Some of these qualities may be conveyed by simple description, as when the speaker tells of his service in the wars. Yet there are other ways to convey character and one of them is by the choice of language. In *Rhetorica Ad Herrenium* (3:52) the author talks about how we may assign to a person language that conforms with his character. Shakespeare does precisely this with Cassius and Brutus in *Julius Caesar*: Brutus is the conspirator, descended of those who first threw off the old kings of Rome, who rebels now to preserve the Republic and the ancient values that it stands for. Brutus uses words that are old even in Shakespeare's day, reflecting his role as the embodiment of the past. Cassius, in contrast, is the modern man. His complaint about Caesar is not born out of any desire to retain the ancient values of the Republic but out of his concern that Caesar will block the ambitions of others, himself included. Cassius' concerns are not to restore what was but to clear the way for what might be. Reflecting this Cassius' language is peppered with neologisms, words first recorded as being used in the 1590s.[4] This is a point vital to acknowledge – Shakespeare's use of language, consistent with classical rhetorical instruction, descends to this level of detail and does so in order to convey matters of character and theme. We ignore the significance of his operating at this level of detail at our peril.

In performance

The key question that *ethos* raises for performance is – what are the things the character offers up as giving them the status in that situation to speak? That tells us about what, if anything, they think the other people present should or will care about. It can be as revealing when they get it wrong – think of Coriolanus trying to persuade the citizens by reference simply to his patrician status and military prowess – as when they get it right – think of Othello speaking of his service to Venice in the wars.

Summary

1   *Ethos* persuades by qualities in the speaker.
2   Although an unreliable guide to the truth, *ethos* is often the most powerful persuader because people want to feel they can trust the arguments that are being made to them.
3   Authority may come from status – moral or personal, from experience – direct or indirect, and from charisma.
4   Authority may be shown in many different ways, by speaking of the things that give us authority or by speaking in a way that conforms to the basis for our authority.
5   What a character thinks gives her authority is a direct insight to that character's perception of herself in the world.

9

Pathos

Pathos, involving as it does the generation of feelings in the audience, requires an understanding of the emotional state of others and what causes those states. Aristotle might have preferred to think that people were best persuaded by reason, but his inclusion of an extensive discussion of the emotions reveals his acknowledgement of their paramount role in relations between individuals and thus in any attempt by one person to persuade another. That was certainly the view of other great rhetoricians. In *The Orator* Cicero (12.53) went so far as to say:

> [T]he virtue of oratory is most effectively displayed in arousing the anger, disgust or indignation of an audience, or in turning them from such excitement of feeling to mercy and pity; and here *no one but a man who has made himself thoroughly familiar with the characters of men, and the whole range of human feeling, and the motives whereby men's minds are excited or calmed, will ever be able to produce by his words the effect which he desires.* (emphasis added)

Developing that understanding and awareness of others was what T. S. Eliot would claim was the essential quality of the dramatist. Indeed, Eliot's raising of Shakespeare over Jonson he attributed not to the former's greater imagination but to his greater sensibility to a range of emotions.[1]

The first book on psychology

In the second book of the *Art of Rhetoric* Aristotle identifies emotional states and what influences or creates them – all for the purpose of allowing the orator to inflame or calm an audience. The Art of Rhetoric has, as a consequence, a good claim to be one of, if not the first, psychological textbooks. Indeed, rhetoric was considered to be the proper basis for study and understanding of emotions, 'until Descartes proposed a "scientific" treatment of them different only in details'.[2]

Aristotle (2.2) presents emotions in many cases as opposing pairs: fear and confidence, friendship and enmity, and anger and calm. In other cases they are presented alone: jealousy, shame, indignation. For example, anger:

> Let us then define anger as a longing, accompanied by pain, for a real or apparent revenge for a real or apparent slight, affecting a man himself or one of his friends, when such a slight is undeserved.

Knowing what causes anger allows the orator to arouse it in others by highlighting the things that cause it:

> It is evident then that it will be necessary for the speaker, by his eloquence, to put the hearers into the frame of mind of those who are inclined to anger, and to show that his opponents are responsible for things which rouse men to anger and are people of the kind with whom men are angry.

The discussion of *pathos* is connected to the discussion of *ethos* because the manner by which one shows one's character depends in part on how the audience is disposed. Aristotle identifies aspects that contribute to the appearance of character: age, wealth, achievement, and in discussing these factors he considers the emotional factors at play within them. For example, he describes the characteristics of different ages: the young being impulsive, hopeful, attaching little importance to money and loving laughter and wit. The old being hesitant, narrow-minded and suspicious. The emotions are similarly analysed and their characteristics considered.

How to play with the emotions

Thomas Wilson (1560: 152) has some advice on the stirring of the emotions.

> Now in moving pity and stirring men to mercy the wrong done
> must first plainly be told.[3]

Have the listeners found themselves in the same position as the person for whom we now plead mercy? Then Wilson asks the judges to remember their own state, how they have been similarly abused, what wrongs evil men have done them, 'that by hearing of their own, they may better harken to others'.

Crucially, Wilson (1560: 153) considers that to convey an emotional state to others we must experience it ourselves.

> Neither can any good be done at all unless we bring the same
> feelings into our own heart that we would have the Judges bear
> towards our own matter. . . . There is no substance that will take
> fire of itself, you must put first into it.[4]

This echoes Quintilian (6) who repeatedly advocates finding ways to make the scene come alive. He suggests retelling it by seeming to address a person, as when one speaks as if to the person who has been murdered, or by exhibiting items that bring to mind the horrid act:[5]

> The blood-stained toga of Caesar, when exhibited in the forum,
> drove the mob of Rome almost to madness. They knew he had
> been killed, and saw his body laid out, yet the sight of his robe,
> drenched in blood, gave such a vivid image of the crime that
> Caesar seemed not to have been assassinated but murdered in
> that very instant.

Quintilian is cautious though, stating that only the best orators should attempt to turn their audience to tears for there is no middle ground. If they attempt to evoke true pity for their client or cause, then either, 'he will provoke tears – or laughter.'

In performance

As Wilson and Quintilian both make clear, the way to stir the emotions is to present the listener with powerful images that make them see, feel and hear the thing we want the listener to care about.[6] The discussion of how to stir the emotions reminds us that rhetoric is concerned about the reaction of others, because, after all, it wants to persuade those others. As is often the case, it is in moments of change that we have the opportunity for the greatest insight. It is when characters in the plays switch from *logos* or *ethos* to *pathos*, from reason or authority to arguments based on emotions, that we learn the most. What is it about the reasoning or the status of the speaker that has prompted this emotional response? What is the image they have then reached for to reflect that emotional state?

Sometimes the answer lies in what is said but equally often it lies in the response of another character to what is being said. It is all too easy when considering a speech in Shakespeare to think that all the prompts for change in a speech are found in the speech itself. But Shakespeare is not so simplistic and understands that the reaction of others can be the reason for change.

As a student of rhetoric Shakespeare is necessarily a student of psychology. That Shakespeare is a particularly perceptive student of character and the emotions hardly needs to be stated. What he understands intimately is that emotional states can be the product of things both internal and external. That is significant for performance because it throws light on the way the energy in a scene comes not just from the words being spoken but the responses they are generating. Therefore, always ask when you see an emotional argument appear, was it what the character said that prompted it or the reaction of the other character to what was being said?

Summary

1   *Pathos* seeks to persuade by emotional force, by showing that what is right is also what matters.

2   The primary concern of *pathos* is to make the listener feel the argument and it draws on imagery and story to make that happen.

3   *Pathos* tries to put the listener into the position of those
    affected by the issue that the speaker is discussing.

4   Consideration of *pathos* reminds us about the importance
    of the reaction of the listener and how that reaction can go
    on to shape the argument. Shakespeare understands this.
    When one of his characters argues, they do not do so
    according to a fixed plan, they respond to the emotional
    reactions their arguments have on those listening and
    change in that response.

10

Disposition

An apt bestowing and orderly placing of things
THOMAS WILSON, *ARTE OF RHETORIQUE*

Once we have worked out what we wish to say, the next question is the order in which we deploy the arguments. For performance the rules of Disposition help us to identify the most important arguments and guide us where to look for arguments of a particular kind.

The classical advice is general in nature, with different authors being more or less prescriptive as to the parts of a speech. All are agreed on the following: there should be a beginning, middle and end. The beginning should seize the audience's attention, establish the speaker's good character and foreshadow where the speaker intends to go in her argument. In the middle the speaker sets out the facts, the arguments in favour and the rebuttals. Finally, the ending is a chance briefly to summarise the case and to leave the audience's emotions stirred.

Within these general rules, however, there is given much leeway to approach matters differently if the circumstances demand it. Ultimately, the only question is what works, and in the *Institutes of Oratory*, Quintilian explains that the orator has three tasks – to persuade, to excite and to please the audience. Quintilian (8.1.7) goes on to explain that persuasion is best achieved by good arguments. Excitement of the audience is best achieved by appeals to the feelings, 'which may be dispersed throughout the speech but should be principally used at the beginning and end'. Finally, pleasing the audience he explains, 'though it depends on both the substance and the words, is chiefly a matter of style'.

More specific advice on Disposition is given in the rhetorical manuals and we set this out below with particular emphasis on perhaps the most important part of the speech, the beginning.

Beginning

There is considerable significance to how one begins. If we don't capture the attention of the judges then all our skill at argument, all our eloquence, is for naught.

The first part of the speech is called the *exordium* or the entrance. Thomas Wilson tells us that, 'victory rests in three points'. First, we must identify the status of the case. Second, we must get the judges to listen with care. Third, we must win their goodwill.

The status of the case

What is 'the status of the case'? It is the point that is actually in dispute. Wilson (1560: 98–99) explains:

> A state then is generally the chief ground of the matter, and the key point that the speaker should devote his thoughts to and the audience chiefly note.[1]

It is the 'issue' and for most of what Aristotle would call 'judicial' or 'forensic' disputes[2] there are three possibilities: Did the thing happen? If it happened, did it meet the legal test that applies? If it happened, and meets the legal definition of the charge, was it nonetheless defensible? Thomas Wilson (1560: 100) calls these three options, 'conjectural', 'legal' and 'juridical'. Cicero's Latin summary of these three possibilities is *'an sit, quid sit, quale sit'* – 'Is it? What kind is it? What quality is it?' It is perhaps easiest to understand the distinction between these three by an example:

Imagine we are to defend Brutus for the murder of Julius Caesar. What is our defence?

- *An sit* – Conjectural – Did it happen? Do we deny the basic fact – that Caesar was killed by Brutus? (No, too many witnesses!)

- *Quid sit* – Legal – What do we call it? Do we deny that, though Brutus killed Caesar, the killing was a 'murder'? (No, it's plainly an unlawful killing.)
- *Quale sit* – Juridical – Was it just? Do we deny that, though Brutus' act meets the legal definition of murder, it was a bad thing? (Yes. It was best for the Republic that he die.)

Defining the status of the case is important for two reasons. It quickly clarifies where we place our argument, allowing the judges to focus their attention on the merits of that argument without distraction. It prevents others, including most notably our opponent, from trying to distract the judges by moving the argument onto different ground. This latter tactic is called 'equivocation' and is well-known even to this day (though we might call it less pretentiously, 'moving the goalposts'). Our opponent, realising that he is losing or that he must argue a difficult point, tries to suggest that the real point of dispute lies elsewhere or even chooses to change the point of dispute half-way through the argument to one that is easier to defend. It was certainly known in Shakespeare's day and a special place in Hell was reserved for such people:

> Knock, knock. Who's there, in th'other
> devil's name? Faith, here's an equivocator that
> could swear in both the scales against either scale,
> who committed treason enough for God's sake, yet
> could not equivocate to heaven. O, come in, equivocator.

> (*Mac* 2.3)

Thomas Wilson (1560: 115) focuses on the first purpose of defining the status of our case, namely, to quickly summarise for the judges where our argument is going.

> Expound it plainly and in brief words ... couch together the whole course of our tale in as small a room as we can ...[3]

First get their attention . . .

If we do not capture the attention of those we are to persuade, our efforts are fruitless. In essence there are three ways to do so, which

Cicero summarises with another of his three-part Latin sayings: *Docere, Delectare, Movare* – Teach, Delight, Move. We can either promise the judges that they will learn something of profit to them or that they will be entertained. Wilson (1560: 115) advises:[4]

> Promise . . . weighty matters . . . promise to talk concerning their own profit or the advancement of their country . . . or . . . we may promise them strange news and persuade them we will make them laugh . . .[5]

. . . then win their goodwill

Of course, to have the attention of the judges is good but not if that attention is focused on dislike of us or of our cause. We must not only seize their attention but also win them over. To do so, we can speak of our good qualities or of the good qualities of those for whom we speak or we can remind them of why they should be well-disposed towards us or those for whom we speak. Thomas Wilson specifically advises that we speak of ourselves and of our service, for example in war, and of our own goodwill towards the judges.

A classic example

We see all this advice taken to heart by Othello. He is accused by Desdemona's father, a senator of Venice, of having stolen away his daughter by witchcraft. He is called to answer the charge and finds himself in a formal court-room environment. It is not surprising, therefore, to find him employing the advice of classical rhetoric. Set out below is the opening part of his speech, the *exordium*.

> Most potent, grave, and reverend signiors,
> My very noble and approv'd good masters:
> That I have ta'en away this old man's daughter
> It is most true; true, I have marri'd her.
> The very head and front of my offending
> Hath this extent, no more. Rude am I in my speech
> And little blest with the soft phrase of peace,
> For since these arms of mine had seven years' pith

Till now some nine moons wasted, they have used
Their dearest action in the tented field,
And little of this great world can I speak
More than pertains to feats of broil and battle,
And therefore little shall I grace my cause
In speaking for myself. Yet, by your gracious patience,
I will a round unvarnish'd tale deliver
Of my whole course of love, what drugs, what charms,
What conjuration and what mighty magic –
For such proceeding I am charged withal –
I won his daughter.

(*Oth* 1.3)

In the first two lines Othello acknowledges and praises the judges
– 'potent, grave, and reverend . . . noble and approved good . . .'. In
the next three lines he sets out the status of the case – he has done
the thing he is accused of, taken away Desdemona, he has married
her. It is not this that he intends to dispute. What he disputes is the
quality of the act – 'the very head and front of my offending has this
extent, no more.' He will show that he did not use unlawful means
to win Desdemona.

Then he returns to the task of winning the goodwill of the judges.
In the first two lines he spoke in praise of them. Now, in the sixth to
twelfth lines he follows Wilson's advice to the letter – he speaks of
himself, and of his service to Venice in its wars. In *Rhetorica Ad
Herrenium* (3.38), the author explains the importance of
understatement where you want to point to something exceptional
but want to avoid appearing arrogant:

For things of this sort, if you handle them indiscreetly, in life
provoke jealousy and in speech antipathy. Therefore, just as by
circumspection we escape jealousy in life, so by prudence we
avoid antipathy in speaking.

The author gives an example: 'I have no right to say – that, by
labour and diligence I have contrived to be no laggard in the mastery
of military science'. He then comments, '[i]f the speaker had here
said "be the best" he might have spoken the truth, but would have
seemed arrogant. He has now said quite enough both to avoid envy
and to secure praise.' The echo of Othello's approach – reminding

the Senators of Venice of his long service while not appearing to boast – is clear.

Finally, conscious that he must keep the attention of the judges but, recalling Wilson's guidance, and seeing that there is little in this personal matter that speaks to things of wider significance or directly to the self-interest of the judges, he promises instead to entertain: 'I will a round unvarnish'd tale deliver of my whole course of love; what drugs, what charms, what conjugation and what might magic.' Othello promises the sixteenth-century equivalent of sex, drugs and rock and roll.

And for performance?

What can the fact that Shakespeare has Othello demonstrate knowledge of rhetoric tell us for performance? In Othello's speech before the senate of Venice we see him display the sophistication of an educated man. That is significant because we know that Shakespeare is quite capable of expressing characters in more robust ways – Dogberry's bumbling malapropisms or Caliban's contorted patterns of speech. That Othello speaks with such eloquence suggests that this is not such a character. He is sophisticated, bold, intelligent and aware. He speaks eloquently and with understanding of human character, of the basis of his love for Desdemona and of hers for him. How then is Iago able to fool such a one? The clues are in the text. We see Othello clearly willing, wanting, to be part of the system that is now challenging him. He doesn't reject the authority of a foreign court, but instead acknowledges that the senators are his 'approved good masters'. When he speaks to build their goodwill it is of his service to the city of Venice. This is a man who wants, desperately, to be part of the system. So much so, that when the system threatens him, he does not respond with threats of his own but meets it on its own terms. There is in Othello a desire to be part of things, to be accepted, even as he is confronted by evidence that he will never truly be accepted. For what is there behind the father's reluctance to accept Othello, Venice's honoured and successful general, but bigotry religious or racial? Is it not in that tension that we see the basis on which Iago will undermine him? Iago finds fertile ground for his lies because Othello cannot quite believe that

Desdemona truly loves him because he does not quite believe it himself.

Look for the ethos

It might be thought from the above example that it is only in formal speeches, ones that have an *exordium*, that we will we find the character's *ethos* clearly set out. That is not so. In such speeches it will be easier to know where to look for the spelling out of the character's *ethos*. That is why such a speech has been chosen to illustrate the point. However, the advice is general and applies to the moment where the speaker is trying to get the judge's attention. If that moment does not come in a formal context but in the course of a conversation then the advice still applies. Though it is, perhaps, harder to spot. We will see, in the discussion of the use of *ethos* as a tool for unpicking character in Chapter 12 how, for example, in *The Winter's Tale* Paulina sets out her *ethos*, her right to be heard, in the course of a conversation as she tries to gain access to Leontes.

Insinuation

The advice to win over the judges and summarise one's argument early on is sound advice in any circumstances and as good today as it was in Cicero's or Wilson's time. Sometimes it is easier to put into practice than others. Wilson distinguishes between two scenarios: In the first, we anticipate that what we have to say will meet with a sympathetic tribunal. In the second, however, the judges are already ill-disposed towards us or our cause. Should we adapt our plan to accommodate these different starting points? Certainly. Here lies the difference between what Wilson calls the 'plain' opening and what he calls 'insinuation'.

Where the judges begin well-disposed the trick is not to lose that goodwill. Wilson suggests that the chief aim – more than actively trying to win – should be to avoid hurting our cause.

Therefore it is wisdom to speak what is needed but also to speak no more than is needful.[6]

More difficult is the situation where one must win one's way into the goodwill of the judges. Here Wilson speaks of 'insinuation'. He advises that the speaker start by speaking only of pleasing things and wait until the audience is calmed before entering into the true matter and then doing so 'little by little'. The speaker should also begin by agreeing with the audience, 'the things the hearer dislikes, we too dislike. Nor should we speak openly against our opponent but instead 'promise to weaken that which the opponent has made most strong for himself'. Alternatively, we can take advantage of some part of the opponent's speech to show that we don't fear it and so that the judges end up thinking, 'they gave rash credit, and were over-hasty in believing the first tale'.

Insinuation in practice

Shakespeare illustrates the effect of this advice perfectly in the two speeches given by Brutus and Mark Antony in *Julius Caesar*. Brutus speaks first and when he speaks it is with the sympathy of the crowd, or at least their neutrality. Mark Antony speaks only after the mob has been whipped against Caesar by Brutus. He has no choice but to adopt insinuation as his method but he then deploys the advice perfectly.

First, Brutus' plain opening: note how he calls for the judge's attention, then attempts quickly to win their goodwill with reminders of his own 'honour' and praise for their 'wisdom'. His point is then shortly made – Caesar's ambition was a threat to Rome and, if you love Rome, then Caesar had to die. Having made it, and concluding with a series of rhetorical questions to which there is only one right answer, he finishes. Short, sharp and to the point.

BRUTUS

Romans, countrymen, and lovers! hear me for my
cause, and be silent, that you may hear: believe me
for mine honour, and have respect to mine honour, that
you may believe: censure me in your wisdom, and
awake your senses, that you may the better judge.
If there be any in this assembly, any dear friend of
Caesar's, to him I say, that Brutus' love to Caesar

was no less than his. If then that friend demand
why Brutus rose against Caesar, this is my answer:
– Not that I loved Caesar less, but that I loved
Rome more. Had you rather Caesar were living and
die all slaves, than that Caesar were dead, to live
all free men? As Caesar loved me, I weep for him;
as he was fortunate, I rejoice at it; as he was
valiant, I honour him: but, as he was ambitious, I
slew him. There is tears for his love; joy for his
fortune; honour for his valour; and death for his
ambition. Who is here so base that would be a
bondman? If any, speak; for him have I offended.
Who is here so rude that would not be a Roman? If
any, speak; for him have I offended. Who is here so
vile that will not love his country? If any, speak;
for him have I offended. I pause for a reply.

ALL

None, Brutus, none.

BRUTUS

Then none have I offended. I have done no more to
Caesar than you shall do to Brutus. The question of
his death is enrolled in the Capitol; his glory not
extenuated, wherein he was worthy, nor his offences
enforced, for which he suffered death.

Enter ANTONY *and others, with* CAESAR's *body*

Here comes his body, mourned by Mark Antony: who,
though he had no hand in his death, shall receive
the benefit of his dying, a place in the
commonwealth; as which of you shall not? With this
I depart, – that, as I slew my best lover for the
good of Rome, I have the same dagger for myself,
when it shall please my country to need my death.

(*JC* 3.2)

Now comes Mark Antony's chance to speak and he must do so
confronted by a mob that was ill-disposed to begin with and has
been whipped up in that belief by Brutus. Antony has no choice but
to adopt insinuation, to begin by appearing to agree with Brutus, to

advance his own argument only slowly and gently and, where possible, to take key points from Brutus and undermine them.

ANTONY

Friends, Romans, countrymen, lend me your ears;
I come to bury Caesar, not to praise him.
The evil that men do lives after them;
The good is oft interred with their bones;
So let it be with Caesar. The noble Brutus
Hath told you Caesar was ambitious:
If it were so, it was a grievous fault,
And grievously hath Caesar answer'd it.
Here, under leave of Brutus and the rest –
For Brutus is an honourable man;
So are they all, all honourable men –

(JC 3.2)

Note that Antony does not disagree with Brutus at this point. Instead he acknowledges that if – observe the crucial conditional – *if* Caesar was ambitious then he was at fault and deserved his fate. However, he goes on to lay his trap – the basis for believing Caesar ambitious is that Brutus says so and relies on his honour as support for his assertion. The charge against Caesar and the question of Brutus's honour are now linked. If the charge fails then, on Antony's argument, it taints Brutus too. True to the advice of Wilson, Brutus does not turn to that question immediately. Instead he explains why he saw Caesar as a friend.

ANTONY

Come I to speak in Caesar's funeral.
He was my friend, faithful and just to me:
But Brutus says he was ambitious;
And Brutus is an honourable man.
He hath brought many captives home to Rome
Whose ransoms did the general coffers fill:
Did this in Caesar seem ambitious?
When that the poor have cried, Caesar hath wept:
Ambition should be made of sterner stuff:
Yet Brutus says he was ambitious;
And Brutus is an honourable man.

You all did see that on the Lupercal
I thrice presented him a kingly crown,
Which he did thrice refuse: was this ambition?
Yet Brutus says he was ambitious;
And, sure, he is an honourable man.
I speak not to disprove what Brutus spoke,
But here I am to speak what I do know.

(*JC* 3.2)

Despite what Antony says at the end of this passage, where he professes not to disagree with Brutus, what has preceded it is a series of examples that contradict the fundamental charge against Caesar – that he was ambitious. Each time, Antony reminds the mob of the connection he has created – between the truth of the charge and Brutus' honour. The contradiction between the charge and the facts is not expressed. Antony lets the mob draw their own conclusions so that they realise they 'gave rash credit' to Brutus.

ANTONY
You all did love him once, not without cause:
What cause withholds you then, to mourn for him?
O judgment! thou art fled to brutish beasts,
And men have lost their reason. Bear with me;
My heart is in the coffin there with Caesar,
And I must pause till it come back to me.
FIRST CITIZEN
Methinks there is much reason in his sayings.
SECOND CITIZEN
If thou consider rightly of the matter,
Caesar has had great wrong.

(*JC* 3.2)

In the play, Shakespeare allows Antony to break off as if overcome with emotion. This rhetorical technique, sometimes identified in Latin as *aposiopesis*, gives the audience a moment to catch up with their own thoughts and we see the consequences of doing so. The mob begins to realise they have been fooled. Antony, noting it, is now in a position to begin to make good on the challenge he slipped in at the outset – if the basis for believing Caesar ambitious is Brutus' word as an honourable man, then if you no longer believe Caesar ambitious you can no longer believe Brutus to be honourable. What follows? The rest of Antony's speech is, again, a textbook example of stirring the emotions of the crowd and directing it towards a course of action. Yet, to be in a position to do so, first Antony had to win the mob round and he does so by following Wilson's advice to the letter. His speech is, in consequence much longer. His beginning is almost as long as Brutus' whole oration, but then Antony has the more difficult task because he cannot just state his argument, first he has to create the trap and do so in a way that allows it to be laid without the mob realising.

And for performance?

What does it tell us of Brutus' character that he speaks so plainly of his own merits and allows Antony the chance to win the mob back round, even though his fellow conspirators have counselled against it? One argument is that it speaks to a certain naivete on Brutus' part. He is so certain of his own honour that he cannot conceive of how others might view him. We can all think of such people – so convinced of their own rightness they cannot conceive of a counterargument. So it seems here: the rhetorical questions he poses admit, at least in Brutus' mind, of no other answer but that he has done the right thing. There is an arrogance too. Brutus does not take the advice of *Rhetorica ad Herrenium* and soften his claim to honour, he simply asserts it, as a given.

As always it is fruitful for assessment of character to consider how Brutus might have handled matters differently. What if he had spoken with greater doubt about his honour and the rectitude of the murder of Caesar? What if he had allowed the mob to come to their own conclusion rather than telling them that they should be grateful because he had saved them from slavery at Caesar's hand? What difference in character would be required for that to have been the speech made? Once one understands the different character that would be needed to make such an argument then we begin to understand something about Brutus the person as he is expressed by Shakespeare.

Here again we see the genius of Shakespeare, for Antony's speech does all of those things that a different Brutus might have. Brutus adopts the technique of rhetorical question but his questions are posed and the answer given too, as if Brutus does not trust the mob to think for itself, or believes he can do their thinking for them. Antony uses rhetorical question too but when he deploys it, no answer is given by Antony. It is left to the mob to draw its own conclusions from the facts. One can easily imagine which is the more persuasive – would you prefer to be told what to think or to be allowed to work through the thought yourself?

Antony's adoption of the rhetorical technique of insinuation speaks to a subtlety of thought, a political cunning, that belies his image as a hot-headed military man.[7] The patience that he shows in allowing the argument to build and his use of his own emotional breakdown to move the mob, all speak to a Machiavellian mind.

What if Antony had approached matters differently, bluntly declaring the mob to be fools and Caesar innocent of the charge of overweening ambition? We sense at once it would have been as disastrous as such speech is for Coriolanus in the eponymous play. More importantly, we sense at once that only a person different in every respect of character to the Antony of the play could or would have done so. The language shows the man: he speaks and we know him.

This too is the genius of Shakespeare, for here at the centre of the play is a pivotal moment of debate in which the methods of the two debaters resemble the central dilemmas of the play: the clash between the political realists and the idealists, between those that think good intentions are enough and those whose politics are tempered by ambition and craft their words to match. Here we see evidence to support the argument that Shakespeare innovates and advances the dramatic form by turning great orations from simply set-piece moments of verbal display that stand apart from the action into integral aspects of character that drive forward the plot.

Our familiarity with his works in the twenty-first century should not disguise for us how new and how engaging this was. It is one of the reasons his plays seem contemporary in a way that his own contemporaries are no longer. For the performer, however, the point is not to marvel at the genius of the man but to note that Shakespeare's use of rhetoric is integrated to the dramatic questions. That is why, in my argument, a knowledge of rhetoric is vital to performance.

Middle

Once one has got the attention of the listeners it is time to lay out one's argument. Various schemes are presented in the textbooks. Thomas Wilson suggests four, sometimes five, parts to a speech. Wilson names them (1) 'narration', (2) 'division', (3) 'proposition', (4) 'confirmation' and (5) 'refutation', but we might say of them – (1) set the scene, (2) outline the argument, (3) say in a sentence why you're right, (4) then spell out your arguments, leading with the strongest, and, if necessary, (5) say why the others are wrong.

End

The final part of the speech is called the 'peroration'. Thomas Wilson explains (1560: 130) the two functions of this part of the speech as summarising the argument and giving an emotional kick in the direction we want the listener to go, and in this he reflects Quintilian. In the *Rhetorica ad Herrenium*, the author suggests the speaker has one further objective for the peroration: to set the argument in the context of general wisdom. The idea is to suggest that the speaker's argument does no more than reflect generally accepted principles of reasoning. By doing so, the listener is left with the impression that to agree is to do no more than accept the obvious and common view as to what is right. Humans are social creatures and prefer, where possible, to go with the social flow.[8]

Rhetorica ad Herrenium suggests that we deploy commonplaces for this purpose. Commonplaces, discussed in Chapter 3, are 'topics of invention' – that is to say, they are patterns of common argument that we can turn to for inspiration in respect of the specific issues we are arguing. *Rhetorica ad Herrenium* (2) suggests we can, in the peroration, draw on one of ten possible commonplace arguments, depending on our role within the argument and the nature of the issue. It is worth briefly summarising them because it helps us in grasping the concept of commonplaces within rhetoric, as prompts to invention of matter for our speech.

1   *Authority* – The first commonplace is to draw on authority – to remind the audience that what we discuss is of concern

to the gods, to our ancestors or how it is a subject addressed by ancient laws.

2   *Scope* – The second commonplace is to recall who is affected by the issue – is it all men? Is it our superiors? Our peers?

3   *Universal Law?* – The third commonplace is to ask what the consequence would be if we were to prescribe from these specific circumstances a general rule that would apply not just to the defendant but to anyone.

4   *Thin end of the wedge* – The fourth commonplace is to argue that if we show mercy on this particular occasion then we will embolden others to think they too can get away with the crime.

5   *Now or never* – The fifth commonplace is to argue that this is the only moment where those listening are in a position to show judgment. If they get it wrong, by which we mean if they decide against us, there will be no chance to remedy that error later.

6   *Deliberate actions* – The sixth commonplace is to argue that the defendant acted in a premeditated way, and that planned crimes demand harsher penalties than things done on the spur of the moment.

7   *Evil* – The seventh commonplace is to talk of the 'foulness' of the crime – cruel, sacrilegious or tyrannical.

8   *Special measures* – The eighth commonplace is to show that the crime in issue is unique, not common, and that by its uniqueness requires an immediate, harsh response.

9   *Comparison* – The ninth commonplace is to compare the crime in issue with other wrongs, either to diminish it or to show how much worse it is than those other wrongs.

10 *Portray* – The tenth commonplace is to spell out in detail the actual events of the crime, so that the listener feels as if they are actually seeing it performed again before them.

As should be apparent, not every one of those ten suggestions will suit every oration. They are particularly directed towards the summation of a judicial matter and, even then, not every one will be appropriate. Rather, they should be thought of as a checklist for the orator when coming up with ideas for how to round out the speech. From the perspective of this book, their importance is in showing how the speaker will have crafted their arguments with regard to the circumstances of their arguing – the concerns of the judge, the nature of the charge. In other words, if Shakespeare has chosen to put particular arguments in the mouths of his characters rather than others, we should ask – why did he think those particular arguments were what the character would choose?

The final goal of the peroration is to stir the emotions. From the perspective of rhetoric this is important because we want to persuade the listener to action. For that reason, we need to leave them understanding why it matters that they agree with us. Thomas Wilson (1560: 130) explains:

> Therefore, when the Orator shall touch any place, which may give just cause to make an exclamation, and stir the hearers to be sorry, to be glad, or to be offended: it is necessary to use Art to the uttermost. . . . to set the judge or hearers in a heat: or else to mitigate and assuage displeasure with much lamenting of the matter, and moving them thereby the rather to show mercy.[9]

Quintilian agrees, saying that exciting the emotions of the judges is the most important function of the peroration because this is the final chance to leave the judges in the right frame of mind for their deliberations and so we should be 'free and full' in trying to rouse their passions. *Rhetorica ad Herrenium* (2.30) on this point turns in particular to how to stir the listeners to pity. Most interesting for our purposes is the final piece of advice:

> The Appeal to Pity must be brief, for nothing dries more quickly than a tear.

Applied

All of this advice is reflected in the peroration from Othello's speech to the senate of Venice refuting the charge of having used magic to win Desdemona. It is, as Wilson suggests, brief and speaks eloquently of the most important thing – that the magic he used was no more than the story of his life, which was enough to make any woman love him.

> Upon this hint I spake:
> She lov'd me for the dangers I had pass'd
> And I lov'd her that she did pity them.
> This only is the witchcraft I have used:
> Here comes the lady, let her witness it.

(Oth 1.3)

Again, for the person playing Othello, what does it tell us that he ends on this note? What does it tell us that it was enough for love 'that she pitied them'? Who is the person that, above all us, craves the love of someone who understands what he has suffered in the service of another? Is this the first person to have done so? Who accepts that someone might love because of the 'dangers I had pass'd'? Who is the person that finishes by calling for her testimony?

11

Using Invention and Disposition in performance

Wave thus to express his disposition.

COR 1.6

The importance of empathy

At the heart of rhetoric is the question of persuasion. What persuades a listener are arguments tailored to them and to their concerns. Key to Invention is, therefore, understanding others and their circumstances. It tells us, for example, whether it is our status or authority that matters most to our listener, or rather our reasons and evidence. The expression of an argument is, therefore, an expression of the speaker's understanding – true or flawed – of their status with and relationship to the listener, of what they think matters to that listener, of what they think the circumstances are in which they speak. Analysing the argument deployed by the speaker allows us to appreciate that understanding, and that, in turn, reveals the character of the speaker.

The basic tool for understanding argument is the Modes of Persuasion. This simplifies all arguments into three kinds: *ethos*, questions of status; *logos*, reasons; and *pathos*, emotional appeals. We can use this simplified model of arguments to quickly grasp the understanding of the speaker. We simply ask a few questions of a piece of text beginning with a process of identification:

- **What is the nature of the argument being deployed at this point:** *ethos, pathos* or *logos?* This allows us to ask why, for example, a character thinks reason will most persuade or why they go straight to an emotional appeal?
- **What matters of status,** *ethos,* **does the character offer?** This tells us how they think they are viewed by the listener.
- **Where does the argument change from one kind to another?** From *ethos* to *pathos,* or from *logos* to *ethos?* This raises the question of what prompted the change: Was it that the first kind of argument didn't work? If so, why not? Or was it that the speaker realised something about the first argument that pushed them in a different direction?
- **What are the images that the speaker draws on?** We will see in the discussion of Style, that rhetoric considers the choice of metaphors and imagery absolutely crucial to the framing of the argument. It allows us to ask why a character uses a personal image or, instead, moves to an impersonal one. Perhaps, in the latter, they are trying to distance themselves from the argument?

The process of identification in each case prompts the question, why? Why this argument, image, change? And from the answers that are given – answers that will reflect the actor's subjective understanding and thus bring out their unique take on the role – we begin to arrive at the character revealed by the text.

The breaking down of the argument forces variety and dynamism into the scene. The actor begins to see the points of change in the speech and to find the reasons why there is change at that point. In performance that prevents a speech or scene being reduced to the playing of an attitude. Instead we see a character alive in the moment, thinking their way through what is happening in the scene.

Quickly we also begin to appreciate how many of the answers only become clear when we factor in not only the speaker but also the spoken to. The changes of argument may be prompted by the response of the listener. The actor playing the listener gains some insight into how the speaker views them. Rhetoric, because it is about persuasion and persuasion about relationships, brings out the drama of a scene.

All this is best illustrated by examples, to which we turn next. Before doing so there are some concerns that may be anticipated.

What of the soliloquy?

Even where we speak to ourselves there is persuasion and a relationship between one part of the mind and another, between desire and reason, between what the heart wants and the head feels it should do. The same analysis brings out the same insights even in soliloquy. Shakespeare often has characters externalise these parts of themselves; allowing the character to address the audience as if they were part of that inner debate. Experience suggests that direct address to the audience is effective in Shakespeare for this reason. But even if a production doesn't want to break the fourth wall, that is no objection to the character vocalising his or her inner debate.

What if the character is mistaken?

It does not matter if the character's analysis of what matters to the listener or understanding of the situation is flawed. That too can be illuminating of the character because we can then ask why? Why did they not see that reason was wasted on the mob or status on the lover? Brutus' ill-judged speech to the mob that leaves him open Antony's counterattack is an example that reveals Brutus' character clearly. Whether the character understands the situation correctly or not, the rhetorical lens focuses us on, gets us to think about, precisely the issues that are central to the dramatic tension of piece: what is the character's understanding of her circumstances and, in particular, her understanding of the person spoken to and what they care about. And all of this is revealed from the simple starting point of asking 'is this argument *logos*, *pathos* or *ethos*?' and proceeding from there.

What if it isn't clearly *ethos*, or *pathos*, or *logos*?

It is rare that an argument is purely one thing or another: reasons are larded with emotional imagery; we draw on our status as a form of reasoning or as a basis for emotional appeal. Ideally, we identify what the primary focus of that argument is but in a sense it doesn't matter. The key is to start thinking about the nature of the argument being deployed and what it tells us about the character who deployed it. In practice, this issue of precise identification, rarely comes up as an obstacle to the insights that rhetoric offers.

Isn't this artificial?

In performance rhetoric provides a scaffold not the building itself. Once rhetorical analysis has revealed its insights for performance we no longer need it and what is left when it is removed is the character living in the moment. The process of exploration in rehearsal has revealed the character, the course of her thoughts, the effect of the others on them, and this becomes the performance. At the end we reach the point made by Peter Hall, 'you've absorbed my note to such a degree that now I'd like to say to you, "just forget it".'

It is important to note that the analysis of the scene or speech is conscious and deliberate in the rehearsal process but that does not necessarily mean that it represents a conscious thought process by the character. Rhetorical analysis is not an approach that holds that the character is thinking (at some level), 'and now for *pathos*', or '*logos* has failed, I shall try *ethos*.' That is not to say that the character is not making conscious choices to shift argument either. Rather, the decision as to whether or not they are doing so is something that will emerge from this very process.

12

Worked examples

Examples gross as earth exhort me.

HAM 4.4

Introduction

The ideas we have been exploring are most easily understood in context. The following two worked examples show how we can use the theory of Invention and Disposition and, in particular, the Modes of Persuasion as a tool for picking apart a text to inform performance. First, an example that focuses on recognition of *ethos:* Paulina in *The Winter's Tale*. Starting here has merit for three reasons. First, because *ethos* is concerned with the character of the speaker, as a result that is directly focused on a key question when it comes to consideration of a text for performance. Second, because it provides a helpful framework for understanding how rhetorical analysis of the Modes of Persuasion can work in rehearsal. Third, because it is understandable to conflate rhetoric with oratory and, in particular, with a set-piece speech, yet that conflation is wrong. Although rhetoric is vital to oratory its principles apply to any use of language to persuade. While such set-pieces are more easily subjected to a rhetorical analysis (and we can see that in the discussion of Othello's speech to the senators of Venice that comes when considering the advice on the beginning of speeches in Chapter 10), the example from Paulina in *The Winter's Tale* demonstrates that rhetorical insights can be found anywhere in the text.

Thereafter, we turn to consider all three modes and how they can be used as a tool for breaking down a speech for performance. This time we look at the character of Helena speaking to the Countess Roussillon in *All's Well That Ends Well.*

The Winter's Tale

The first example is concerned with resolving a thematic question for a production. Resolving that thematic question prompts and guides characterisation in performance. The example takes an issue from *The Winter's Tale,* a play full of questions for the director, actors and, ultimately, the audience to answer.[1] One question arises in the pivotal trial scene in Act 3. Hermione, overcome by the news of her son's death, faints and is taken from the court. Paulina follows her and, returning, tells Leontes that Hermione is dead. Only at the end of the play do we discover that Hermione is not dead at all. This then is the question, at that moment does Paulina know that Hermione is not dead? Or does she, at that instant as she confronts Leontes, believe it to be so?

Consider the two Paulinas created by answering that question one way or the other:

- One knows that Leontes, already remorseful, has not lost his wife even as he has lost his son but this Paulina still pretends Hermione is dead and uses that death as another rod with which to punish Leontes.

- The other Paulina is distraught at the death of her friend and her own inability to prevent it, to prevent the disaster that has overcome the Court. Her harsh words reflect that distress but do not compound it by the lie that Leontes' wife is also dead.

Which is it?

Answering this question matters not only for the character of Paulina but also for Hermione. When she returns after sixteen years what is it that prompts her return at that moment? Is it something of Leontes? Is it his remorse? Why was the remorse shown in the previous sixteen years not enough? Is he forgiven at all, or is it simply that, Perdita returned, Hermione wishes to see her daughter? If we knew if Hermione was conscious at the moment that Paulina decided to return and declare Hermione dead we might have some insight into Hermione's own character and views. Equally, if she was not conscious but presented with a *fait accomplis* by Paulina after the event, how does this change her reaction in the final scene when Paulina restores her to Leontes? Let me indicate how a rhetorical analysis of the play might provide us with an answer.

Paulina's words at this juncture in the play (3.2), seem to speak of a certain cruelty. Part of that cruelty must be informed by anger and Paulina's hot blood. But is there more than that at work? In an earlier scene Paulina has tried to confront Leontes and in demanding to be heard says this:

> Myself your loyal servant, your physician,
> Your most obedient counsellor;
>
> (*WT* 2.3)

This is not a passage from a set-piece of oratory. There is no formal courtroom moment where she can deliver a defence of Hermione. Paulina is struggling to get her words in amongst a general conversation. Yet she follows the precepts of rhetoric. She sets out her *ethos*, her right to be heard, and it is the authority of the physician that she calls out to. If she sees herself in that light, is she not then a doctor who is cruel to be kind? The surgeon who cuts off the limb to save the body? She doesn't come with the soothing bedside manner of a GP but with the high-handed, know-it-allness of the Consulting Surgeon, true. Yet she is honest in saying that she is 'loyal' and 'obedient', but to his higher good:

> I come to bring him sleep. 'Tis such as you,
> That creep like shadows by him and do sigh
> At each his needless heavings – such as you
> Nourish the cause of his awaking. I
> Do come with words as medicinal as true,
> Honest as either, to purge him of that humour
> That presses him from sleep.
>
> (*WT* 2.3)

Again, note the medical imagery: not only are words medicine but they will alter his very character, purging him of the humour that keeps him from sleep. This is not humour in the modern sense of the word but that of the ancient physician Galen and his theory of four humours that governed the body and the emotions: melancholic, phlegmatic, choleric, sanguine.

If Paulina sees herself as physician this, perhaps, explains why she enforces the 'cure' of sixteen years of silence. It is strong medicine but as she says to the attendant Lords:

> You that are thus so tender o'er his follies
> Will never do him good, not one of you.

> (WT 2.3)

In 3.2 when Hermione falls to the ground, Paulina leaves with her. Is Paulina going with her because she is the Doctor of the court? Certainly, when she comes back it is Paulina that pronounces Hermione's condition – dead – and no one challenges her pronouncement, for example by calling for a (or even *another*) doctor's opinion. To the contrary, Leontes sees Paulina as the physician and expressly asks her to, 'tenderly apply to her some remedies for life'. If she is the doctor figure, as the evidence of these lines suggest, is it likely that she would mistake fainting or catalepsy for death? If she is the doctor figure, is she in a position to dose Hermione so as to make her appear dead? Paulina confidently offers to let others view the body:

> I say she's dead – I'll swear't. If word nor oath
> Prevail not, go and see. If you can bring
> Tincture or lustre in her lip, her eye,
> Heat outwardly or breath within, I'll serve you
> As I would do the gods.

> (WT 3.2)

The answers that rhetoric gives

The arguments that Paulina presents in her cause, how she frames her *ethos*, tell us that of the two Paulinas we considered at the outset, the first seems better fitted to the text. It also suggests answers to other questions in the play. For example, Paulina clearly understands Leontes as unwell: his belief in the affair between Hermione and Polixenes not based on reality but on the fevers of his brain. Crediting Paulina as qualified to make that diagnosis gives strength to that interpretation of the truth of what has happened. I do not suggest for one moment that this is the only interpretation that is open. I do suggest that it is a plausible interpretation, that frames clear character choices, and does so not out of any arbitrary conceit about what the play should be about but drawing on the words that Shakespeare deliberately chose. Since any production must make such choices, to be able to do so drawing on the text for support, gives confidence to the coherence of the resulting performance.

All's Well That Ends Well

From a focus on *ethos* alone and on broader thematic questions for performance, we turn to consideration of all three Modes of Persuasion and what they may suggest for the particulars of dramatic interpretation of a speech. Our example is taken from *All's Well That Ends Well*. Helena, who is speaking, is hopelessly in love with Bertram, the son of the Countess Roussillon, to whom she is speaking. The love is hopeless because Bertram and the Countess are far above Helena in station. In this moment Helena, realising that the Countess now understands all, tries to explain herself.

Helena's speech begins, as every good *exordium* should, with an identification of the status of the case and an appeal to the goodwill of the Countess:[2] as she explains, her argument does not turn on whether the thing happened or a quibble over its nature. She loves Bertram, yes, and her defence, as is usually most interesting in drama, turns on the question of the value, or quality,[3] of that love. To that question she argues that it is an honest love and she herself, honest. In doing so she wraps up the question of her standing, her *ethos*, with the justification she proposes to give:

> Then, I confess,
> Here on my knee, before high heaven and you
> That before you, and next unto high heaven,
> I love your son.
> My friends were poor, but honest; so's my love:

> (*AW* 1.3)

From the *exordium* we pass to the argument itself and in this speech the argument changes four times. The first argument is one of *logos*, of reason, for Helena begins by proposing that one should only be offended by a love that would cause Bertram harm, but hers does not.

> My friends were poor, but honest; so's my love:
> Be not offended, for it hurts not him
> That he is lov'd of me: I follow him not
> By any token of presumptuous suit;
> Nor would I have him till I do deserve him;

(AW 1.3)

Why does Helena lead with an argument of reason? Does she think that the Countess is most concerned with the consequences for Bertram and so seek to show that there are none? If so, why does she think that the Countess, of whom Helena is the ward, is most concerned by Helena's status and poverty? Perhaps it is because Bertram himself seemed most concerned by these things. Perhaps it is because these are the things that are foremost in Helena's own mind. As we have seen, the argument we reach for first is that which is easiest to grasp, namely the one in our own mind. Rhetoric is pushing us to ask some questions that are interesting for characterisation: What kind of person puts forward her poverty as part of her *ethos*? A woman both defensive of that status and seeing it as part of her argument? Or, in loving, is so conscious of how that poverty is a barrier to what she wants?

Note the change

Whatever her reasons, Helena does not persist in this line of argument but moves to another. This time not one of reason but one of emotion, *pathos*:

> I follow him not
> By any token of presumptuous suit;
> Nor would I have him till I do deserve him;
> Yet never know how that desert should be.
> I know I love in vain, strive against hope;

Yet, in this captious and intenible sieve
I still pour in the waters of my love,
And lack not to lose still.

(AW 1.3)

Her second argument is that the love is hopeless. This is an argument
that calls for sympathy for the speaker – don't be angry with me
when I am the one that suffers. Why this shift? At least two possible
explanations present themselves:

The first is that Helena has, in that moment, come to appreciate
the truth of her first argument, that she loves in vain. That soul-
crushing truth, now realised, is what turns her from a focus on
persuading the Countess that there is no real danger to a plea for
pity that is driven by her own need for it. That would be consistent
with the identification of her *ethos*, but also with the lines that
follow immediately on:

Thus, Indian-like,
Religious in mine error, I adore
The sun, that looks upon his worshipper,
But knows of him no more.

(AW 1.3)

Another explanation is that Helena sees that her first argument has
not landed and that, perhaps, the Countess is not concerned with
the question of whether Helena is a real threat to Bertram's prospects
and dignity. The existence of this second possibility is a reminder
that the course of an argument is dictated by the listener as much as
by the speaker. All acting is, as the old saying has it, reacting, and it
is, perhaps, in the reaction that we find the prompt to the change of
course.

Of course, both explanations may be at work at once. The
purpose of this discussion is not to choose between them. It is to
show how the mere process of asking whether we are dealing with
logos or *pathos* has thrown up a range of interesting questions for
the performance. These questions have already suggested something
about the dynamic of the speech and the action. They have already
suggested points of inflection in the speech as we note where its
course changes in important ways.

A digression about change

Digressing briefly here, there are, of course, certain speeches in Shakespeare where the character has prepared his or her words and so that preparation should be marked in its own way, perhaps by the smooth flow of the delivery. Often, however, when Shakespeare has the characters begin with a set piece their emotions then drive them off course. An example of this happens in *The Winter's Tale* when Hermione confronts Leontes in the trial scene (my suggestion as to where the change from prepared to spontaneous speech occurs is marked):

> Sir, spare your threats:
> The bug which you would fright me with I seek.
> To me can life be no commodity:
> The crown and comfort of my life, your favour,
> I do give lost; for I do feel it gone,
> But know not how it went. My second joy
> And first-fruits of my body, from his presence
> I am barr'd, like one infectious. My third comfort
> Starr'd most unluckily, is from my breast,
> The innocent milk in its most innocent mouth,
> Haled out to murder: myself on every post
> Proclaimed a strumpet: with immodest hatred
> The child-bed privilege denied, which 'longs
> To women of all fashion; lastly, hurried
> Here to this place, i' the open air, before
> I have got strength of limit. Now, my liege,
> Tell me what blessings I have here alive,
> That I should fear to die? Therefore proceed.
> <u>But yet hear this:</u> mistake me not; no life,
> I prize it not a straw, but for mine honour,
> Which I would free, if I shall be condemn'd
> Upon surmises, all proofs sleeping else
> But what your jealousies awake, I tell you
> 'Tis rigor and not law. Your honours all,
> I do refer me to the oracle:
> Apollo be my judge!

> (*WT* 3.2)

The first part of Hermione's speech is clearly prepared, consisting of an escalating and numbered trio of punishments that she has already experienced and from whose torments death, the threatened sentence, would be a relief. It is a dignified defence and ends with Hermione commanding as if she were the judge, 'therefore proceed'. But Hermione is unable to leave matters there. The desperation and injustice she feels cannot be contained and bursts it way out. The considered argument, so carefully structured that it ended on the line break and the words were coordinated with the metre, is then followed by a single sentence six lines long, full of subordinate clauses, where all the thoughts run over the ends of the lines, each thought being qualified and refined as it is expressed. The shape of the passage itself reflecting the sudden overflowing of emotion and the unprepared nature of the outburst.

Change and change again

Returning to Helena's speech, her third argument is again one of reason, *logos*: Helena's love is unsurprising. After all the mother loves the son; is it any surprise that another also loves him? It would be inconsistent to praise one and condemn the other. This an argument of reason, yes, but of course one that also calls for empathy because it reaches out for the parallels between Helena and the Countess.

> My dearest madam,
> Let not your hate encounter with my love
> For loving where you do:

> (*AW* 1.3)

Rhetoric is again causing us to ask important questions for performance, about character, about the dynamics of the scene: How does the Countess feel about both the logic and the call to empathy? Is she still considering or does Helena's argument strike her immediately? Has Helena moved to this comparison between her state and that of the Countess because she has seen in the Countess's reaction to her former argument some sign of sympathy?

Double-down

What we see is that Helena compounds that call for empathy by her
fourth argument, which plays more strongly on the emotions by
asking the Countess to put herself in Helena's place.

> but, if yourself,
> Whose aged honour cites a virtuous youth,
> Did ever in so true a flame of liking
> Wish chastely and love dearly, that your Dian
> Was both herself and Love; O! then, give pity.

$$(AW\ 1.3)$$

Again we see shifts from reason to emotion, from the logical
consequences to the personal circumstances. Perhaps this is Helena
struggling to keep control of emotions that threaten to overwhelm
her even as she wants to show that she is in control of them.

The peroration

Certainly, in the end the emotional appeal dominates in the
peroration, which, consistent with the advice in the textbooks
contains the greatest emotional appeal and also a summary of the
argument:

> O! then, give pity
> To her, whose state is such that cannot choose
> But lend and give where she is sure to lose;
> That seeks not to find that her search implies,
> But, riddle-like, lives sweetly where she dies.

$$(AW\ 1.3)$$

The speech has, therefore, six parts each of which is marked by a
separate rhetorical purpose and to which different emphasis can be
put and to which different emotions can be attached. This though
the objective remains the same throughout – to ensure the Countess
is not angry with Helena. The six different parts are all revealed by
consideration of a single question: which mode of persuasion
dominates at this moment?

What does this analysis offer the performer?

First, the rhetorical analysis avoids the trap that the singular objective to the speech, persuade the Countess to forgive her, colours the entire performance with the result that the speech is treated as a single moment with a linear course, perhaps rising to a crescendo at the end. Instead rhetoric focuses the analysis on the dynamics of the argument with positive consequences for liveliness.[4]

Second, it brings alive the question of the reaction of the listener and reminds us how central that reaction is to the overall appreciation of the scene. Of course, the focus tends to be on the speaker but that is not where the drama lies. It lies in the tensions between speaker and listener. Asking how the listener feels about the argument brings that tension out.[5]

Third, these two factors combine to help express to the audience the shape of the speech and the movement of the thoughts. That is so even without the shape and movements of thought being reflected physically. Once there is clarity in the minds of the actors, that clarity is inevitably conveyed to the audience. Shakespearean language is notoriously difficult for the unfamiliar ear to grasp. There is a duty to try to clarify and it is the trait of all great Shakespearean performances that they do so.

Fourth, and relatedly, the explanation of the different arguments and why they have been deployed, as well as why the character has moved from one to the other, explains and justifies the different emotions that are connected to these arguments and shifts of argument. That means the actor has a reason for making the emotional gear-changes they suggest. Again, in performance that is compelling as well as comprehensible to the audience.

So, returning to our example, the production can mark the six inflection points in some way. This may be substantial, a move by the speaker, or subtler, some shift in the stance of the listener. It need not be physically marked at all as long as it is mentally noted. The value of rhetoric for unpicking a text is not that it suggests the answers but that it shows us where important questions are being asked, questions that need an answer that works within the production. In this, the rhetorical lens proves immensely fruitful.

Henry V

A final example, this time from *Henry V*, Act 3 Scene 3. Henry is before the walls of Harfleur seeking to persuade the citizens to surrender their city before he has to make a final assault. The dangers with a speech like this are two-fold: First, because it has a single overarching theme – surrender the city or face destruction – it can become one note in performance. Second and relatedly, because its imagery is so violent it can start at a high pitch and leaves itself nowhere to go. The rhetorical analysis leads us away from both dangers and, in its course, makes us ask vital questions about Henry and how he sees himself. A significant question at the outset is who, during the various passages of the speech, is Henry addressing? The men of Harfleur, yes, but also perhaps Essex? And also himself?

> How yet resolves the governor of the town?
> This is the latest parle we will admit;
> Therefore to our best mercy give yourselves;
> Or like to men proud of destruction
> Defy us to our worst: for, as I am a soldier,

This first part of the speech lays out all of the argument: surrender or be destroyed. It is an argument of *logos* but it mixes in a little *pathos* with its description of the men of Harfleur as 'proud of destruction'. This becomes a theme in the speech – it is not Henry who will bring about the destruction but others. Henry distances himself from the violence. The question we must ask is why? Note that the final part of the argument ends in the middle of the line and suddenly Henry turns to himself and to his *ethos*. Why that sudden change mid-line? Some response from the men of Harfleur? Some concern in Henry that he had not made clear his serious intent? Some lingering doubt about his own maturity and certainty of purpose? Or, simply a boast?

> for, as I am a soldier,
> A name that in my thoughts becomes me best,
> If I begin the battery once again,
> I will not leave the half-achieved Harfleur
> Till in her ashes she lie buried.

This reiteration of the threat seems to have been prompted by something in the reaction the initial threat received. Why else repeat but this time under-scored by martial name?

> The gates of mercy shall be all shut up,
> And the flesh'd soldier, rough and hard of heart,
> In liberty of bloody hand shall range
> With conscience wide as hell, mowing like grass
> Your fresh-fair virgins and your flowering infants.

Now Henry paints a vivid picture of what will happen. This is all *pathos*. What prompts him to these images? Does he, standing before besieged Harfleur, see unfleshed soldiers, dead from the fighting, their bones covered in blood? The sight of something such as this might prompt the move from *logos* to *pathos*? As the horrid imagery increases there is a sense that Henry is himself feeling the growing horror of what is to come. Note again that distancing – it is not Henry who will wreak this havoc but the soldier, rough and hard of heart.

> What is it then to me, if impious war,
> Array'd in flames like to the prince of fiends,
> Do, with his smirch'd complexion, all fell feats
> Enlink'd to waste and desolation?

Now Henry has separated himself fully from what is to come. It is an anthropomorphised War that will do the evil deeds. Why does Henry move from his own personal role, to that of the soldier, and finally to something apart from himself utterly? Why does Henry continue to make threats? The stark choice was clear in the first few lines, so to repeat these threats needs a reason. Is it that he is trying to ram home the point to a doubting citizenry? Is it for the benefit of his soldiers? Or, is it now, to himself? That last option would chime with the distancing of the imagery. The sin that is to come is not on his head. He doesn't want it. It will be War that does it, not him. If this line is taken it is an opportunity to come down from the heightened delivery of threats shouted to men atop a wall and find the personal, the reflective even in the midst of this speech.

> What is't to me, when you yourselves are cause,
> If your pure maidens fall into the hand
> Of hot and forcing violation?

This is an argument of *logos*. Who is it to? Why can Henry not bring himself to say 'rape' but disguise it in these terms? It seems almost as if it is Henry reasoning to himself. If so, why? What is it that in the previous part of the speech, or in the reaction to it, has prompted this introspection? Note that the question line is short, it misses a beat, does he pause to think of his own answer?

> What rein can hold licentious wickedness
> When down the hill he holds his fierce career?
> We may as bootless spend our vain command
> Upon the enraged soldiers in their spoil
> As send precepts to the leviathan
> To come ashore. Therefore, you men of Harfleur,

Here Henry gives his own answer: The course of war has its own demands and he will not be able to control it. Is this to the men of Harfleur? Does persuasion of them call for this kind of argument? It seems part of that introspection we saw in the earlier passage. Note again that the final part of the argument ends in the middle of the line. Again, what causes him to turn to direct address of the men of Harfleur? Is it that he has fully envisioned the horror to come? Is it that he is now desperate that the citizens should surrender and spare themselves? If so, it is a reason to come out of the quieter and more reflective mode and turn again to demand action of the men atop the walls of the city.

> Therefore, you men of Harfleur,
> Take pity of your town and of your people,
> Whiles yet my soldiers are in my command;
> Whiles yet the cool and temperate wind of grace
> O'erblows the filthy and contagious clouds
> Of heady murder, spoil and villany.

There is an air of desperation to this passage, which speaks less of threat and more of pleading, as if Henry feels the horse beginning to pull at the reins and he is conscious of only having a moment or so more before it is beyond his control. Stylistic elements seem to confirm it for the words that describe his control are in careful pairs with polysyllabic parts – 'cool and temperate', 'filthy and contagious'. But then we have them break into a triad of horrors.

> If not, why, in a moment look to see
> The blind and bloody soldier with foul hand
> Defile the locks of your shrill-shrieking daughters;
> Your fathers taken by the silver beards,
> And their most reverend heads dash'd to the walls,
> Your naked infants spitted upon pikes,
> Whiles the mad mothers with their howls confused
> Do break the clouds, as did the wives of Jewry
> At Herod's bloody-hunting slaughtermen.

This choice of imagery is significant, for in it Henry is Herod and his soldiers those who killed children indiscriminately. That choice suggests that Henry does not want the role, fears it, fears the sin inherent in it. That lends credence to the idea that he has begun with threats but ends with a desperate plea that the men of Harfleur save not only themselves but also Henry from the horrors that are to come. Who is the Henry that tries to distance himself from the horrors of war even as he commits to carrying them out? How is it reflected in later scenes, such as the moments of prayer before the battle of Agincourt?

> What say you? will you yield, and this avoid,
> Or, guilty in defence, be thus destroy'd?

This final passage is a rhyming couplet. That connection between the two alternatives, each of which forms the final word of the line, conveys a sense in which calm has returned because Henry realises these are the only two options open.

What went before is only my own analysis but hopefully it makes clear how breaking the speech down in the way I have suggested forces questions that, answered, then lend insights for both the performance itself and for the character of Henry. Though prompted by and anchored in the text, your own answers to the questions will give your unique take on the text.

Further work

Even though these worked examples show how rhetorical analysis can be employed, inevitably words on a page struggle to convey the effect of applying a rhetorical lens to the performance. For that reason, in Chapter 13, I suggest specific ways of bringing rhetoric into the rehearsal room. Used once in practice, seen once to have unlocked a passage that seemed to lie weak on the stage, the power of rhetoric as a tool for performance will be quickly appreciated.

Summary of the theory

Relationships

1   Identifying the arguments that characters are deploying (or not deploying) is a starting point for identifying how those characters view their circumstances and relationships.

2   We start from the premise that the character is deploying a particular argument because the character thinks (consciously or subconsciously) that it will be persuasive. Asking if the nature of the argument is one of *logos*, *pathos* or *ethos* tells us the character is thinking with their head, their heart or with their dignity in mind or that the character believes that matters of head, heart or experience are those most important to the person they are trying to persuade.

Inflection points

1   Just as interesting is to see the nature of the argument change. A character that begins with arguments grounded in reason or the presentation of facts but shifts to emotional appeals is doing so for a reason and exploring the basis for the shift of appeal and its timing at the point in the scene or speech can be illuminating and suggestive for the direction of the scene.

Balance

1   Focusing our analysis of the text on the nature of the
    argument being deployed strikes a helpful balance between
    over-generality and over-granularity. Too general a
    consideration of the speech or scene can lead to playing an
    attitude rather than engaging with the light and shade, the
    active and reactive, that makes drama so engaging. Too
    detailed attention to the meaning and choice of each of the
    words on the other hand, apart from consuming time that
    may not be available in the rehearsal process, can result in
    the scene losing clarity and focus. By looking at the level of
    the nature of the arguments being deployed we get a rapid
    investigation of the course of the scene that is more than
    one-note, that tracks the changes in the dynamics as the
    scene progresses, but keeps the clarity of the argument in
    the scene.

13

Invention and Disposition in rehearsal

And made the most notorious geck and gull
That e'er invention play'd on? Tell me why?

TN 5.1

In Chapters 5 to 10 we looked at what classical rhetoric taught about coming up with arguments and how to order those arguments. Then in Chapters 11 and 12 we looked at how those lessons might inform performance. In this chapter, we look at specific suggestions for using Invention and Disposition in the rehearsal room.

Who is this chapter for?

The contents of this chapter are primarily intended for group leaders: directors, teachers, company leaders. It aims to give them ways of introducing rhetorical ideas and how they can inform performance to others. It assumes that the person leading the session has some knowledge of rhetoric and its potential use in performance. When I say, 'some knowledge', there is sufficient information in Chapter 3 to allow the process to begin. However, the director or teacher that is guiding others will find it beneficial to have also read the preceding Chapters 5 to 12, which delve into these issues in greater detail. The suggestions put forward are only that – suggestions. They are based on my experience and on feedback from directors and teachers I have worked with. There are, however, many ways of drawing on rhetoric in the rehearsal room and the following is only one way.[1]

What if I am an actor?

If you are an actor working solo, the best way to gain an understanding of Invention and Disposition and bring it into your performance is simply to begin to apply the teaching of the earlier Chapters to texts you are working with. However, you may find the discussion that follows illustrative of how to work your way into a text.

The plan

There are two parts to what follows:

- First, developing a sufficient understanding of the principles of Invention and Disposition to make use of them in rehearsal.
- Second, tying the principles of Invention and Disposition into particular issues in rehearsal.

As to this second issue the worked examples in the previous chapter show there are two ways in which rhetoric applies to rehearsal:

First, rhetoric allows for puzzles in the text to be unpicked. The answers rhetoric gives are objective, in the limited sense that the source of the answers lies in the text itself.

Second, rhetoric provides a method for breaking apart the words and understanding the structure and flow of the argument. Seeing that structure and flow creates a basis for giving light and shade, liveliness and clarity, to the performance itself. In particular, it allows us to identify 'inflection points'. By this I mean the significant moments of change in a speech or scene. The change can be of any kind – a shift of argument, of energy, of position, of addressee – but we are concerned with dramatically significant changes only. For example, almost invariably, a change of argument – say from one of reason, *logos*, to one of emotional appeal, *pathos* – will mark an inflection point in the speech and scene.

Exercises for understanding Invention

First, exercises to start people thinking about argument and what it can reveal.

What has persuaded you in the past?

The exercise

The session leader asks the actors or students to consider, drawing on their own experience, the kind of things that they have found persuasive in the past. The group discusses these examples, examining why they are persuasive. The session leader then draws the discussion together by introducing and explaining the Modes of Persuasion.

Discussion

This exercise starts participants thinking about *how* words persuade.

It allows the leader to draw the threads together at the end by introducing the three Modes of Persuasion and showing how the varied answers may all be categorised as one of the three Modes of Persuasion.

The session leader should be alert to ensure that the answers given are explored fully: bringing out not only *what* was the occasion on which someone was persuaded but also *why* it was persuasive. So, for example, among the answers given will often be a variant of – 'I was told by someone I admired or respected', 'someone was passionate about the topic', 'the speaker had been through the experience themselves'. These are classic examples of *ethos* and it is important to bring out why the quality of the speaker was persuasive, which is usually about providing some basis for trusting them. Explore: Why does trust matter to persuasion? It isn't inherently connected to the truth of any question or to the wisdom of any course of action. So why do we look for it? By considering the nature of the qualities in a speaker that we are looking for, the participants are prepared to consider later rhetorical techniques that are intended to convey trustworthiness (see for example the discussion of *diacope* on page 111).

If you were trying to persuade a judge, would you emphasise *logos*, *ethos* or *pathos*? If you were trying to persuade a mob, which would you lead with?

The exercise

The session leader facilitates a discussion based on the contrast between the answers to these two questions. The session leader aims to bring out the point, discussed in Chapters 11 and 12 at page 80, that it is what matters to the audience that is important to persuasion.

Discussion

It is usually apparent that a judge, who must produce a written judgment, would be best persuaded by rational arguments and evidence, *logos*. In contrast, a mob will be best persuaded by an emotional appeal or by an appeal to the authority of the speaker.

Sometimes it is objected that you would also rely on emotional appeals or authority with a judge. That is true and if the point is made the session leader has an opportunity to emphasise that the Modes of Persuasion are just a tool to help us think in a manageable way about argument. In the real world we never rely on one of the Modes to the exclusion of the others. Moreover, even though true, it doesn't detract from the main point, namely that we emphasise one of the three Modes because of the circumstances of the listener: The judge is particularly constrained to provide reasons and so you need to give her reasons to work with. The mob is too emotionally charged to listen to reason and so we need to give them something else, emotion or authority, to work with. All this provides the session leader with the opportunity to show how a key concern of rhetoric is to understand the relationship between speaker and spoken to and why that is of value in drama.

Sometimes it is objected that whether you would lead with *logos*, *pathos* or *ethos* with the judge depends on who that judge is. That is correct. Again, it allows the session leader to emphasise that what matters to persuasion is not what the speaker thinks but what the listener thinks. We adapt our argument (if we are sensible), to the listener. Often we fail to persuade because what we do is put forward arguments that have persuaded us, the speaker, but which do not bite on the values or concerns of the listener. Again, there is an opportunity to show that argument is about relationships, as is drama.

Mini-debates

The exercise

The session leader asks participants to engage in a series of short debates. After the debate the participants consider the nature of the arguments that were proffered. Did they reflect the interests, values and concerns of the person being spoken to, or, in fact, those of the speaker?

Discussion

Ideally, the topics for debate are trivial or mundane – where to go on holiday, what to have for lunch tomorrow and so forth. They are kept mundane to avoid any true controversy in the topic overshadowing the exercise and to ensure that everyone can participate irrespective of their knowledge of current affairs.

Each debate should be short, each speaker arguing for no more than a minute. They are kept short because the purpose of the exercise is not to demonstrate genius in debate. The purpose is to demonstrate, as will usually though not always be the case, that the arguments put forward are not based on consideration of the values of the person being persuaded. Usually, the speaker reaches for arguments that are closest to their own concerns because these are the easiest to bring to mind and were persuasive for the speaker. They will usually do so even if the participants have just completed the previous exercise that is intended to bring out how it is the audience's perspective that matters most for persuasion.

Once it is appreciated that persuasion requires the speaker to work out what matters to the listener it is often asked: How do we work that out? And, relatedly, what if there is more than one person in the audience and the multitude have different concerns? Again, in answering these questions,[2] the focus is less on the particular answers to these questions than on getting the participants to begin to ask such questions. In doing so they are beginning to consider persuasive speaking at a deeper level, as an art form.

Anthropomorphising

Exercise

To check understanding and to embed the idea of three Modes, the participants are asked to think how they might anthropomorphise the modes in order to teach them to children.

Discussion

Session leaders might wish to give a starting example: Think of *ethos* as like Captain Kirk, *logos* as like Mr Spock and *pathos* as like Dr McCoy. Or if that is too dated a reference, *ethos* might be Harry Potter, *logos* Hermione Granger, *pathos* Ron Weasley. Or, even consider an analogy with Shakespearean characters – *ethos*, Lear; *pathos*, Cornwall; *logos*, the Fool.

This exercise can be done in small groups to allow for discussion as to the possible combinations. The discussion process will bring out points of uncertainty and of interest.

Exercises for application to Shakespeare in performance

Having introduced and embedded the concepts of Invention and Disposition and the Modes of Persuasion it is possible to turn to showing how we can apply them to a piece of dramatic text. The following exercises serve as a starting point for doing so:

The Modes of Persuasion

Exercise framework

Take Helena's speech from *All's Well That Ends Well* that is addressed in Chapter 12 at page 79 and following. Review the analysis of the argument in that chapter in preparation for the discussion to follow.

Ask one of the participants to deliver it, either reading it or, if time permits, having memorised it. Make sure the performer has a Countess Roussillon to play to: this is so that the point about the potential significance of the reaction of the listener to the course of the argument (see page 81) may show itself.

When the participants have seen the speech performed once, engage in the following questions:

(A) What is the argument of the speech?

Exercise

Engage in a group discussion that seeks to recall Helena's argument.

Discussion

Usually, after this first reading it proves difficult for the participants to recall the argument of the speech made by Helena at all; let alone to articulate there are, in fact, a number of different arguments being deployed within the speech. Usually what is recalled is simply a generalised notion of how Helena feels, unhappy or scared, and what she wants, to soothe the Countess. But if the argument is articulated in full and in detail, ask what made that possible.

Discuss what might make the meaning of a speech clear to an audience that is hearing it for the first time.

Discuss whether that initial read sufficiently conveyed the way in which the thought processes of the character are happening – or indeed that they are happening at all.

Look out for moments of change in the performance of the first read. Praise and draw attention to them. Discuss why the performer made those changes and what prompted them.

(B) What is Helena's purpose in speaking?

Exercise and discussion

Explore the following questions with the participants:

- How does Helena feel?
  This question should be considered at each stage of the argument. It may be an opportunity to note how easily we fall into giving a single answer for the whole speech rather than checking to see if those feelings change as the speech progresses. If there are changes as the speech progresses, what has prompted them?

- How does Helena think the Countess feels?
  Discuss how that belief may have informed Helena's choice of argument. Also, discuss whether Helena's belief changes during the course of the speech.

- Is it notable that Helena's first response is to swear to her own honesty?
  The imagery throughout the speech draws heavily on religion, which appears to be Helena's go-to position. Does that suggest anything about Helena the person? Or about what she thinks are the Countess's values? Discuss what the choices of argument suggest about Helena's character and her relationship to the Countess.

Parts of the speech

Exercise and discussion

Ask the participants to identify the beginning (*exordium*) and ending (*peroration*) of the speech. Where do they think the meat of the argument begins? What, if anything, do they think distinguishes the beginning and the ending from the body of the speech? What is Helena trying to bring out in the first part of the speech? Would it be fair to say that Helena is summarising her argument in the ending? Why does she bother to do so?

Repeat performance

Exercise

Following on from these first discussions, ask the performer to give the speech again.

It is useful now to compare and contrast the impression of the audience after the first reading with the more granular understanding that comes once we begin to break the speech down.

Discussion

- Do the participants agree that not only is the speech richer than it might first appear but there are more changes of tone and mood in it than a first hearing suggests?
- Do the participants think the previous discussions informed the performance?

While a more nuanced performance is an almost inevitable difference between a first read and a second, has rhetorical analysis contributed?

Draw attention to the fact that the inflection points that are being discovered through these discussions are all ones that require no more input than consideration of the text itself.

Identify the different arguments that Helena deploys

Exercise

Go through the speech identifying where each argument begins and ends. (Again see the discussion in Chapter 12 at page 79 and following for suggested answers.)

Begin to explore those arguments.

Discussion

- In each argument which Mode of Persuasion is dominant?
- Do the participants agree there are four key arguments and six parts? Or do they think there are more or less?
- Why do the Modes of Persuasion change between the arguments? Is the change the result of some part of Helena's thought process? If so, what? Or is it the result of some response by the Countess Rousillon? If so, what is that reaction and how does Helena interpret it? How, if Helena is changing course in response to a reaction from the Countess, is that change supposed to reflect the reaction from the Countess?
- What other arguments might Helena have deployed instead of these? Why do we think that Helena doesn't take these alternative arguments as her starting point? What does it tell us about her as a character that these were the arguments that she deployed?

What insights have we gained?

Exercise

Compare and contrast the answers to the initial questions about objective and about Helena's feelings and perception of the Countess Rousillon with those that have been given to the most recent set of questions.

Discussion

How do they differ? What do we learn about Helena's character from the answers? What do they suggest for the dynamics of the scene?

Informed replay

Exercise

Replay the scene again, now drawing on the further analysis that has been undertaken. See how, if at all, it alters the playing.

Discussion

Was this version of the speech clearer? Easier to follow? More interesting? If so, why?

Exercises of general application

Finally, here are some exercises that build on the understanding of argument, and how it may be applied to a text, any text.

Initial approach to the text

With the actors or students armed with an understanding of Invention and Disposition they are able to go away, in their own time, to review the script and ask of their speech, of any particular, scene: What is the nature of the argument in this moment? Why is an argument of this kind being deployed?

Directors and teachers approaching a script will find this process of review helpful too. It immediately suggests a series of inflection points: where the argument is introduced, where it ends, and where within the argument there are shifts from *logos* to *pathos* to *ethos*. Those inflection points then become opportunities to consider the energy in the scene and where it comes from, where the characters are in relation to each other at that point and why changes are occurring at those moments.

The table read

Another opportunity for this process is at the initial table read.[3] This has the advantage of allowing the analysis to be collaborative and, ultimately, consensual. The disadvantage is that the table read doesn't easily or always provide the time and space for exploring the questions rhetoric raises or for the iterative process of trying on some answers to see how they fit overall and discarding those that don't and trying new answers. It may be more fruitful therefore to tackle key scenes on their feet and then seeing how the answers fit in to the play as a whole in the table read. Equally, rhetorical analysis may be used later in the process for specific scenes or speeches or used as a way of breaking through a scene or speech that has become muddy or stuck.

Actors should be encouraged to look for situations where the character is consciously debating (even if only with themselves or the audience) because such moments are likely to express questions of *ethos* in a more easily identifiable way. What are the matters of experience or authority that a character calls to in those moments? Another situation to look out for *ethos* is in moments where a character is being challenged by another.

Inflection points

The following exercises are intended to bring out the inflection points and see what they may prompt. The starting point is to review the scene and note the nature of the arguments within it in terms of the parts of the argument, exordium, peroration, and in terms of the Modes of Persuasion, *logos*, *ethos* or *pathos*:

1   Play the scene or speech with the actors deliberately changing their physical position within the space at the inflection points; thus physically marking the moments of change.

2   In a variant of the above, the actors could consciously change physical position at those moments, going from standing to sitting, or from stillness to movement.

3   In a variant of the above, the actors could consciously change energy levels as they move from *logos* to *ethos* to *pathos*. The aim should be to exaggerate the changes so that *logos* is distinct from *pathos*. There should be no concern for naturalism in this exercise. Its purpose is to bring out the changes and to suggest a feel for the movement of the energy in the speech or scene. If it helps, possibly in echo of the earlier anthropomorphising exercise, have them move from character to character – from being played by, for example, Captain Kirk to Mr Spock to Dr McCoy.

Counterfactuals

The following exercises are intended to emphasise the significance of the choices that have been made by bringing out the counterfactuals:

1   Take the scene or speech and having identified the
    exordium, the formal beginning, and *peroration*, the formal
    ending, replay the scene omitting them. What has changed
    about the energy of the speech? If this was how the speech
    was to be played what would be different in performance?
    Usually this will bring out the emotional peaks contained
    between the *exordium* and *peroration*. It should also show
    how the beginning and ending of the arguments helps
    understanding by summarising the theme.

2   Take the scene or speech and, having identified the Modes
    of Persuasion in each argument, come up with a new
    argument with the same objective but one that consciously
    adopts a different Mode of Persuasion at each point. For
    example, where a character starts with *logos* have them
    offer an argument that emphasises *pathos*, where *ethos* now
    emphasise *logos*, where *pathos* now emphasise *logos*.

3   A variant of the previous exercise keeps the same arguments
    as given by Shakespeare but changes the order in which they
    are presented. How does that affect the impression of the
    speaker? (For example, what if Helena began with *pathos*
    and then moved to *logos*? Does it change the impression of
    her character if she leads with the argument that calls for
    personal pity? Does it make her seem whiny, self-indulgent?)

4   A further variant of the previous exercise asks simply, what
    other arguments are available to the character? Doing so
    allows the follow up question, if these other arguments are
    available, why does the character go with these? (For
    example, Othello could have denied the authority of the
    Senate of Venice but chooses not to, why?) There are many
    possible answers – something about their understanding of
    what matters to the person they are speaking to is one, or
    something about their own thinking on the point is another.
    Giving consideration to the path not taken illuminates that
    actually adopted.

5   After the scene or speech has been run once or twice to
    establish a starting point, it can be replayed with the person
    who is being persuaded at any particular point (for example
    the Countess Roussillon in Helena's speech), giving out loud
    their response to each of the arguments as the speech

unfolds. Initially this can be the actor's personal response. Later they can do the exercise giving their character's response.[4] In neither case should the responder attempt to respond in Shakespearean English! The immediate reaction, briefly expressed, is the aim. The purpose of this exercise is to highlight the reactions by verbalising them. By making them express and vocal, the speaker (for example Helena) should respond as if they can hear the verbalising. This is a chance to see if the argument adapts to the response of the other character. The exercise helps both parties to note and respond to the inflection points.

14

Style

*Applying apt words and sentences to the matter, found
out to confirm the cause*

THOMAS WILSON, *ARTE OF RHETORIQUE*

What is Style?

Style[1] is a reference to the way in which we express our ideas. The
aim of Style is summarised in the Roman orator Cicero's phrase,
'*docere, delectare, movare*' – to teach, to delight, to move.[2] That is
to say, we want ways to express our ideas clearly, so that we can
teach them to others, we want to do so in an engaging and
memorable way, to delight them, and in a manner that makes those
words resonant, because ultimately we want to move our listeners
to action. Style is the part of rhetoric where we study how to achieve
these effects. It looks to both what words we choose and, just as
importantly, how we order those words.[3]

The classical and even modern texts on Style devote much of
their teaching to consideration of specific patterns of words,
rhetorical techniques called 'tropes' and 'figures'. We will look at
these rhetorical techniques in Chapter 15 (see page 121 and
following). But there are also overarching themes to the study of
Style that concern the *purpose* to which these rhetorical techniques
are to be put. It is these themes that are of greatest interest and
use to the performer. Identifying these themes is the focus of
Chapter 15.

What is the significance of Style?

When we speak, what we say and the manner in which we say it reflects our emotional state: angry, calm, happy, sad. That manner may also make manifest whether what we say is a considered thought or something we've conjured up on the spot, whether we think we're superior to our audience or inferior, or whether we think we can get what we want by direct command or only by sly appeal. These are all matters relevant to the performance of a character. The words in the play's text will, therefore, reveal who a character thinks she is, how she feels in that moment, what she thinks her relative status is, as well as what she wants.

Often how the character speaks is the *only* source of information about these matters. Were the author living we might ask her, and modern playwrights sometimes include copious side-notes to guide performance, but with Shakespeare we have only the text to draw on. Fortunately, Shakespeare adopts consistent patterns of speech to signal particular answers to these questions. The patterns he adopts are those set down in the theory of classical rhetoric.

This is not accident. It is deliberate. Shakespeare's contemporary, Ben Jonson (1641), explained the point in his *Timber*, his notes on writing:

> *Oratio imago animi* – Language most shows a man: Speak, that I may see thee. It springs out of the most retired and inmost parts of us, and is the image of the parent of it, the mind. No glass renders a man's form or likeness so true as his speech. Nay, it is likened to a man; and as we consider feature and composition in a man, so words in language; in the greatness, aptness, sound structure, and harmony of it.

Ben Jonson's words capture the point of studying Style. It tells us that Elizabethan playwrights expected us to look to the choice of words to reveal character. They tell us that character was to be revealed not only by the ideas the character expresses but also by the selection of the words they chose to express those ideas and by the way they are arranged. It tells us that, to an Elizabethan playwright, these choices of technique are not incidental, accidental or superficial; they are an integral part of the writing process precisely because they reveal character.

What don't people understand about Style?

This explanation of Style contains two ideas that are not always fully appreciated and yet are of the greatest importance and explain its relevance to performance:

1   The purpose of Style is not simply to make words beautiful, memorable or to show emphasis, though it does all those things. Stylistic choices are part of how we convey meaning and emotion.

2   Style works not just with the words chosen but also with the order and structure of those words. You can convey what you mean as much by *how* you say it as by *what* you say.

An example of Style in practice

It helps to illustrate all these points by an example that shows how Style is used to express character and to create emotion in the audience and how it does so by changing the way the words are set down. Below is a passage from a speech by Barack Obama made in 2004 before he became President.[4]

> Tonight, we gather to affirm the greatness of our Nation – not because of the height of our skyscrapers, or the power of our military, or the size of our economy. Our pride is based on a very simple premise, summed up in a declaration made over two hundred years ago:
>
> > We hold these truths to be self-evident, that all men are created equal, that they are endowed by their Creator with certain inalienable rights, that among these are Life, Liberty and the pursuit of Happiness.
>
> That is the true genius of America, a faith – a faith in simple dreams, an insistence on small miracles; that we can tuck in our children at night and know that they are fed and clothed and safe

from harm; that we can say what we think, write what we think, without hearing a sudden knock on the door; that we can have an idea and start our own business without paying a bribe; that we can participate in the political process without fear of retribution, and that our votes will be counted – at least most of the time.

Take a moment to look at that first sentence. You may notice a number of interesting stylistic things in it but for the moment I want to draw your attention to just two of them.

Every speaker wants their audience to be actively engaged with what they are saying. Senator Obama creates that active engagement by adopting a particular form for his argument, offering a riddle for his audience to solve: he states he wants to talk about what makes the USA great but does not immediately do so. Instead he proceeds to list three things that might be considered good answers to the question but which he says are not. This way of expressing himself,[5] not simply giving the answer but beginning by rejecting plausible answers, creates a sense of anticipation in the listener: if it isn't these things then what is it? The listener's expectation that this is the answer is constantly met and dashed and that creates an intriguing mystery: why is this not the answer? What *is* the answer? The listener now hangs on his words because they want the riddle solved. It is a fundamental of human nature to want answers to questions, to want solutions to problems, to be curious. This is the reason why television channels put questions just before an advert break with the promise of an answer afterwards. They know that the desire to have that curiosity sated will keep the viewer hooked.[6] It is the reason for rhetoric's love of the question form. And this active mental state is something that Senator Obama has created through Style; through the form in which he expressed himself. He could have said simply and directly, 'the greatness of our nation is a faith in simple dreams', but doing so would not have created the same sense of anticipation and active engagement. This is the true power of Style, not its ability to beautify language, but to directly affect the mental and emotional state of the listener.

Note also that the stylistic technique is concerned with *how* he put his argument and not with the words that he chose. That is to say, it is by putting his argument in riddle form that he has created a mental state in his listeners and not by, for example, saying, 'pay attention to this' or 'you should be curious as to what the true genius of America is . . .'

This use of Style is not accidental on Senator Obama's part. We can see that from the fact he uses another rhetorical technique in the same sentence that has a similar effect to the first we have discussed and which emphasises and amplifies the result. You will have noticed that he gives a list of three things that are not the basis of America's greatness. Ordinarily, when one lists things out, the final item in the list is indicated by a conjunction, a word that connects parts of a sentence such as 'but' or 'and'. Thus we have A, B *and* C, as in 'Life, Liberty *and* the pursuit of Happiness'. That final conjunction is an audible cue that tells us to expect that the end of the list has been reached. There is an expected pattern to the words; an audible pattern.

What happens then when the expectation is played with? Here Senator Obama does not use one conjunction but two, not A, B or C, but A *or* B or C.[7] The result of adding in this initial 'or' is to change the cue, and to turn the list from a complete one to something that could go on and on. The listener no longer knows where Senator Obama is going to stop and this implies that the list of things to which America might lay claim as the basis of its greatness but which are, in fact, not goes on and on and on. It serves to heighten the sense of anticipation too – when is he going to tell us what the correct answer is? This technique therefore compounds the effect of the riddle technique.[8] Again, it is not a result of the meaning of the words – the dictionary definitions of the words does not alter between examples – but of the way that they are ordered. The structure of the sentence has changed the meaning. The addition of the extra conjunction alters the rhythm of the sentence and also where the attention of the listener is placed. You can, and should, test that for yourself by saying the sentence out loud both with and without the first 'or'. You will hear how it changes the meaning, not only creating anticipation but also lending strength and emphasis to the examples that are being given.

You can hear that it is a function of the rhythm rather than the meaning of the words by taking another example of a list. (Usually these lists are in sets of three because a complete set of things seems to have at least three items in it.)[9] Consider 'truth, justice and the American way' as an example: What if we remove that final, expected 'and'? The phrase, 'truth, justice, the American way', not only sounds different,[10] it also seems to convey a different message about how the speaker feels about these three things or about how the speaker wants the listener to feel about it. This is no longer a complete and considered group but, perhaps, some of the ingredients in a more general set of things. Without its conclusive 'and', the list sounds almost doubtful. Is this really all? Why these three things? Now contrast that with a multiplicity of 'ands' instead, as in 'truth and justice and the American way'. Now the doubt is gone, instead there is an emphasis, a strength to the list, as if there can be no other combination worthy of consideration or as if the list is the complete answer to some profound question. Crucially, nothing has changed in the list. The same three items are set out but, in each of the three examples, the meaning is different because we have played with the rhythm by adding or removing conjunctions. That is the power of Style.

Now look at the first sentence of the final paragraph of the passage above that begins, 'That is the true genius of America . . .' Again, there are many things going on but I want to draw attention to two rhetorical techniques that are being used to convey something about Senator Obama's own emotional and mental state. If we look for something unusual in this sentence we note that he has repeated the words, 'a faith'.[11] Why has he done so? To understand the answer speak the sentence aloud both with and without the repetition. You will hear a difference in tone that results. In the version with the repetition of 'a faith' there is an impression of spontaneity. It is as if Senator Obama has become caught up on his own words, as if he is saying '. . . a faith (yes, that's right, of course!), a faith . . .'. No doubt Senator Obama wrote this important speech some time before delivering it, no doubt he practised it many times before the performance of it, how then to convey to his audience when he finally gives the speech? How to get over his own passion and excitement at the idea as he first had it? By expressing the core idea in a way that sounds as if he himself is noticing its importance at the same time we do.

That this is what he intends becomes clear from the next words, '. . . in simple dreams, an insistence on small miracles . . .'. Here we have a list of two things and, ordinarily, such lists are set out with a conjunction, 'and', between them. It is omitted here.[12] That omission changes the rhythm of the phrase, giving it an urgency and, again, a spontaneity that is consistent with the effect of the earlier repetition of '. . . a faith, a faith . . .' The overall effect is to replace any impression of a cynical, polished politician's speech with the true passion of a believer who is caught up on his own ideas and who has no time to carefully order the list of things because it is so important to him to get out the ideas themselves.

Style and theme

In Senator Obama's speech stylistic technique is used to convey meaning and emotional state. This is a large part of the power of Style. These stylistic techniques tell us, and are meant to tell us, both something about the speaker, his passion and excitement, but also how the writer intends the words to be spoken. It is because stylistic choices give us such clues that they are so valuable in preparation for a performance.

Theme

There is one further point to bring out: not only can stylistic choices tell us about the emotions of the speaker, they can also point out dramatic themes. Consider that technique of repetition of the words '. . . a faith, a faith in simple dreams, an insistence on small miracles'. It draws attention to the main theme of Senator Obama's speech, namely that the greatness of America is not in its showy displays of economic or military might, but in the everyday dignities of the rule of law and democracy. These things are secured by the people's belief in them – their faith in them.

Structure also

There is another modern example of the use of repetition both to convey mental information and to identify a theme that springs immediately to mind: that of Martin Luther King in the Dream speech:

I still have a dream. It is a dream deeply rooted in the American dream. I have a dream that one day this nation will rise up and live out the true meaning of its creed: 'We hold these truths to be self-evident: that all men are created equal.'

I have a dream that one day on the red hills of Georgia the sons of former slaves and the sons of former slave owners will be able to sit down together at a table of brotherhood.

I have a dream that one day even the state of Mississippi, a desert state, sweltering with the heat of injustice and oppression, will be transformed into an oasis of freedom and justice.

I have a dream that my four children will one day live in a nation where they will not be judged by the color of their skin but by the content of their character.

I have a dream today.[13]

Martin Luther King uses the repetition of 'I have a dream' at the start of each example[14] to indicate that each of them is connected to the opening idea. The repetition helps the listener mentally map the structure of the argument within the speech. That is an important further point about Style: listening to someone speak and fully following what they have to say is hard. It is hard because it calls on the listener to memorise the points as they are presented, to see how the argument unfolds and how the points are related to the argument. Unlike in a conversation or when reading a paper, there is limited opportunity for review. In a conversation we can stop the speaker and ask for clarification or to be reminded of how the point relates to the argument. Similarly, if we are reading a paper or a book and do not understand a passage we can go back and re-read it. The audience for a speech, or a play, does not have those routes to understanding open to them. The wise orator, or playwright, therefore provides alternatives that show the shape of the argument, that give opportunities for review, that connect parts of an argument together. Of course, this shouldn't be done clunkily but in a way that is true to the theme, to the character of the speaker – Style provides the tools to do so. At its best, this use of Style also serves to reinforce the theme of that speech, here that only true equality honours the mythical founding principle of the United States, the American Dream.

Dramatic themes

Shakespeare makes considerable use of these same techniques of repetition for stylistic effect. When he does so it can also be to highlight a dramatic theme. As Sister Miriam Joseph (1947: 88) puts it:

> In his best work, Shakespeare employs the figures of repetition with easy mastery to achieve varied artistic effects. Yet even in his early plays he seldom uses them merely as verbal embroidery. When they are so used, they usually serve by that very fact to characterise the speaker. The repetition often accentuates an idea dramatically significant, as in 2 Henry VI (1.3), where the repetition of Lord Protector galls Queen Margaret, who wishes Henry to rule, and who accordingly schemes to get rid of the Lord Protector.

Great rhetoric often draws on stylistic technique for the dual purpose of conveying emotion, emphasis or mental state, as well as to identify theme. So it is with Shakespeare, a master of rhetorical technique, who uses these Stylistic choices to bring out the character's and the play's themes.

Reverse engineering

Once we are alert to the idea that Stylistic choices are deliberate clues by the author as to character, emotional state, and dramatic theme then we can mine those Stylistic choices for answers to questions that arise in a production or a performance. In effect by looking at Stylistic choices to determine character, we are reverse engineering the work of the author.

Placing ourselves in Shakespeare's position for a moment as he writes: He has a character that he wishes to convey is thinking about an issue for the first time or has come to a conclusion spontaneously because of something she has just learned. He will draw on the theory of rhetoric to employ techniques such as the repetition of words to suggest as much. Four centuries later: the actor notes that use of repetition of words and understands it is often used to show spontaneous thought and reflects on how that might inform her performance.

Now we imagine that Shakespeare wishes to convey a mind disordered. He recalls that rhetorical theory suggests that to convey emotional excitement you can have the speaker omit expected words or have the speaker pile point on point in rapid succession.

Four centuries later the actor notes that pattern in the speech and concludes that it may suggest Shakespeare wanted the lines spoken with great agitation.

This is not a new idea but central to the teaching of rhetoric. This reverse engineering process is the same exercise that Shakespeare would have carried out at school to learn how to write. A pupil approaching a passage of Cicero would have been asked not just what technique is Cicero using here, but why is Cicero choosing this particular technique out of all the ways he might have expressed himself? It is through this process that the pupil learned how different techniques worked and how he could apply them to his own writing.[15]

The labour and the reward

It is almost always true to say of the use of a rhetorical technique that it beautifies the language or that it makes the ideas more memorable or serves to create emphasis. This level of analysis – it beautifies, makes memorable, shows emphasis – is, in my experience, the usual stopping point in rehearsal but misses most of the significance and value of identification of the techniques. It is by considering *the way in which* they make things memorable, *the kind* of emphasis that they generate, that we see how rhetorical technique can become a key for unlocking how a character is feeling in a particular moment. This is harder to do. In part because it is less familiar, but this book and the exercises it suggests will help overcome that unfamiliarity.

Should you put in that effort? I suggest that Shakespeare expects you to do so because he is engaging with language at this deep level to show character. The example I offer to illustrate this is his choice of language for Brutus and for Cassius in *Julius Caesar* that was discussed when considering *ethos* at page 47. Shakespeare gives to Brutus only words that were old in Shakespeare's day, reflecting Brutus as the conspirator who looks to restore the glories of the past. In contrast, Cassius, the new man, the conspirator who seeks Caesar's overthrow not to restore the glories of the Republic but to clear the path for his own triumphs in the future, uses words new minted in Shakespeare's day. If Shakespeare considers that we can learn about the characters not just by what they say but from awareness of when the words they use were coined, how much more must he expect us to learn by observing other details of how they speak? That is particularly so given that, at the time Shakespeare wrote, the understanding of classical rhetoric was more widespread than it is now.

Speak that I may see thee

Shakespeare's attitude reflects the theory of rhetoric that he would have learned at school. It runs like a golden thread through all the great works: Whether it is Aristotle's pronouncement in the *Art of Rhetoric* that the choice of the words, of the images, of the maxims shows the speaker's character and that it is that character that serves most to persuade, or Cicero's theory of '*res in verba*' – matter cloaked in words, or Ben Jonson's note in his *Timber* that greeted us at the opening of this chapter.

Indeed, we may go so far as to say that it is because Style conveys meaning and reveals character that we find truth in the observation made in many of the Elizabethan textbooks on Style[16] that one *needs* to study and understand Style if one is to understand what the writer meant. Henry Peacham goes so far in his book on Style, *The Garden of Eloquence*,[17] as to state:

> The knowledge of [rhetorical techniques is] so necessary that no man can read profitably or understand perfectly either poets, orators or the Holy Scriptures without them;[18]

Another example, this time Shakespearean

The promise of Style in performance is that by looking at the Stylistic choices we learn something about Shakespeare's characters. Again, it helps to illustrate how this works with an example. We have already seen that certain rhetorical techniques are associated with heightened emotions and with anger and agitation (and will learn more of this later) – figures of repetition and of omission and of amplification. Others we will see are associated with considered thought, with reasoning and with logic. We should, therefore, expect that the former kind are to be found in passages where the character is agitated but not the other kind, and vice versa. If we were uncertain whether, in a particular moment, a character is rational and considered, or excited and passionate, or even playing at being excited, then we might look to see the stylistic techniques being deployed and ask whether they suggest an answer.

The madness of Hamlet, whether feigned or real, and the degree to which it is manifest at any moment, are key questions for both the production and performance of that play. One particular moment when these questions come to the fore is in the scene when Polonius and Claudius put Ophelia before Hamlet to see if she is the cause of his unhappiness. In the following example we can witness the increasing anger and excitement of Hamlet as his confrontation with Ophelia progresses and, consistent with our theory, an increasing shift towards rhetorical techniques that convey agitation. Their use argues for a real agitation on Hamlet's part, as opposed to feigned for the observers' benefit. It also pushes toward the expression of strong passions in performance rather than resignation or muteness.

At first Hamlet is still enough in control to deploy a sophisticated argument and to structure it in a complicated way – having the words in the first part of the sentence reflected back in the second.[19] Further sophisticated word patterns are to be seen, such as the way that Hamlet mirrors one idea with another, matching the sentences in length and form even as the ideas contrast:[20] beauty sooner corrupts honesty, than honesty purifies beauty.

HAMLET
> Ay, truly, for the power of beauty will sooner transform honesty from what it is to a bawd than the force of honesty can translate beauty into his likeness. This was sometime a paradox, but now the time gives it proof. I did love you once.

OPHELIA
> Indeed, my lord, you made me believe so.

> (*Ham* 3.1)

As Hamlet's fury builds we see him shift away from these carefully constructed and layered patterns to the questioning form, interrogating Ophelia but not pausing for answers. Now we begin to see increasingly unusual word order[21] – not, 'I did not love you', but 'I loved you not.'[22] He piles a list[23] of adjectives, onto himself without troubling with conjunctions.[24] Read the line out loud and hear the difference – 'I am very proud, revengeful, ambitious' versus 'I am very proud, revengeful and ambitious' – which sounds more agitated? Which more ordered and considered? To this list he then tacks on another without pause, not naming the offences but rather listing their effects upon his thoughts, his imagination and his actions. There is yet more unusual word order[25] – not 'we are all arrant knaves' but 'we are arrant knaves all'. Again, speak the two versions of the line out loud and note the differences you hear. Which appears more considered? Which more agitated? Which thought appears to have been grasped in the moment and which to have been brooded on for some time only to be expressed now?

Note how in both instances where Hamlet speaks with an unusual word order the change allows Shakespeare to give Hamlet a word of emphasis with which to finish. In the first case, ending with the negation abruptly changes the meaning of the sentence and reflects the sudden change from loving to not loving within Hamlet. In the second case, the 'all' is arguably redundant because the use of 'we' encompasses everyone in the first place. Adding it allows Hamlet to emphasise the universality of his pronouncement. In both cases, the power of the technique can only be appreciated by speaking out loud the lines both with their usual word order and then with the unusual word order Shakespeare has given them.

This is an important point: sometimes we only note the significance of the effect by considering what alternative might have been employed. If you find yourself stuck on the meaning or expression of a passage of Shakespeare it is often worth trying to rewrite it with the same words but in a different word order in case the contrast sheds light on why the words were in that order in Shakespeare's version.

HAMLET
You should not have believed me. For virtue
cannot so inoculate our old stock but we shall relish
of it. I loved you not.

OPHELIA
I was the more deceived.

HAMLET
> Get thee to a nunnery! Why wouldst thou be a
> breeder of sinners? I am myself indifferent honest but
> yet I could accuse me of such things that it were better
> my mother had not borne me. I am very proud,
> revengeful, ambitious, with more offences at my beck
> than I have thoughts to put them in, imagination to give
> them shape, or time to act them in. What should such
> fellows as I do crawling between earth and heaven? We
> are arrant knaves all – believe none of us. Go thy ways to
> a nunnery. Where's your father?

> (*Ham* 3.1)

Now in full spate we see words omitted again[26] because Hamlet's emotional turmoil allows him no time for the usual conjunction between, 'chaste as ice [or] as pure as snow'. His speech is clipped and the thoughts spat out half formed so that he has to return to them and amplify them – no sooner having told her to go, and then repeated the command, than he returns to his theme, the treachery of women driving men to madness, larding it with repetition of words and the key words all starting with the same letter[27] – marry, men, monsters. Again, it is vital to test the analysis by speaking out loud the alternatives. To hear Hamlet's lines with the 'or' replaced and then again with it removed, is to witness the remarkable power of a rhetorical figure to convey emotion by a simple change of rhythm.

OPHELIA
> At home, my lord.

HAMLET
> Let the doors be shut upon him, that he may
> play the fool nowhere but in's own house. Farewell.

OPHELIA
> O help him, you sweet heavens!

HAMLET
> If thou dost marry, I'll give thee this plague for
> thy dowry: be thou as chaste as ice, as pure as snow,
> thou shalt not escape calumny. Get thee to a nunnery.
> Farewell. Or, if thou wilt needs marry, marry a fool, for
> wise men know well enough what monsters you make
> of them. To a nunnery, go, and quickly too. Farewell.

> (*Ham* 3.1)

Summary

1   An idea cannot be separated from its expression. How
    someone expresses the argument shapes that argument.
    Therefore, looking at *how* a character expresses themselves
    tells you as much about them as *what* they say.

2   Elizabethan playwrights consciously and deliberately
    applied rhetorical Style to bring out character.

3   Style is concerned with the choice of words and their
    arrangement. Both reveal character.

4   Stylistic choices can show emotion or mental state in the
    speaker and create emotional or mental states in the listener.
    Both are important for performance.

5   Stylistic choices can reveal dramatic themes.

6   We can reverse engineer Stylistic choices in order to
    understand what the author intended to bring out about a
    character.

15

The purposes of Style

I know from whence this same device proceeds.
TA 4.4

Style in practice

Style, as we saw in the previous chapter, is used to create or convey certain mental and emotional states through the way language is used. It is valuable to the performer because the presence of the stylistic technique hints at the intention on the part of the author, i.e., as to the intended mental or emotional message. Recognising that intention guides performance and can answer difficult questions in the text.

How do we turn that theory into practice?

To get to that point of recognition we need to introduce general concepts of Style and show how classical rhetoric suggests these concepts can be put to use. The patterns of words we discuss will almost certainly already be familiar to you in one form or another but in what follows I will attempt to clarify those that are not and, even where they are already known to you, bring into focus how recognising them can help in characterisation and performance.

Categorisation

To assist in that process of recognition I have grouped categories of rhetorical techniques by reference to the purpose that underlies them:

1 Techniques that convey or create an emotional state;
2 Techniques that convey or create a mental structure to the argument; and
3 Techniques that give the illusion of logic.

Within these three categories I have identified individual techniques. The idea here is that by naming particular patterns we will be better able to recognise them, to use them consciously, and to understand why they have been deployed.

Naturally, the three categories I have identified are not hard edged. The idea behind their use is simply to encourage actors and directors to see stylistic techniques in terms of the purpose they serve. By starting at a high level of generality, emotion, mental structure, logic, it becomes easier to grip onto the idea of purpose as the defining question to ask of Style. In so doing I hope it moves us away from seeing Style as simply about beautifying or making words memorable or showing emphasis. Again, it is not that Style doesn't want to achieve these three things, it is that these aspects of Style are not what make it so valuable for performance.

Why not simply name and list the rhetorical techniques with examples?

The sheer number and range of rhetorical techniques can seem intimidating and impenetrable. Does one need to know them all to make use of Style as a tool in performance? Absolutely not. In fact, there is no need to know the specifics of any of them, let alone the Latin or Greek names that are given to them. To appreciate Style is simply to note the point that it is not just *what* is said that gives clues for performance but also *how* it is said and hear the effect. As a practical matter for those approaching Shakespeare in performance the question, therefore, is not, 'what is this rhetorical technique?'

but, 'what significance does it have that Shakespeare chose to form the words in this way rather than another?'

That said, there are reasons why, if one is sufficiently interested to do so, it may assist to be familiar with specific rhetorical techniques:

First, there was a common understanding – recorded in the classical and Elizabethan texts – as to the effects produced by these rhetorical techniques. It follows that, to a certain extent, if we know the expected effect then we have some insight into why Shakespeare chose to adopt it at that point.

Second, noting that a rhetorical technique is in use draws attention to the ways in which meaning may be conveyed by more than the definitions of the words used.

Finally, awareness of the use of a technique draws attention to the alternatives that might have been used but were not. In so doing it makes visible that which is not always clear, namely the path not taken. Character choices become clearer when we consider the counter-factuals – what was an option for this character but rejected by the author?

A dead language

Before continuing, an apology: in what follows I have set out the Latin and Greek names for the rhetorical techniques and figures. I do so in a book whose avowed intent is to avoid jargon for three reasons.

First, one must have a name for a thing if one is to easily and concisely identify it. The Latin and Greek names are traditional and as good as any other for this purpose. Since other authors have used them it also makes cross-referencing between those authors and this book easier.

Second, there is a significance to the fact that we can use these terms drawn from old and largely dead languages to refer to techniques and forms of language that are still in use today. Modern life would be unrecognisable to an Ancient Greek or Roman, or an Elizabethan, who would marvel at our cars, phones, electric lights and dentistry. Yet, though the world around us has changed, we humans have not changed greatly in the same time: the same patterns of thought still arise, the same aesthetic pleasures still strike a chord. By continuing to use the same terms that those people in times so remote and different to our own employed for the same effect of language we are reminded of these continuities.

Third, the use of their formal and ancient names gives the user an air of knowledge and gravitas because it contributes to an aura of expertise. This is a rhetorical technique called *aureation*, from the Latin word for gold – I gild my teaching with the use of jargon to make me appear more expert. The use of a rhetorical technique in the teaching of a rhetorical technique is a satisfaction in itself.

A rose by any other name . . .

It is one thing to name a technique, it is another to do so without controversy. My second apology is, therefore, for generating any such disputes but it is a muted apology because, first, there has never been agreement on the identification of techniques and, second, and more importantly for our purpose – rhetoric in performance – any such controversy matters not at all.

What matters, says Quintilian repeatedly in Books 8 and 9 of the *Institutes of Oratory*, is not the name of the technique but the effect that it has in rhetoric. Thus, speaking of the technique of irony (9.1.17, emphasis added):

> As regards *irony*, I shall show elsewhere how in some of its forms it is a trope, in others a figure. For I admit that the name is common to both and am aware of the complicated and minute discussions to which it has given rise. *They, however, have no bearing on my present task. For it makes no difference by which name either is called, so long as its stylistic value is apparent, since the meaning of things is not altered by a change of name.*

In what follows, if I have described a technique by reference to a particular term and you or another learned fellow thinks it better described by another term, so be it. On this I am, again, with Quintilian (8.4.15) himself:

> I am not a stickler for exact terminology, provided the sense is clear to any serious student.

A map for the lost

I have not sought to be comprehensive in this book. If you want to delve deeper into Stylistic techniques there are plenty of books that do so and I have suggested further reading at the end of the book. What is needful, in my opinion, is not another dictionary of rhetorical techniques but an understanding of *why* those techniques are being deployed.

For that reason, I have sought to provide various forms of reverse dictionary as a guide to identifying and exploring the techniques as you encounter them in one of the plays:

1 In the 'Reverse Dictionary', I have set out patterns that you might recognise in a text and then suggested where in this book that pattern's purpose is discussed.

2 The glossary also attempts to provide brief definitions of traditional terms and references the further guidance to be found in the book.

16

Emotional state

The first discussion is concerned with how Style may convey or create emotional states.

The significance of rhythm and metre

Many aspects of Style are the result of rhythm and metre.

What are rhythm and metre?

When we talk about rhythm[1] and metre we mean by this simply that the number of beats[2] in a line and the positions of stress given to the words can be significant for meaning. It is the combination of these two that gives the musical quality to spoken English. We are familiar with rhythm and metre from verse where they are used explicitly to convey meaning but they are important in prose too, though sometimes less prominent, less visible. In truth, whether in prose or in verse, you will find we have an intuitive, natural, understanding of them because the English language relies for its meaning on the concepts that underlie rhythm and metre – syllables and stress.[3]

1 Syllables are the individual pronounced elements of a word and are identified by the vowel sounds:

- 'Not' is a word with a single syllable and a single beat when spoken. So is 'scratched'; although it contains many more letters than 'not', including two vowels, it still contains but a single vowel sound.[4]

- 'Certainly' is a word with three syllables, three vowel sounds in it – 'Cer-tain-ly' – and thus three beats to it. 'Idea' is also a word of three syllables, though much shorter than 'certainly' – 'I-de-a'.

2   Stress is about which syllable or syllables we place the emphasis on when speaking the word out loud. There is an agreed point for that stress in usual pronunciation[5] (which I show here by putting the point of stress in capital letters), thus 'CER-tain-ly', not 'cer-TAIN-ly'.

Rhythm and metre in verse

Every word has at least one syllable. Where the word has more than one syllable, there is usually one or more syllables that receive particular stress. These are not things of verse or prose but of English. However, in verse we apply strict rules about the numbers of syllables and placement of the stress in each line. One such form of verse is that used regularly by Shakespeare, iambic pentameter. An 'iamb' is a pair of syllables where the stress comes on the second syllable in a pair, for example, 'to BE / or NOT / to BE' is three iambs in a row. We can string together iambs in any number but where we do so in sets of five that is a 'pentameter'.[6] For example, the opening line of Sonnet 2 is in perfect iambic pentameter, 'When FORty WINters HAVE beSIEGED thy BROW.' Where, even though using iambic pentameter, one does not try to create rhymes for the end words this is called 'blank verse'. Blank verse is said most naturally to resemble the rhythm of spoken English, which is why Shakespeare uses it so often.

The question

Why use verse at all? Obeying the rules that the verse form dictates makes the process of writing harder and more involved. If the aim is ultimately to sound natural, then why not simply stick to prose?

The answer

The rules of verse help the author guide both the actor and the audience as to meaning by highlighting questions of rhythm, expectations of stress and word order. For example, the rules of iambic pentameter provide clues as to the way the line is to be spoken:

First, and perhaps most commonly, by influencing where the stress, and thus the emphasis, is to be placed. The words that are significant for theme, or for emotional or mental state are usually those on which the stress falls.

Second, the use of a pattern (such as iambic pentameter) creates an expectation in the audience as to where the stress will fall and the writer can use that expectation. For example, because the audience knows that in iambic pentameter the lines have five pairs of syllables the fact that one has reached the end of the line becomes audible; the writer can then place particularly significant words at that end point.[7] There is an example in Hamlet's soliloquy: 'Oh that this too too solid flesh would melt'. The rhythm of the line, TA-dum[8] ta-DUM ta-DUM ta-DUM ta-DUM, gives emphasis and power to the final word, 'melt', which is the final stress of the line: 'OH that this TOO too SOLid FLESH would MELT'.

The expected rhythm can also be used to create different effects not by meeting but by *breaking* from that expectation. Hamlet's famous soliloquy does precisely that by finishing what is an otherwise conventional iambic pentameter not with a pair of syllables but with three syllables, the last one of which is unstressed: To BE / or NOT / to BE / that IS / the QUEStion . . .[9] The effect of doing so can be heard; it makes audible Hamlet's doubt because where completeness seems just within grasp it is suddenly lost. It promises conventional iambic pentameter and then breaks that promise – audibly, by giving a feminine ending.

Similarly, one can alter the beginning of the line. Again from Hamlet's soliloquy:

Whether 'tis nobler in the mind to suffer

Here, instead of the pair of syllables with the second syllable being stressed (as in 'to BE'), Shakespeare reverses it and makes the first syllable the one that carries the stress, 'WHETHer'.[10] The rest of the line carries on in standard iambic pentameter finishing with that same triple syllable: 'WHETHer / 'tis NO/bler IN/ the MIND /to SUFFer'. The changed stress of the first part of the line highlights a word that foreshadows a question and puts the focus on the choice that is to be set out – is it nobler to endure life's suffering or bravely to end that suffering by suicide?

Wood for the trees

It is possible to descend speedily into increasing technical detail about verse and to deploy increasingly complicated identification of different kinds of stress from iambs to trochees to amphibrachs, from pentameter to hexameter and on. None of that is necessary for our purpose. What we need is simply to note that rhythm and metre are tools in and of themselves for conveying meaning quite apart from the dictionary definition of the word to which they apply. Or perhaps we might say, more importantly, we need to note that Shakespeare understands that we can use rhythm and metre to convey meaning and intends that we should.[11]

A powerful example is to be found in *Macbeth* (2.2).[12] Throughout this scene there are broken-backed lines, short lines and ambiguous metrical connections between Lady Macbeth's lines and those of Macbeth. They suggest pauses, reflective and awkward, the verse is as disjointed as the thoughts of the speakers.

> LADY MACBETH   Had he not resembled
> My father as he slept, I had done't.
> My husband?
> MACBETH   I have done the deed.

That line, 'My father as he slept, I had done't', is a broken-backed line. There is a missing beat in the middle. It is as if at that point Lady Macbeth is pausing to reflect on why she didn't, or perhaps on how she could have done. Similarly, Lady Macbeth and Macbeth share the line, 'My husband? I have done the deed.' But there are only eight beats and so a pause appears somewhere in the line, presumably between query and response. It suggests that Lady Macbeth has to get her husband's attention and he only slowly becomes aware of her query. The metre is suggesting pacing in the performance and, through that pacing, mental state for the character.

Prose too

Because there are rules to the use of rhythm and metre in verse, use of verse more readily alerts us to the presence of deliberate decisions by the author about them – which word to finish the line on, which word to use in order to maintain or break the metrical system and so on. We are then alert to the consciousness of the choice of what word to use and where to put it. But rhythm and metre are also present in prose because they are a feature of syllables and stress and these are aspects of words whether those words are being used in prose or poetry. Verse simply exploits these features explicitly by adding in the idea of specific rules for their use.

With verse the rules come from the form but there are also rules of this kind in prose. We encountered one of these in the example from the speech of Senator Obama, given in Chapter 14: the presentation of lists. As noted in that example, lists are usually presented with the final item of the list identified and set off by a conjunction (a joining word such as 'and', or 'but'). This creates a rule that affects the rhythm: 'A, B and C' – here four beats, the stress on the list items and the conjunction unstressed. This rule about the usual way to present a list, and the expectation it creates in the listener, can then be played with to alter the meaning. Imagine, for example, that we wanted to suggest some surprise at the presence of the last item being included in the list – we might change the stress to convey that surprise: 'a, b AND C?' Again, as noted in the example from Senator Obama, we can go further to change the rhythms and the points of stress, for example by adding more conjunctions[13] or by removing them altogether:[14] 'A and B and C', or, 'A, B, C'. The power of these techniques is particularly audible when using algebraic notation as we do here instead of real words. To speak even these examples out loud is to hear the effect of the change on the rhythm and stress that is produced, and that, as a result, it changes the emotional content.

Ways to play

One of the ways we can play with rhythm and metre to convey emotional states is by using repetition, particularly where the repetition is of a single word or phrase. Repetition inherently alters the rhythm and, by the repeated use of the same word or phrase, calls attention to the choice to alter the rhythm even as we drive home particular words. As *Rhetorica ad Herrenium* (3.14) explains:

> [The figures serve to] make it possible for the same word to be frequently reintroduced not only without offence to good taste but even so as to render the style more elegant . . . . There inheres in repetition an elegance, which the ear can distinguish more easily than words can explain.

Epizeuxis

Epizeuxis is the repetition of the same word, again, again, again. It often appears in threes, sometimes with the final part of the triplet slightly set off:

> A horse! A horse! My kingdom for a horse!
>
> (*R3* 5.4)

It functions as a verbal hammer blow, drawing attention to the particular word but also to the speaker's state of mind. The emotional state is frequently heightened, agitated – great fear, anger or determination, as in these examples from Shakespeare:

> Reputation, reputation, reputation! O, I have lost
> my reputation! I have lost the immortal part of
> myself, and what remains is bestial. My reputation,
> Iago, my reputation!
>
> (*Oth* 2.3)

> O horror, horror, horror! Tongue nor heart
> Cannot conceive nor name thee!
>
> (*Mac* 2.3)

Sometimes it is used to indicate an urgent command to action:

> Come, bustle, bustle! Caparison my horse!
>
> (*R3* 5.3)

> O, treachery! Fly, good Fleance, fly, fly, fly!
>
> (*Mac* 3.3)

It can also be used to indicate weariness but, crucially, in order to do so the rhythm must be still further played with by drawing out the process of repetition. This is achieved by inserting additional conjunctions into the phrase, *polysyndeton*.

> To-morrow, and to-morrow, and to-morrow,
> Creeps in this petty pace from day to day
> To the last syllable of recorded time,
>
> (*Mac* 5.5)

In this example Shakespeare even tells us the effect he hopes to achieve – the creeping in, syllable by syllable. In all this, the repetition reflects Thomas Wilson's (1560: 231) explanation:[15]

> The oft repeating of one word much stirs the hearer and makes the word seem greater as though a sword were oft digged and thrust twice or thrice in one place in the body.[16]

Diacope

The repetition of the same word or phrase with a few words in-between is called *diacope*. The repetition is often of a pair. We encountered its use in the example from Senator Obama discussed in Chapter 14 at page 111 and following. The introduction of the intervening words into the repetition allows the speaker to use diacope to convey a certain spontaneity – as if they spoke first without thought but, hearing their own words, catch on them, and stop to mull them.

> I am dying, Egypt, dying; only
> I here importune death awhile, until
> Of many thousand kisses the poor last
> I lay up thy lips.
>
> (*AC* 4.15)

> O Romeo, Romeo, wherefore art thou Romeo?
>
> (*RJ* 2.3)

> O Cressid! O false Cressid! false, false, false!
>
> (*TC* 5.2)

Conduplicatio

An extended version of *diacope*, where the interruption between the repeated word or phrase is greater, is called *conduplicatio*. The repetition of the word can be simply to serve to highlight an argumentative theme as in this example from Brutus' speech in Julius Caesar.

> Who is here so base that would be a
> bondman? If any, speak; for him have I offended.
> Who is here so rude that would not be a Roman? If
> any, speak; for him have I offended. Who is here so
> vile that will not love his country? If any, speak;
> for him have I offended. I pause for a reply.
>
> (*JC* 3.2)

In the repetition of the word or phrase there is often the suggestion of a certain intensity on the part of the speaker, as if the idea contained in the word is troubling them, they cannot let it go, it works upon them as much as it is used to convey the theme to the listener.

> Lie with her! lie on her! We say lie on her, when
> they belie her. Lie with her! that's fulsome.
> – Handkerchief – confessions – handkerchief! – To
> confess, and be hanged for his labour; – first, to be
> hanged, and then to confess. – I tremble at it.
>
> (*Oth* 4.1)

> There I have another bad match: a bankrupt, a
> prodigal, who dare scarce show his head on the
> Rialto; a beggar, that was used to come so smug upon
> the mart; let him look to his bond: he was wont to
> call me usurer; let him look to his bond: he was
> wont to lend money for a Christian courtesy; let him
> look to his bond.
>
> (*MV* 3.1)

Epanalepsis

The repeated word or phrase can be put at the beginning and the end of the passage. This is called *epanalepsis*. It can be used to

create a sense of exhortation as in the examples from Othello and
Henry V below or to highlight that what seemed separate is, in fact,
one as in the example from Richard III below.

Work on,
My medicine, work!

(Oth 4.1)

Once more unto the breach, dear friends, once more.

(H5 3.1)

And being seated, and domestic broils
Clean over-blown, themselves, the conquerors.
Make war upon themselves; blood against blood,
Self against self:

(R3 2.4)

Word order

The discussion of rhythm in prose and verse, and of the number of
beats and the placement of stress in a line of verse, or how repetition
alters the rhythm in prose, inevitably brings into focus the question
of word placement.

Beginnings and endings

In verse, the placement of words is never arbitrary because it affects
the metre. That is why we look with such care at the words that
start and end verse lines because Shakespeare has taken care over
the choice of what goes there. However, like rhythm and metre,
word placement is not a thing of verse only.

Beginning and endings are always important. Quintilian, advising
in the Institutes of Oratory, suggests that in prose the beginning
and ending of passages in particular require careful thought. He
offers the following pointers: The ends should fall where one would
take natural breath. Going too long risks losing the listeners
attention. Pausing not only allows for breath but also for the listener
to absorb what has been said. Similarly, the beginnings of passages
also require care because the audience is primed to listen to them
more carefully than what follows.

Note how Shakespeare follows this advice – the beginnings and endings of lines are of particular importance for meaning and theme.

Expected word order

Quintilian goes on to explain in the *Institutes of Oratory* that the positioning of words has a significance all of its own quite apart from whether they begin or end passages. His first point is that in some cases images must be built up by taking the parts and proceeding to the whole.[17] Shakespeare often follows this guidance. In the following example, we start from the materials, proceed to one of the things made from them, then the building made from that part, then to the earth itself on which the buildings sit and from there to 'all which it inherit'. The expansion of scope to its very limit serves by its scale to enhance the contrast when, at the end, it disappears:

> And, like the baseless fabric of this vision,
> The cloud-capp'd towers, the gorgeous palaces,
> The solemn temples, the great globe itself,
> Ye all which it inherit, shall dissolve
>
> (*Tem* 4.1)

No uncaused cause

Quintilian then speaks of how there is a natural order to the placement of things that reflects our perception of their causal order: the example he gives is that night follows day, not the other way round.[18] The sun rises and sets, it does not set and then rise. This expectation that things will be presented in a particular order means that when it does not happen it creates a sensation:

> Yet I'll not shed her blood,
> Nor scar that whiter skin of hers than snow . . .
>
> (*Oth* 5.2)

We normally connect the adjective to the simile (that skin of hers whiter than snow), but here the breaking of expectations and the separation of adjective from the simile is part of what conveys the sense of disorder in Othello's mind and of disorder in the world. His focus is on the scarring of her skin, not on the whiteness of it.

The audible highlighter pen

Finally, there are words that can have extraordinary significance and yet would be lost if they were placed in the middle of a sentence where they would become obscured by all that surrounds them. Placed at the end they are called to the hearer's attention and burnt into her mind. Here are three examples where Shakespeare moves the emotionally or thematically significant word to the end, that it may strike the bell loudest.

> You should not have believ'd me; for virtue cannot so inoculate
> our old stock but we shall relish of it. I loved you not.
>
> *(Ham* 3.1)

> How he did shake: 'tis true, this god did shake;
> His coward lips did from their colour fly,
>
> *(JC* 1.2)

> Well, heaven forgive him! and forgive us all!
> Some rise by sin, and some by virtue fall:
>
> *(MM* 2.1)

Note also how, in these last two examples, it is not just by putting the significant word at the end that Shakespeare guides us. He also uses rhythm and metre to convey his thinking to the actor and, ultimately, to the audience by putting the emotionally and thematically important words on the points where the stress in the iambic pentameter should fall. When Cassius mocks Julius Caesar's fit the contempt falls on the contrast between the HE that SHAKES, and between the GOD and the SHAKING. Or, look at Escalus' warning, which again sees the moments of stress falling on the contrast – 'some RISE by SIN' versus, 'by VIRtue FALL'.

Unexpected word order

Rhetorical technique often places words in an unexpected order to draw attention to those very words.[19] In part unusual word order has its power because English often has clear expectations about sentence structure and so defying those expectations is immediately noticeable even in prose. Consider:

> Uneasy lies the head that wears a crown.
>
> (*2H4* 3.1)

Ordinarily in a sentence we identify subject and then state what happens to that subject – the head that wears the crown (subject) lies uneasily (verb and adverb). Shakespeare, in that example, takes verb and adverb and pushes them to the front of the sentence and in doing so shows at once the focus of the thought, highlights the unease, and – serving as echo to the thoughts of the character, the form of the sentence is itself uneasy. Again, note Quintilian's advice about beginnings and endings is being heard, the sentence form allows the key concepts to top and tail – 'uneasy' and 'crown'. The unusual sentence structure, adverb, verb, subject alerts us to the thought, the conscious effort, the author has put into the structure of the sentence.

As with verse lines so with prose, when we see that something unusual has happened as a result of Shakespeare's deliberate choice the question is always, why? The subject of the sentence is hidden at the end, why? The object of the sentence is brought to the front, why?[20] Consider another example:

HENRY BOLINGBROKE
> I thought you had been willing to resign.

KING RICHARD II
> My crown I am; but still my griefs are mine:
> You may my glories and my state depose,
> But not my griefs; still am I king of those.
>
> (*R2* 4.1)

In this passage, the placing of 'my crown' at the front of his answer[21] allows Richard to distinguish between the office of state and the man himself. It also allows him to distinguish between the two things that matter to him. The unusual word order makes plain the character's mental focus.

The point of emphasis is usually to be found in moments of the unexpected. As in the following passage where the sudden inversion of adjective and noun, from 'beautiful tyrant' (adjective then noun) to 'fiend angelical' (noun then adjective) shows the shift in focus and the character's realisation of the paradoxes inherent in the unobtainable but desired.

> O serpent heart, hid with a flowering face!
> Did ever dragon keep so fair a cave?
> Beautiful tyrant! fiend angelical!
> ... O that deceit should dwell
> In such a gorgeous palace!
>
> (RJ 3.2)

Enough theory – what about the practice?

Pause over this last example from *Romeo and Juliet* to consider how we might make that insight useful to performance. The danger with a speech like this one is that it becomes simply a flow of images around a single idea, without thought or emotion differentiated through the lines. That danger is particularly great where, as here, the four images have a common theme. To avoid that danger we have to ask why four images all with the same message – the paradox of a beautiful outward show when evil lurks within?

No doubt part of what is going on here is that Shakespeare is giving the audience four beats to notice and understand that idea:[22] A first to register that there is an idea in play. A second to say, have you understood the idea? Here is a different way of expressing it. A third to allow the now attentive audience fully to understand the image and the final one to allow the actor to play out his feelings about the idea with the audience now attentive.[23] Of course, although there is commonality there is also difference: the first time, we have the character notice the idea, with the second, the character asks the audience if they have noticed it too, with the third, the character rails against it and with the fourth, the character marvels at it. Each of these four are different in thought, emotion and emphasis – and can be played differently.

Yet even within those moments there is still further difference, as in that third line and its unusual word order. When we notice the unexpected word order we are also noticing a moment Shakespeare has given to the character to demonstrate the shifting of thought and emotion. In performance it should be marked in some way. How it is marked is for the particular production and actor – a movement, a gesture, an expression or just something internal to the actor's own thinking – but it should be marked. The gift Shakespeare makes the actor is to offer something in the writing that justifies that shift of thought and emotion, that moment of change, and the creation of interest for the audience that results from seeing and hearing the thoughts happen in the moment.

Conclusions: Word placement

The choice of *where* to place a word has a significance of its own. It can serve to draw attention to themes but also to show off the character's emotional and mental state. In part this is because the word placement effects the rhythm and metre. However, word placement can also work with rules that exist in English, or can break those rules, to create a particular effect.

Again, the key is to note where Shakespeare has done something unusual or unexpected because that is a deliberate choice on his part and, therefore, one that he considered significant as to the effect it created.

Ancient wisdom

These are not new arguments. We have already seen that Quintilian discusses word placement in the *Institutes of Oratory*. He also discusses the power of rhythm and metre. Quintilian begins with an observation from Cicero – 'the whole beauty of a speech consists in its rhythm'. Quintilian then discusses how certain rhythms and metres, and the matters that affect them, are appropriate to certain contexts and achieve certain effects. He observes, for example, that long syllables have a greater impressiveness and weight, that short syllables mixed with long may seem to run but short syllables continued in unbroken succession seem to bound, that long syllables are more suited to grave subjects and that statements of fact require slower and more modest metre. Whether the specifics of these observations are as true of English as they were of Latin is not clear but the idea of syllable length affecting the energy and pace of a speech is certainly true.

As I have sought to do, Quintilian emphasises that this matters for both prose and for poetry. He also acknowledges that it can be harder to work with rhythm and metre in prose because in that context its use is less explicit (Quintilian 9.4):

> [Cicero] is criticised in some quarters for seeming to want to bind prose down to rhythmical rules ... They attack Cicero, among others, when he says – the thunderbolts of Demosthenes would not have vibrated with so much force if they had not been hurled and driven by rhythm ... But it should be noted that the management of the beats is much more difficult in prose than in verse: first, because verse is usually composed of shorter sentences than prose, second because verse is often working to a uniform rule but prose, unless it is varied, offends by monotony and becomes stilted ...

Whatever the practical difficulties of doing so in prose, the great Roman orator Cicero considered rhythm and metre essential parts of rhetorical art. Indeed, in his book, *The Orator*, Cicero (6.70) unfavourably compares poets and orators, holding orators have greater freedom to play with rhythm and metre:

> For the poet is very near akin to the orator, being somewhat more restricted in his rhythms, though freer in his choice of words, but in many of his methods of ornament his fellow and almost his equal.

We may now raise an eyebrow on seeing Cicero's concession to the poet of near equality to the skill of the orator – to think that there was a time when there was a class of wordsmiths considered to have a finer appreciation of how to play with words than poets! Yet our surprise is itself revealing. It shows how, since Cicero's time, we have limited our appreciation of what can be done with words outside of verse. Shakespeare's understanding is closer to Cicero's own.

Summary: Rhythm, metre and word order

1   There are expectations about word order and where and on which word stress should fall.

2   That is true for both verse and prose. With verse, the expectations arise from the rules of the verse form. In prose, the expectations arise from custom, grammar and the way words relate to mental models we have the about world (e.g., that cause is followed by effect).

3   Those expectations can be used by the author to identify points of emphasis, themes, or create or convey emotional or mental states. They can be used both by working with the expectations and by doing something unexpected.

4   For performance the value of this knowledge lies in looking out for unexpected word order or rhythm and asking why this has been done. And in looking to the places that we would expect important matters to be found (e.g., beginnings and endings, words where the stress falls, etc).

The central importance of imagery

One set of rhetorical techniques is particularly prominent in rhetorical theory and valuable for guiding performance, transformations: Words are replaced with different, more evocative ones; ideas are replaced with analogous ones that bring out important comparisons; parts are made to stand for the whole because the thematic aspect is clearest in the part; and so on. Although these techniques all have in common some kind of transformation the effects they produce vary wildly. In this category, in particular, the same rhetorical technique may be deployed for emotional significance, to indicate structure, or to identify theme.

Chief among these transformations is metaphor; both for variety and for power of effect it has no compare. A metaphor is a transformation by analogy, it is the application of an image or idea to something to which it cannot literally apply but which brings out something by the figure of it. Consider Romeo's line on seeing Juliet, seeming dead:

> Death, that hath suck'd the honey of thy breath,
> Hath had no power yet upon thy beauty:

(RJ 5.3)

Here there are multiple such transformations: Death is first transformed into a creature, a bird or bee perhaps, that sucks the nectar from the flower. Living breath is become sweet as honey. Breath is transformed and made to stand for life itself. Death then becomes a conquering army that has not yet seized Juliet's beauty, which is itself transformed into territory that will be conquered and laid waste. In these transformations lie not just beauty but meaning. At once we have the idea of life as sweet, of life as something that is stolen away, of life as something that has been, here at least, snatched away by an unwelcome conqueror. Not bad for two lines and twenty syllables.

Classical guidance

Because transformations are so powerful and so widely applicable, there is extensive discussion of the theory behind their use in the classical texts on rhetoric. Cicero, in *The Orator*, puts into the mouth of the historical figure of Crassus[24] (considered by Cicero the greatest orator apart from himself), an explanation of how, when and why to use metaphor. That explanation is worth summarising because it unpicks why metaphor is considered so desirable by rhetoric.

Crassus begins by explaining that although it is important to speak clearly and properly, so that we are understood and not mocked for our strange speech, that is not what gains the orator praise and admiration. Speaking ornately – in a style distinctive yet straightforward, showing brilliance in thought and language – this is the mark of the great orator. One must be careful though not to exceed good taste. This exhortation to brilliance is followed by a clear warning against excessive style, which cloys.[25] Rhetorical techniques are like salt and spice to the stew, a little gives flavour and interest to the meal, too much ruins it. Striking the balance isn't easy. Yet, according to Crassus, you must try because it is through rhetorical technique that we bring variety, light and shade, into the speech and this is what maintains the audience's interest.

Crassus then explains that the chief significance of style is in the arousing of emotion and the greatest achievement of eloquence is in amplifying and adorning that which one speaks about. In achieving these goals Crassus advises that opportunity is to be found both in individual words and also in their combination; therefore, the orator should consider words individually first and only then in combination.

In choosing individual words, while avoiding cliché, one should use richly expressive language. Doing so relies on a trained ear that recognises the richness and calls for the possession of a decent vocabulary to supply options. There are three approaches to creating the desired eloquence:

1   One can use unusual or little encountered words but Crassus advises us to do so sparingly.

2   We can use new coined words but, again, we should do so only occasionally. Crassus advises creating them by combining known words.[26]

3   Finally, we can use metaphor and this, according to Crassus, is a technique one may use frequently.

The three uses of metaphor

Three uses are given by Crassus for metaphor: clarifying ideas, revealing hidden connections and brevity of expression.

1   According to Crassus metaphor should clarify meaning by transferring words on the basis of the sought-for similarity e.g., 'the sea shudders' conveys the image of a person with a chill running across her back.

2   Metaphor may also be used to communicate some secret meaning, for example if we say that someone 'builds a fortress with deceit' we convey by the choice of image not just that they lie but that their lies are intended to protect them.

3   Sometimes they are a way of expressing something briefly, e.g., 'the weapon flees his hand.' Here the weapon is not literally running away but we quickly grasp the idea that the sword is not the wielder's to command but rebellious to his wishes.

The threefold value of metaphors

Cicero also has Crassus explain the threefold value of metaphors to the orator. The first is that is that the use of metaphors makes the orator appear ingenious for having found the connection. Useful to note if you ever plan to give a speech but of little interest to us for performance. It is the second and third that explain the importance of metaphor to characterisation in performance:

Clarification and revelation

The second value given to metaphor by Crassus relies on the three practical effects to which metaphors may be put: clarifying, revealing and doing so briefly. These mean that metaphors allow the speaker to say something additional without the train of thought being lost. This is, unsurprisingly, essential to the dramatist's art and Shakespeare makes vast use of its power to illustrate and amplify characters' mental and emotional states, as well as to bring out dramatic themes. We have seen this in action in the example from *Romeo and Juliet* above (see page 142 and following).

Arousing emotion through appeal to the senses

Cicero has already had Crassus speak of the special power of metaphor to arouse emotion. Cicero even has Crassus state that this is the *purpose* of metaphor. That metaphor has this power is a common theme in rhetorical manuals and there it is connected to the third advantage that metaphor offers, namely that it appeals to the senses and especially sight, the sharpest sense. Metaphor, Cicero has Crassus tell us, is designed to move the feelings because it makes things distinctive and places them vividly before the eye. Again, we have already seen this in the example of Romeo's words above (see page 142 and following). The image that Romeo chooses for life is honey and it is, therefore, an image that allows us to see the golden liquid and taste the sweetness of life, it turns an abstract idea into something visible, tangible. Modern neuroscience has confirmed that when we are presented with images that appeal to the senses, the parts of our brains that are associated with those senses fire. The figurative becomes the literal in our brains.[27]

Making the abstract real

What this third advantage tells us is that not all images are equal. As Quintilian explains a simile or metaphor can clarify but, what is presented for the sake of clarifying something must be clearer than what it clarifies. If I try to explain how I stand in relation to my family, I can say that I am the Sun around which my wife, the Earth, revolves and around her, moons, my children. Such a metaphor has explanatory force, perhaps hinting at a slightly stultifying home life, but it doesn't generate or communicate any emotional power. The images that do so are the ones that appeal to the senses because they immediately generate a physical response in the audience. This is why Cicero tells us not only that metaphor's purpose is to arouse emotion but also that it does so most powerfully and effectively by speaking to the senses. Because a metaphor allows us to make a transformation it allows us to turn abstract ideas and thoughts into physical sensations. In this way, emotionally important but abstract ideas like love, hatred, desire, can become embodied.

An excellent example of Shakespeare applying this theory is found in *The Merchant of Venice*, albeit using simile rather than metaphor, when Portia seeks to generate pity and explain the significance of mercy:

> The quality of mercy is not strain'd,
> It droppeth as the gentle rain from heaven
> Upon the place beneath:
>
> *(MV 4.1)*

The comparison of mercy with the image of gentle rain is powerful precisely because the audience can immediately recall the physical sensation of cooling rain on a hot day. The relief that is inherent in the abstract nature of mercy is made real. Martin Luther King employed similar imagery in his 'I Have A Dream' speech. Seeking to convey the oppression of segregation in the southern states of America he spoke of Mississippi metaphorically:

I have a dream that one day even the state of Mississippi, a desert state, sweltering with the heat of injustice and oppression, will be transformed into an oasis of freedom and justice.

Again, that image immediately conveys a physical impression of the impact of the abstract concept of equal rights for all people. It is, as a result, better able to stir the emotions. Note that the important aspect is the appeal to the senses. In neither case would it be suggested that mercy was simply like feeling cooled when a bit hot, or the nature of the oppression akin to simply being sweaty on a humid day. The transformation or comparison works not because of the equality of image to concept but because the image makes the abstract concept real and, most importantly, felt. Again and again in Shakespeare's works it is images of these kinds he calls on:

> If not, why, in a moment look to see
> The blind and bloody soldier with foul hand
> Defile the locks of your shrill-shrieking daughters;
> Your fathers taken by the silver beards,
> And their most reverend heads dash'd to the walls,
>
> (H5 3.3)

The imagery that Henry deploys to persuade the men of Harfleur to surrender is visual, tactile and audible. The hands are sticky with blood, the hair of the daughters is pulled, they shriek and their mothers howl, their fathers' beards are turned red with blood and we hear the knock as they are smashed against the walls. We see the consequences of resisting Henry set before us.

As the author of *Rhetorica Ad Herrenium* explains, such imagery

. . . is very useful in amplifying a matter and basing on it an appeal to pity, for it sets forth the whole incident and virtually brings it before our eyes.

'. . . aut quia significantius est . . .'

In performance, therefore, Shakespeare's metaphors are not to be treated idly. They are not simply imagery for imagery's sake, to make different an otherwise dull scene. Or at least, not only that. As

Quintilian explains in *Institutes of Oratory*, we use metaphor out
of necessity, or to decorate or because the choice of metaphor is
significant – '. . . *aut quia significantius est* . . .'.[28] Significant because
it makes our meaning clearer. The choice of image is intended to
build the scenery, to make the abstract real and to reveal the
crucially important aspect of the idea that is being conveyed by
metaphor.

Mark the change

The significance of imagery is particularly apparent when
Shakespeare has a character change or correct the image.[29] It is as if
at such points Shakespeare is saying, the image matters and that is
something that the character is conscious of and so should you be.
Take this example from Hamlet:

> O, that this too too solid flesh would melt
> Thaw and resolve itself into a dew!
>
> (*Ham* 1.2)

Hamlet is speaking after Claudius has denied his request to leave
for Wittenberg, forcing him to remain and confront the vision of his
mother and his uncle, now husband and wife. He begins, in the first
line, with an image of his flesh melting. What melts? Ice? A candle?
It could be either but the distinction matters because in one image,
that of ice melting, Hamlet thinks himself frozen to begin with and
the heat brings him up to room temperature, to the temperature of
normal people. In the other, the candle-wax melting, Hamlet is
normal to begin with but is being consumed by great heat.
Accordingly, which of the two images Hamlet has in mind tells us
something about where Hamlet thinks he starts from. But then the
second line immediately, in its first word, shifts sense. Now he is
thawing, as ice would do but not a candle. That suggests that
Hamlet recognised the ambiguity in the image of the first line and
sought to clarify it by saying that he thought himself cold to begin
with and not so much melting as thawing. However, with this
clarification the image becomes in need of further clarification, it is
not an injunction simply to feel, to unfreeze, but to go further, to
lose himself, to evaporate.

The confusion, the attempt to clarify, over the course of the two
lines reflects Hamlet's own troubled mental state. It is no coincidence
that the first line ends with one image 'melt' and then immediately
clarifies itself in the first word of the second sentence. We have
already seen in the discussion of rhythm and metre, the importance
given to endings and beginnings of lines. This is Hamlet noting his
own confused thinking, seeking to clarify it, but in doing so moving
through different emotions with incredible rapidity. This sense of
unsettled thought, touching on an idea and immediately refining it
is then present throughout the rest of the soliloquy, see for example:

> That it should come to this!
> But two months dead – nay, not so much, not two –
>
> *(Ham* 1.2)

Consideration of the choice of metaphor has guided us to questions
that open up Hamlet's inner thoughts. It has also given us moments
of reflection within the lines. The actor can show the change of
thought in his or her performance. Shakespeare has helped us to do
so by placing the point of the change of thought at a natural break,
that between end of line and start of new one.

Too much, too much

Cicero warns us that these advantages are undone by the use of
metaphors that jar. He has Crassus give us the examples of using big
images for small ideas or vice versa, or the use of implausible images.
At the same time, it is clear that a striking image – one that requires
a little thought to understand – can be powerful precisely because
the listener must engage with it to appreciate it. Thomas Wilson
makes this point in the second book of the *Arte of Rhetorique*:

> Vehemence of language helps the matter forward better when
> more is gathered by thinking than if the thing spoken of had
> been set in plain words . . . . When we say that a woman spits
> fire, we understand immediately that she is a devil.[30]

Naturally the skill lies in knowing when one is producing a jarring
image or simply a striking one.

Catachresis

Catachresis is the use of a startling metaphor, one where there is perhaps not a natural connection between the two things compared.[31] It is all the more noticeable for that and, perhaps, reflects the disturbed state of mind of the speaker.

> Or to take arms against a sea of troubles
> And by opposing end them.
>
> *(Ham* 3.1)

>   I do not ask you much,
> I beg cold comfort;
>
>   *(KJ* 5.7)

>   . . . methinks he
> hath no drowning mark upon him; his complexion is
> perfect gallows.
>
>   *(Tem* 1.1)

Let the part stand for the whole

A particular kind of metaphor is called 'synecdoche'. This is where the metaphorical comparison involves treating the whole of a thing as represented by a part. There are numerous examples in Shakespeare:

> Friends, Romans, Countrymen, lend me your ears.
>
>   *(JC* 3.2)

> Take thy face hence.
>
>   *(Mac* 4.3)

As Quintilian explains:

What I have said above applies perhaps with even greater force to synecdoche. For while metaphor is designed to move the feelings, give special distinction to things and place them vividly

before the eye, synecdoche has the power to give variety to our
language by making us realise many things from one, the whole
from a part, the genus from a species, things which follow from
things which have preceded; or, on the other hand, the whole
procedure may be reversed. It may, however, be more freely
employed by poets than by orators.

Synecdoche is a particularly important form of metaphor. It is
used by Shakespeare to describe the character through choosing
those aspects that are the most important for the drama purpose. It
can also be used as a figure of emphasis in which a person is taken
to be represented by one quality, the one to which the speaker
wishes to draw attention:

Farewell fair cruelty

(TN 1.5)

Shrug'st thou, malice?

(Tem 1.2)

Symbolism

Another kind of metaphor is where one concept is made to stand
for another; as where an invention is indicated by its inventor or
a thing possessed by its possessor. Quintilian gives the example,
'sixty thousand were killed by Hannibal at Cannae.' We do not
mean in saying so that Hannibal did the killing but rather that
Hannibal stands as a reference for the army he commanded. This
kind of metaphor is called *metonymy* and one can see it is akin to
synecdoche.

Metonymy's power comes from the symbolism that it permits.
Like *synecdoche* it allows an author to throw the spotlight on the
aspects of the thing described that are dramatically important. It is
as if, through the device, the author is saying – or having the
character say – this is how I see things, no other element matters. So
it is in Hamlet's description of what followed on his father's death,
where the incestuous sheets stand for the marriage of his mother to
Claudius:

O most wicked speed! To post
With such dexterity to incestuous sheets!

(Ham 1.2)

We see it in use in the sonnets, where true love is compared to the north star:

It is the star to every wand'ring bark,
Whose worth's unknown, although his height be taken.

(Son 116)

Summary

1   Transformations such as metaphor allow Shakespeare to bring out, beautifully, efficiently, and strikingly, important aspects of the drama.

2   Because they allow Shakespeare to convert abstract ideas into physical things transformations can be powerful sources of emotional power.

3   This power and versatility is well known to rhetoric and, unsurprisingly, to Shakespeare. In performance, therefore, the choice of imagery should never be overlooked. It is deliberate and significant.

Amplification

For Thomas Wilson (1560: 132) the chief rhetorical technique was amplification.

Among the figures of rhetoric there is none that so much helps an oration and beautifies the same with delightful ornament as does Amplification. For if we aim to make our story more vehement, more pleasant or well storied with variety, it is in amplification that we must seek help, where help is chiefly to be had and not elsewhere.[32]

The chief value of amplification is the moving of emotions. As Wilson explains we call on it to create, 'a stirring of the mind, either to desire or to detest and loathe a thing more vehemently than by nature we are wont to do'.

There are a number of methods of amplification. We can divide them into two groups. Those that amplify by altering the original and those that amplify by making a comparison of some kind.

Alterations

Among the techniques of amplification that achieve their effect by alteration of words are *exaggeration*, *congeries* and *pleonasm*.

Exaggeration

Exaggeration is changing a word to amplify the meaning. In the *Arte of Rhetorique*, Thomas Wilson describes it as the first form of amplification: Where we wish to amplify matters we choose a greater word, where we wish to diminish, a lesser. Wilson (1560: 139) gives the following example:

> When I say a man is beaten, to say instead that he is slain. When I call a naughty fellow a thief or hangman when he is not known as such.[33]

Wilson explains that we can make the amplification seem even greater by correcting our sentence as we speak it, adding ever greater exaggeration.[34] He uses the image of a staircase to explain the technique, 'we shall seem as though we went up the stairs not only to the top of a thing but above the top.' We can see this technique at play in the opening lines of Sonnet 129 (where it is combined with *comma* and *congeries* to further suggest the ever more excited nature of the poet):

> Th' expense of spirit in a waste of shame
> Is lust in action; and till action, lust
> Is perjured, murd'rous, bloody, full of blame,
> Savage, extreme, rude, cruel, not to trust,

> (*Son* 129)

We see it here in King Richard's exhortation to his army:

> Remember whom you are to cope withal:
> A sort of vagabonds, rascals, and runaways,
> A scum of Bretons and base lackey peasants,
> Whom their o'ercloyed country vomits forth

> (*R3* 5.3)

Congeries

This piling up of adjectives or nouns seen in both these examples of *exaggeration* is an example of the rhetorical technique called *congeries*, which simply means heaping. There is a spontaneity evoked by such heapings because where one word should do the character finds in the saying of that word too little for her meaning and is driven on to find another, better word. That driving on not only suggests spontaneity but indicates the rising of passions.

For our purpose in performance the significance of this rhetorical technique is again to focus on the importance of the particular image chosen by Shakespeare for the character. How does the image vary from the facts? Why does the character choose to amplify matters or diminish them? And what aspect of the act is being picked out for amplification or diminishment?

Pleonasm

Pleonasm is the immediate repetition of an idea in different words, as when we say that something is available free, gratis and for nothing. It is a form of amplification, a version of exaggeration where to ram home the point of the amplification the author doubles down on the alternatives.

Shakespeare can be seen using *pleonasm* for characters who are searching for ways to understand their own state, perhaps marvelling at it, trying to find the right way to express it:

> Then comes my fit again. I had else been perfect;
> Whole as the marble, founded as the rock,
> As broad and general as the casing air:
> But now I am cabin'd, cribb'd, confined, bound in
> To saucy doubts and fears. But Banquo's safe?

> (*Mac* 3.4)

How weary, stale, flat, and unprofitable
Seem to me all the uses of this world!
Fie on't, ah fie, 'tis an unweeded garden
That grows to seed,

(*Ham* 1.2)

The examples above are in verse. When we meet it in prose, however, it is often in the mouths of clowns who by their verbiage show their minds cluttered or reveal themselves to know the principle of rhetorical copiousness but without the ear to handle it wisely.

But, masters, here are your parts, and I am to entreat you, request you, and desire you, to con them by tomorrow night; and meet me in the palace wood, a mile without the town, by moonlight;

(*MND* 1.2)

Where, I mean, I did encounter that obscene and most preposterous event that draweth from my snow-white pen the ebon-coloured ink, which here thou viewest, beholdest, surveyest, or seest.

(*LLL* 1.1)

The last example is from a letter written by Don Armado, who is taken by Shakespeare to be a fine example of those that understand the theory of rhetoric but do not have the ear for its practice. He is frequently to be found following the precepts by rote and without judgment. The result is an embarrassment.

Comparisons

The other form of amplification works through the making of comparisons. The chief of these comparative techniques is metaphor in all its forms, which we discuss above, but to it we may add *addition*, *comparison* and *simile*.

Addition

Addition is where we amplify by adding to the matter under discussion a reference to something that is the greatest example of that thing. Thomas Wilson gives this as his second form of amplification and his examples are all of the form – there is no greater thing than this except X, which is the greatest of them all. The amplification works by tying the thing discussed to a concrete example. It does not matter if the listener agrees that the concrete example is the best. Even if they disagree then, mentally, they are already making comparisons of the kind that the speaker wants them to make. It is not much met in Shakespeare.

Comparison

Comparison takes a lesser example and asks the hearer to consider it first and then compares it to the thing actually being discussed and asks the hearer to appreciate how much greater their reaction must be to this compared to the first.

Wilson calls this the third form of amplification and gives an example from Cicero's speeches against Catiline where he asks, 'If my servants fear me as the citizens of Rome fear you, I should quit my house.' The implication being that Catiline should quit Rome. As Wilson explains:

> By using the least first, this sentence is increased: few servants are compared with all the citizenry, slaves compared with free men, Cicero, their master, compared with Catiline, the traitor, and Cicero's house compared with Rome.

An example can be found from Brutus in *Julius Caesar* 4.2:

> Judge me, you gods; wrong I mine enemies?
> And if not so, how should I wrong a brother?

Another example is to be found in *Coriolanus* 3.2 when the hero is asked to repent to the citizens of Rome.

> I cannot do it to the gods,
> Must I then do't to them?

Another example is Jaques' speech in *As You Like It*:

> All the world's a stage,
> And all the men and women merely players;

They have their exits and their entrances;
And one man in his time plays many parts,
His acts being seven ages.

(AYL 2.7)

The comparison may be simpler and look to contraries. Such comparisons seek to make a dark outline starker by setting it against a white background or vice versa.

My mistress' eyes are nothing like the sun;
Coral is far more red than her lips' red;
If snow be white, why then her breasts are dun;
If hairs be wires, black wires grow on her head.

(Son 130)

Simile

Similes are where we say one thing is like another. They are a common form of comparison and allow significant imagery to be introduced (see page 144 and following above). In *Rhetorica Ad Herrenium* (3.49) the author suggests that similes are particularly useful for praise or censure – as when we say a hero entered combat like a bull or of someone that he glides through the forum like a serpent. Perhaps for that reason *simile* is well suited to the insult.

This woman's an easy glove, my lord, she goes off and on at pleasure.

(AW 5.3)

Structures of emotion

The discussion of the general concepts of rhythm and metre, and of metaphor has shown how Style may contribute emotional meaning through technique. In the course of the discussion we looked at the specific use of repetition of words to alter the rhythm and metre to achieve particular emotional effects and at techniques of amplification. There are many other ways of conveying emotion through technique than this. Below I consider five: *Comma*, *Aposiopesis*, *Paralepsis*, *Metanoia* and *Apostrophe*.

Drumbeats

Comma is when you take single words and set them apart by pauses in staccato speech. Quintilian gives the following examples:

> By your vigour, voice, looks you have terrified your adversaries. You have destroyed your enemies by jealousy, injuries, influence, perfidy.

The rhythm that this creates allows for different forms of verbal violence. On the one hand, where the list comes first, one can seem to be gathering up the storm to hurl at one's opponent, on the other, where we end with the list, it can seem like a series of swift, sharp jabs. Either way the effect is forceful, violent:

> I am very proud, revengeful, ambitious, with more offences at my beck than I have thoughts to put them in, imagination to give them shape, or time to act them in.
>
> *(Ham 3.1)*

This line is spoken by Hamlet in his confrontation with Ophelia. The initial urgency of the line contrasts with the earlier passages in their dialogue in this scene where Hamlet uses more complex rhetorical techniques. By this point in the scene arguably the emotions are beginning to overcome his schooled wit and he is falling into the grip of his passions. The list of offences, given as a *comma* are like whiplashes against Hamlet's own back. Compare and contrast the rhythm and sound of the line with a conjunction added to the list (shown in bold):

> I am very proud, revengeful, **and** ambitious, with more offences at my beck than I have thoughts to put them in, imagination to give them shape, or time to act them in.

The emotional effect is different, now the list appears more considered because it seems as if Hamlet knows the list in advance and where it ends. Whereas in the original, these are things bubbling spontaneously out of Hamlet's excited mind.

Dramatic pauses

Aposiopesis is a sudden breaking off mid-speech. Commonly we do so because we are overcome by emotion. Another reason for doing so is that we realise that the thing we are about to say ought not to be said either as a matter of discretion or because silence is more eloquent since it lets the imagination of the listener will fill in the blank. In this example from Shakespeare both reasons are at play:

> No, you unnatural hags,
> I will have such revenges on you both,
> That all the world shall – I will do such things, –
> What they are, yet I know not: but they shall be
> The terrors of the earth.
>
> (*KL* 2.4)

Almost invariably in Shakespeare the use of *aposiopesis* indicates that the character is in the grip of strong emotions, barely containable but that the character fears to give full vent to for fear that all control will be lost.

> Bear with me;
> My heart is in the coffin there with Caesar,
> And I must pause till it come back to me.
>
> (*JC* 3.2)

> Must I remember? Why, she would hang on him
> As if increase of appetite had grown
> By what it fed on. And yet within a month
> (Let me not think on't – Frailty, thy name is Woman)
>
> (*Ham* 1.2)

In *Richard III*, *aposiopesis* signals how Richard has been unnerved by news of Richmond and Buckingham's advance, as he breaks off to chide Catesby for not acting at once on his orders.

RICHARD
> Some light-foot friend post to the Duke of Norfolk:
> Ratcliffe, thyself – or Catesby. Where is he?

CATESBY
  Here, my good lord.
RICHARD   Catesby, fly to the Duke.
CATESBY
  I will, my lord, with all convenient haste.
RICHARD
  Ratcliffe, come hither. Post thou to Salisbury
  When thou comest thither –
  [*To* CATESBY]   Dull, unmindful villain,
  Whystay'st thou here, and go'st not to the duke?

                                        (*R3* 4.4)

Denials

Paralepsis is to call attention to something by specifically saying you
will not mention it. *Rhetorica ad Herrenium* (4.27) explains its
value thus:

> This figure is useful if employed in a matter which is not pertinent
> to call specifically to the attention of others, because there is
> advantage in making only an indirect reference to it, or because
> the direct reference would be tedious or undignified, or cannot
> be made clear, or can easily be refuted. As a result, it is of greater
> advantage to create a suspicion by paralepsis than to insist
> directly on a statement that is refutable.

In recent years it has been much beloved of President Trump.
Speaking of North Korean leader Kim Jong-un:

> Why would Kim Jong-un insult me by calling me 'old', when I
> would NEVER call him 'short and fat'?

It is clear why President Trump employs the figure. The question
that arises where Shakespeare has a character do so is which of
these reasons applies in that scene. Is it simply a sly dig? Or is it
thought in some way undignified and, if so, why? Antony uses it
so he may raise the point without appearing to thrust it onto the
mob – letting them draw it from him.

Have patience, gentle friends, I must not read it.
It is not meet you know how Caesar loved you.
You are not wood, you are not stones, but men:
And being men, hearing the will of Caesar,
It will inflame you, it will make you mad.
'Tis good you know not that you are his heirs,
For if you should, O what would come of it?

(*JC* 3.2)

Corrections

Metanoia or *epanorthosis* is the retraction of what was first said
and its replacement with something deemed more suitable. A
deliberate correction serves to create the impression of spontaneity:
as if the speaker is not simply delivering a pre-prepared speech but
considering the matter in the moment and engaging with it as she
speaks. As Quintilian (9.2.59) explains:

> For by making our speech appear plain and unstudied, they
> render us objects of less suspicion to the judge.

Shakespeare uses it to create precisely that sense of spontaneity

> . . . thence I have follow'd it,
> Or it hath drawn me rather.

(*Tem* 1.2)

That correction shows Ferdinand's uncertainty as to what has
happened and draws attention to the confusing state of affairs and
to Ferdinand's own state of confusion. In the next example its use is
designed to show that Henry is not seducing Katherine using a pre-
prepared speech but saying something he genuinely believes and
that he is considering and refining as he expresses it.

> . . . but a good heart, Kate, is the sun and the
> moon; or, rather, the sun, and not the moon; for it
> shines bright and never changes, but keeps his
> course truly.

(*H5* 5.2)

The speaker's apparent engagement with the issue will prompt the audience's own: was the speaker right the first time round or right now in how they put matters? It also has the advantage of being unexpected, which draws the listeners' attention to the point being discussed.

> Come not within these doors; within this roof
> The enemy of all your graces lives.
> Your brother, no, no brother; yet the son –
> Yet not the son, I will not call him son –
> Of him I was about to call his father,
> Hath heard your praises,
>
> (*AYL* 2.3)

Finally, by setting up a contrast between that word first chosen and the one finally rested on you draw attention to the contrast. As the *Rhetorica Ad Herennium* (3.26) puts it:

> The thought is such that in rendering it by an ordinary word you seem to have expressed it rather feebly, but having come to a choicer word you make the thought more striking. But if you had at once arrived at this word, the grace neither of the thought nor of the word would have been noticed.

Sometimes, that emphatic correction is intended as a rebuke or to pick up on the difference in thinking between one character and another:

> Seems, madam? Nay, it is. I know not 'seems'.
>
> (*Ham* 1.2)

Of course, it can also be used for humour, as in this threat, which is turned instead into an insult:

> You are not worth another word, else I'd call you knave.
>
> (*AW* 2.3)

Interrogation

Apostrophe is a direct questioning of a person or place or object. It allows the speaker immediately and effectively to convey grief or indignation: In a speech directed as if towards a specific person the challenges made or the emotional pleas within it are no longer abstract, they have become personal. That allows the audience to see and feel those challenges and appeals directly. They are given the chance to see the scene rather than having to infer it. Its use is explained in *Rhetorica ad Herrenium* (3.15) thus:

> If we use Apostrophe in its proper place, sparingly, and when the importance of the subject seems to demand it, we shall instil in the hearer as much indignation as we desire.

Hamlet uses it when confronting Gertrude:

> Frailty, thy name is woman
>
> (*Ham* 1.2)

It is also frequently used by characters to berate or encourage themselves, as Marc Antony does when viewing Caesar's murdered body.

> That I did love thee, Caesar, O 'tis true:
> If then thy spirit look upon us now,
> Shall it not grieve thee dearer than thy death
> To see thy Antony making his peace,
> Shaking the bloody fingers of thy foes?
> Most noble in the presence of thy corse,
>
> (*JC* 3.1)

Or in *Cymbeline* when Iachimo summons courage before Imogen:

> If she be furnish'd with a mind so rare,
> She is alone the Arabian bird, and I
> Have lost the wager. Boldness be my friend!
> Arm me, audacity, from head to foot!
> Or, like the Parthian, I shall flying fight;
> Rather directly fly.
>
> (*Cym* 1.6)

Occasionally, *apostrophe* is the means by which Shakespeare is able to have a character express his thoughts out loud:

Come, seeling night,
Scarf up the tender eye of pitiful day
And with thy bloody and invisible hand
Cancel and tear to pieces that great bond
Which keeps me pale.

(*Mac* 3.2)

17

Structures of thought

The second of our general categories are those techniques that are intended to assist with creating the right mental structures in the listener. Within this category are two sub-categories: those techniques that try to ensure that our listener is attentive, and those techniques that try to ensure our listener is able to follow along with the argument.

Active vs passive

An orator's audience inherently tends to the passive. Generally, they sit and wait for the speaker's words. In contrast, in a conversation both parties are necessarily involved, waiting for the pause that indicates it is the next person's turn to speak and quailing when, instead, a silence falls. This inherent passivity is dangerous for the speaker, and the playwright, who may lose the attention of the audience in it. As a counter, rhetoric offers a number of techniques whose purpose is to turn the audience back to an active mode of listening – by thrusting a question at them or by unexpectedly altering the course of the speech or by appearing to show a conversation in mid-flow.

Questions

Using the question form as a rhetorical technique for expressing oneself is well known. If a question is made of you then – even knowing that no answer is needed – you will sit up and pay attention. People hate unresolved questions and wait eagerly to hear them answered. As *Rhetorica Ad Herrenium* (3.16) explains:

> This figure is exceedingly well adapted to a conversational style, and both by its stylistic grace and the anticipation of the reasons, holds the hearer's attention.

As well as making the expression more active and engaging, posing a thought as a question allows one to express it with a colouring of emotion. That is well illustrated by the following two examples, where it is used by Shakespeare first to have Laertes express horror and sadness and disbelief, and second by Lady Macbeth to show anger and contempt:

> O heavens, is't possible a young maid's wits
> Should be as mortal as a poor man's life?
>
> *(Ham 4.5)*

>   Was the hope drunk
> Wherein you dress'd yourself? Hath it slept since?
> And wakes it now, to look so green and pale,
> At what it did so freely? From this time
> Such I account thy love. Art thou afear'd
> To be the same in thine own act and valour,
> As thou art in desire?
>
> *(Mac 1.7)*

Assertion by denial: Litotes

Litotes is the assertion of something by the denial of its opposite. It is a rhetorical technique frequently encountered among certain of the English who, on being asked, 'how are you?' Reply, 'not bad.' Why embrace this approach rather than simply making the point one wants to make? Perhaps it is embarrassing to make that point. One doesn't want to appear too enthusiastic, too committed to the idea. We see that in this modern example:

> But the Royal Navy has immediately attacked the U-boats, and is hunting them night and day, I will not say without

mercy – because God forbid we should ever part company
with that – but at any rate with zeal and not altogether without
relish.

(Winston Churchill, Radio Address,
1 October 1939)

Sometimes it is used to suggest a common understanding with the
listener. The element of understatement in litotes relies on the idea
that the listener recognises that what is being stated does not reflect
the true position.

> He hath not fail'd to pester us with message,
> Importing the surrender of those lands.

(Ham 1.2)

Sometimes it is used to create a sense of anticipation by setting up a
question and then by denying that one of several potential answers
is the right one. The anticipation keeps the audience's attention and
focuses it on the speaker's answer. Hearing good answers voiced
and rejected, there is a native desire to hear the 'true' answer.[1]
Isabella uses it in *Measure for Measure* when trying to persuade
Angelo to show mercy.

> No ceremony that to great ones 'longs,
> Not the king's crown, nor the deputed sword,
> The marshal's truncheon, nor the judge's robe,
> Become them with one half so good a grace
> As mercy does.

(MM 2.2)

Road maps

In considering how to stir the emotions we looked at repetitions
of a single word or phrase in a single sentence. Now we turn to
the repetition of words or phrases at the beginning of adjoining
sentences, *anaphora*, *epistrophe*, and *symploce*. The distinction
between repetition within a sentence and across them might seem
minor but the effect is markedly different. Now the repetition is
less concerned with conveying emotion and more about making

the structure of the speech clearer and highlighting themes in the argument.

Anaphora

Anaphora occurs where the first word or words of the phrase are repeated with each successive phrase.

The use of *anaphora* serves to link the phrases together. That is useful where the speaker wants to indicate that all the different phrases are connected to one idea. It might, for example, be used for a succession of examples that are said to be illustrations of, or exemplifications of, the point made at the outset. As well as this sign-posting function, the repetition of the phrases creates a drumbeat of emphasis, and thus creates a sense of purpose and of power. Each starting phrase serves as the ring of a hammer's blow. *Rhetorica Ad Herrenium* says of it, 'this figure not only has much charm but also impressiveness and vigour in highest degree'. It may be used to indicate an amplification is coming – the first phrase starting with the smallest example and working its way up to the crescendo. Often it is a conscious and considered rhetorical technique, in the sense that the audience understands that the orator knows they are using *anaphora* because the orator must be remembering the phrase to repeat it. As a result, it suggests a character in a considered frame of mind, not flustered, not uncertain but confident of their point. We see that here in this moment from *Richard II*, where the king has taken the decision to abdicate:

> With mine own tears I wash away my balm,
> With mine own hands I give away my crown,
> With mine own breath release all duty's rites:
> All pomp and majesty I do forswear

(R2 4.1)

Sometimes the repeated word is picked up from what has gone before and then the reason for the repetition is not considered use of stylistic technique but rather that the character is unable to let that particular word go because of its emotional significance. We see that in Constance's repetition of 'gone' in *King John*, which seems to have been prompted by something the messenger she is responding to has said:

Gone to be married? Gone to swear a peace?
False blood to false blood join'd. Gone to be friends?

(KJ 3.1)

Epistrophe

Epistrophe is the sister to *anaphora* and is the repetition of a word or phrase at the end of sentences or passages (where *anaphora* was the repetition at the start).

Epistrophe serves, like its sister, to tie together sentences or passages. It helps a listener to understand that this is linked material, perhaps the examples serving the same point. It can also be used to show that something stays the same while other things change, and so emphasise the unchanging commonality:

... that government of the people, by the people, for the people, shall not perish from the earth.[2]

The repeated phrase serves as a point of emphasis and creates an impression of strength, power and considered thought. In this it is similar to *anaphora* but the placing of the repeated phrase at the end makes it's effect play more subtly on the ear than *anaphora*. The listener is not confronted by the hammer blows but has to wait till the end of each phrase to realise the pattern exists. It is, perhaps, the more insistent and insidious in its power as a result. It is a noticeable feature of insults, but insults where the criticism emerges only after thought. (One thinks of Cyrano de Bergerac composing a poem as he duels – 'And touch you at the final line.') It is a consciously considered rhetorical technique and is, therefore, unlikely to be used by a character in the midst of chaos or uncertainty.

To say nothing, to do nothing, to know nothing, and to have nothing, is to be a great part of your title, which is within a very little of nothing.

(AW 2.4)

I will buy with you, sell with you, talk with you, walk with you, and so following: but I will not eat with you, drink with you, nor pray with you.

(MV 1.3)

Sometimes we see it used by characters who are distressed but are trying to reason themselves back to calmness. Constance in *King John* does this when she tries to justify to herself her hope that she might have misunderstood or misheard the messenger's terrible news by reminding herself that she is prone to unnecessary fears. However, her use, by linking together all the examples of fears, only serves to give an impression of barely controlled hysteria:

> For I am sick and capable of fears,
> Oppress'd with wrongs, and therefore full of fears,
> A widow, husbandless, subject to fears
> A woman, naturally born to fears;
>
> *(KJ* 3.1)

Symploce

Symploce is *anaphora* and *epistrophe* combined: the repetition of a phrase at the beginning of a passage together with repetition of a phrase at the end of a passage. *Symploce* serves similar purposes to *anaphora* and *epistrophe*. It links together parts of a speech to show them all part of a connected idea. However, the multiplication of repetitions now serves to create in the ear a less deliberate air. It can be used to give the impression of someone who's mind is in a whirl, fixed on an idea and circling round and round it.

> That Angelo's forsworn, is it not strange?
> That Angelo's a murder, is't not strange?
> That Angelo is an adulterous thief,
> An hypocrite, a virgin violator,
> Is it not strange and strange?
>
> *(MM* 5.1)

> O, what men dare do! What men may do! What men daily do, not knowing what they do!
>
> *(MA* 4.1)

Summary

1   Audiences have difficulty following arguments. The form makes them inherently passive, just listeners, and this means

they may lose attentiveness. The inability to review or question what has been said means they may lose the thread of the argument. Rhetoric seeks to compensate for both difficulties through Style.

2 Certain structures prompt an active role in the listener, for example, rhetorical questions, or the creation of puzzles for the audience to resolve.

3 Structures in the language can make apparent the structure of an argument. They do so primarily by using repetition to show that passages are connected to an initial idea.

18

Illusions of logic

We come then to the third of the general categories of rhetorical technique – those whose purpose is to give the impression of deep logic or wisdom at work. In considering the previous category, we discussed one of the figures of repetition used by Martin Luther King in his 'I Have A Dream' speech, *anaphora*, where all the sentences begin with the same word or phrase.[1] Its use was, in part, to make clear the structure of the speech by indicating that each of the phrases was connected to the same point. Rhetorical techniques can also be used to give our words the impression of logic itself. Often this is because the techniques structures the words so that they mimic a recognised pattern of reasoning; in other cases it is because a structure or connection in the words is used to suggest that there is also a logical structure or connection in the thoughts.

Stories and ancient wisdom

One of the simplest ways we can give the impression of underlying logic through Stylistic choices is to make our point through the telling of stories, allegories and fables. Aristotle considered this created the impression of logic by mimicking the form of inductive reasoning.[2] That is to say, by telling a story of similar events we give the impression – so it was in the past, so it will be in the future. Or by the cunning of a good allegory (think of the tale of the hare and the tortoise),[3] we give the impression of some deeper wisdom at play because it appears as if there is some idea that is either generalisable to an allegorical form or such a profound truth as to be the subject of ancient story.[4]

That impression of ancient wisdom, of something being true simply because it sounds right, can also be seen in rhetorical techniques that use symmetry as a way of standing in for reason.

Reflections

Consider the following example of symmetry used to imply truth:

> Suit the action to the word, the word to the action,
> (Ham 3.2)

Here, to allow Hamlet to suggest that this is the true, the only, way of acting, Shakespeare has reflected the words in the second half of the sentence back from the first half. This technique, where it is the words that are mirrored, is called *antimetabole*. Another of these symmetrical techniques is called *chiasmus*. Here it is the *idea* in the first half that is reflected back in the second half, though not necessarily in the same words. See this example:

> But, O, what damned minutes tells he o'er
> Who dotes, yet doubts, suspects, yet strongly loves!
> (Oth 3.3)

Antimetabole and *chiasmus* have been responsible for some of the most memorable lines in oratory:

> Ask not what your country can do for you, ask what you can do for your country.
> (John F. Kennedy, Inaugural Address 1961)

> I have wasted time and now doth time waste me.
> (R2 5.5)

The two are often confused because of their obvious parallels. Distinguishing between them is not important for our purpose. What matters is why they are used: The repetition with inversion of the words or ideas suggests, by the symmetry, that there is some form of inherent logic at work in what is said:

The hand that hath made you fair hath made you good:
the goodness that is cheap in beauty makes beauty
brief in goodness

(*MM* 3.1)

That there is not, in fact, any inherent logic is apparent from the
Witches' use of these techniques in *Macbeth* to create a deliberate
paradox:

Fair is foul, and foul is fair
Hover through the fog and filthy air.

(*Mac* 1.1)

That absence of true logic is also unimportant for our purposes.
The character perceives there to be a connection: the dethroned
king, Richard, in his cell sees that his earlier dissolution has led him
to the prison where he languishes. Othello is tormented by the twin
emotions of love and doubt that circle within him at once. Even the
Witches are demonstrating their twisted world view by their
reasoning that black is white, fair is foul.

Shakespeare uses these figures regularly, not only playing with
them, but even commenting on them and their false impression of
logic:

VIOLA
So thou mayst say the king lies by a beggar if a
beggar dwell near him, or the church stands by thy
tabor if thy tabor stand by the church.
FESTE
You have said, sir. To see this age! A sentence is
but a cheverel glove to a good wit: how quickly
the wrong side may be turned outward.

(*TN* 3.1)

Because they look to the logic of the arguments being used these
figures also allow the tensions and emotional reversions of a scene
to be summarised. They do so by the focus that they give to the
existence of the contrast:

My husband lives that Tybalt would have slain
And Tybalt's dead that would have slain my husband.
All this is comfort. Wherefore weep I then?

(RJ 3.2)

For this same lord

I do repent, but heaven hath pleased it so
To punish me with this, and this with me,
That I must be their scourge and minister.
I will bestow him and will answer well
The death I gave him. So again goodnight.
I must be cruel only to be kind.
Thus bad begins and worse remains behind.

(Ham 3.4)

Antithesis or contraries

A similar technique is called, *antithesis* or *contraries*, and is the presentation of two opposites to emphasise, by their contrast, the significance of one or both.

And let my liver rather heat with wine
Than my heart cool with mortifying groans.

(MV 1.1)

These contrasts can be used to create an impression of logic. The two opposing ideas may be presented one after the other so that the one proves the other. An example given by Quintilian is: 'Now how should you expect one who has been hostile to his own interests to be friendly to another's?' *Rhetorica ad Herrenium* advises that this figure be kept brief and confined to a single sentence. It works because it gives force to the reasoning within it[5] by appearing to compel it through the contrast:

It is not only agreeable to the ear on account of its brief and complete rounding off, but by means of the contrary statement it also forcibly proves what the speaker needs to prove and from a statement which is not open to question it draws a thought which is in question, in such a way that the inference cannot be refuted, or can be refuted only with much the greatest difficulty.

Brutus uses this figure of speech in the question he poses to the mob when trying to justify the killing of Caesar:

> Had you rather Caesar were living, and
> die all slaves, than that Caesar were dead, to live
> all freemen? As Caesar loved me, I weep for him;
> as he was fortunate, I rejoice at it; as he was
> valiant, I honour him: but as he was ambitious, I
> slew him.
>
> (*JC* 3.2)

Alliteration and assonance

Another set of rhetorical techniques rely on some connection between the words or phrases to suggest that a logical connection exists between the ideas. *Alliteration* and *assonance* are such techniques.[6] *Alliteration* is the repetition of a common consonant sound, usually at the beginning of words, whilst the words themselves then shift:

> 'Tis safer to be that which we destroy,
> Than by destruction dwell in doubtful joy
>
> (*Mac* 3.2)

> And I have built
> Two chantries, where the sad and solemn priests
> Sing still for Richard's soul
>
> (*H5* 4.1)

The repetition of these consonants is pleasing to the ear but also suggests something deeper at work.[7] The considered use of the same consonant makes the phrase that includes them appear more solid and profound. It is as if the fact that words can be found that share the consonants in this way reflects a deeper, fated truth. So powerful is the effect that phrases that have no meaning beyond their alliteration have sprung into common parlance: 'curiosity killed the cat' is a warning against sticking your nose where it is not needed. Yet there is no reason to attribute this failing to cats in particular. Moreover, as Mark Forsyth points out in *The Elements of Eloquence*, the phrase was originally, 'care killed the cat' – in the sense that overfeeding did so. That at least makes sense to any cat owner. That it has morphed and still retained its seeming profundity is not due to any truth within it. It is due to alliteration.

The power of the sound of words to convey a certain mental sense goes beyond the use of common consonant sounds. Into Cicero's mouth Quintilian puts lessons as to the effect of certain parts of words: Open vowel sounds are said to have something soft about them that indicates the speaker cares more about the subject of his speaking than about the words used. Monosyllables used too often in succession are said to sound harsh, as if the speaker spoke in stops and starts. Yet a succession of long words will make sentences seem heavy and slow. The sound of Latin is not the same as English and the emotional message of any particular combination of sounds may be different from that found in Latin. But the idea that combinations of sounds have their own emotional resonance is the same: 'Full fathom five thy father lies', has, by virtue of its use of alliteration, by the fullness of the repeated FUH and FAH sounds, a profundity that is not to be found in 'Thy father lies thirty feet down', even if the semantic meaning is identical.

In *A Midsummer Night's Dream* Shakespeare again reveals his consciousness of rhetorical technique. He uses overdone alliteration for comic effect in Quince's prologue for the rude mechanicals' play:

Whereat with blade, with bloody blameful blade,
He bravely broach'd his boiling bloody breast;

(*MND* 5.1)

The vowel equivalent of *alliteration* is *assonance* – as in the next example's 'OW' sounds:

Now are our brows bound with victorious wreaths

(*R3* 1.1)

It is considerably harder to spot assonance in Shakespeare, in large part because of the changes in pronunciation over time, to which vowel sounds are more prone than consonants.

If this be error and upon me proved
I never write, nor no man ever loved

(Son 116)

The final couplet of Sonnet 116 no longer rhymes in modern English pronunciation. Did it once? If so, how many other vowel sounds and accompanying assonance are we missing? The difficulties in identifying assonance make it of less interest than alliteration for those seeking to draw on it for performance.

Keep the word but change it

Another way we can use repetition to suggest a connection is to repeat the word but change its form, for example taking it from verb to noun, or adjective to verb. Changes of this kind, i.e., to the case of the word, is called *polyptoton*.

The Greeks are strong, and skilful to their strength, fierce to their skill, and to their fierceness valiant . . .

(TC 1.1)

With eager feeding food doth choke the feeder . . .

(R2 2.1)

Another kind of change is to use words having a common stem and this is called *metabole*:

A little more than kin, and less than kind.

(Ham 1.2)

Using the same word in an altered form highlights the idea that the two ideas can be in opposition to each other and by the connection of the words gives the impression of a connection in the ideas.

. . . society is no comfort
To one not sociable . . .

(Cym 4.2)

The use of words repeated but altered can signal a central dramatic question as, I suggest, in the examples below:

> I am a man
> More sinned against than sinning
>
> (*KL* 3.2)

> The tempter or the tempted, who sins most, hah?
>
> (*MM* 2.2)

> . . . love is not love
> Which alters when it alteration finds,
> Or bends with the remover to remove.
>
> (*Son* 116)

Metabole is often combined with *antithesis* to aid in the sense, invoked by *antithesis*, that something fundamental, some deeper truth, is in play. The way that the words work together compounds the contrast to suggest that the sentiment expressed is recognising a deeper connection.

> Unheedful vows may heedfully be broken
>
> (*TGV* 2.6)

Symmetry

In certain figures the structure of the words used can itself seem to suggest logic is at work. It does so in one of two ways, either by the symmetry of the phrases suggesting that there is some inherent connection or by the overall shape mimicking patterns of argument.

Colon

An example of pattern mimicking is found when we string together three incomplete thoughts to make a whole. A *colon* is a grammatically complete sentence that does not express a whole thought. It is almost never met alone but followed by another that completes the thought. Better yet, the thought is only completed over the course of three cola, because groups of three have a sense of completeness to them.[8] The use of groups of three[9] is called *tricolon*. I give Quintilian's example of a *tricolon* below, with each *cola* separated by a comma.

> *Colon*: 'On the one hand you were helping your enemy.
> Two *cola*: 'On one hand you were helping your enemy, and on the other you were hurting your friend.'
> *Tricolon*: 'You were helping your enemy, you were hurting your friend, and you were not consulting your own best friend.'

The use of the *colon* in the form of *tricolon* as in the last example above mimics the appearance of a logical syllogism, an argument of the form: If A and B, then C. There is, however, in the use of *tricolon* no necessity of logic, it is simply the appearance created by the structure.

Isocolon

An *isocolon* is a clause where the individual phrases, the *cola*, replicate each other in length and structure.[10] As an example, 'While the father met death in battle, the son planned marriage at home.' Another illusion of reason is created by the matching of length in each *cola* – it seems as if there is an essential rightness or connectedness between the two ideas though the connection is only one of length and form of the phrase used to express each. The use of *isocolon* can be extended as in this example:

> What must the king do now? must he submit?
> The king shall do it: must he be deposed?
> The king shall be contented: must he lose
> The name of king? O' God's name, let it go:
> I'll give my jewels for a set of beads,
> My gorgeous palace for a hermitage,
> My gay apparel for an almsman's gown,
> My figured goblets for a dish of wood,
> My sceptre for a palmer's walking staff,
> My subjects for a pair of carved saints
> And my large kingdom for a little grave,

> (*R2* 3.3)

Period

In contrast to the use of *cola*, some thoughts are advantageously expressed by cramming the thought into a single sentence, referred to as a 'period' in the classical texts. *Rhetorica Ad Herrenium* (3.19) suggests that it is particularly suited to the maxim, the contrast and the conclusion. In each case, by the compactness of the expression of the thought the form again suggests the essential rightness of the idea. It gains the appearance of a universal law.

> Serve God, love me and mend.
>
> (*MA* 5.2)

Note again the use of a list of three.

> Friends, Romans, countrymen, lend me your ears:
>
> (*JC* 3.2)

Three is the magic number

As we saw with *tricolon* above, groups of three appear to have a special status. The ear hears a set of three as a complete list. A, B and C. Lists of two things, though perfectly logically possible, do not have that sense of completeness. Instead they suggest choices, two paths that diverge in the wood. So strong is this effect that, when dealing with lists that contain only two items, in order to indicate that they are the complete list – despite there only being two of them – we often foreshadow that fact by a precursor, e.g., 'Both', 'neither'. Since a group of three has the appearance of a complete list it suggests a wholeness of thought or example, whether or not that is so.

> Love all, trust a few,
> Do wrong to none
>
> (*AW* 1.1)

> Be bloody, bold, and resolute.
>
> (*Mac* 4.1)

Equally, as we saw in the discussion of Senator Obama's speech at page 108 and following and his use of multiple 'or' connectors, *polysyndeton*, the expectation that lists will consist of three items allows us to play with that expectation and, in particular, to generate a desire to hear more in order to hear the list completed.

The ending is also the beginning

Another structure that gives the appearance of logic is where the ending of the first part of the phrase is then repeated as the beginning of the next part of the phrase, which in turn has its ending become the beginning of the next phrase. This is called *anadiplosis*. The linking of the phrases by their beginnings and endings audibly connects the thoughts in each part. In doing so it imbues what is said with a sense of logic that it may not otherwise have. It suggests a chain of causation:

> Husband win, win brother,
> Prays, and destroys the prayer; no midway
> 'Twixt these extremes at all.

(AC 3.4)

The effect can be made more noticeable by having the conclusion of the reasoning depart from the pattern, which highlights that there was such a pattern to begin with. As with any ladder effect, it is naturally suited to passages that build to a climax and extended *anadiplosis* is called '*Climax*'.

> The love of wicked men converts to fear;
> That fear to hate, and hate turns one or both
> To worthy danger and deserved death.

(R2 5.1)

Here the use of *anadiplosis* conveys the sense of causal inevitability in Richard's argument. Finishing with a line full of *alliteration* compounds this sense of fatefulness by providing an element connecting the outcomes – danger leading to deserved death.

Refining

The previous examples have shown how, by the structure of what we want to say, we can give an impression of logic. Sometimes, though, we want to show the thought process of the character at work. *Refining* is the term given to describe the way we return to a subject seeming to say something new upon it. We can return by repeating it, not precisely but with changes. Those changes can be to the words, to the delivery or to the treatment of the idea. Returning allows the speaker to dwell on a topic without becoming boring. It also allows the speaker to vary the imagery and examples employed so that the experience of different people may be touched upon. For these reasons, Shakespeare uses returning as a way of ensuring that he has managed to get his point across without becoming dull. Shakespeare has Hamlet returning to the idea of how a person with a true motive for passion would act, first drowning the stage with tears, then roaring so as to make mad, appal, confound, amaze the eyes and ears:

> What would he do,
> Had he the motive and the cue for passion
> That I have? He would drown the stage with tears
> And cleave the general ear with horrid speech,
> Make mad the guilty and appal the free,
> Confound the ignorant and amaze indeed
> The very faculties of eyes and ears. Yet I,
> A dull and muddy-mettl'd rascal, peak
> Like John-a-dreams, unpregnant of my cause,
> And can say nothing.
>
> (*Ham* 2.2)

Summary

1 Rhetorical techniques may be used to create a sense that there is logic in what is being said, or profundity, or rightness.

2 Whether such logic is actually present is less important than the fact that the character speaking it believes there is or wants others to believe there is.

3   Some rhetorical techniques seek to make the thought
    process audible so that the audience can follow along. The
    repetitions that this often involves may appear clunky
    viewed on the page but are vital for aiding the
    comprehension of an audience that will only hear the ideas.

4   Some rhetorical techniques seek to make the thought
    process audible so that, without boredom, we can hear the
    character working through the idea.

5   The use of patterns is a key feature of creating that sense of
    logic, profundity or rightness. A pattern in the language
    (same consonant, same phrase length, same root word, etc.)
    is taken to represent an underlying logic.

19

Style and Tone

Finally, another aspect of Style that is addressed in the classical texts is the overarching tone of a speech. By 'tone' I mean the feel of the language that is being used – for example, is it grand or common, full of fine words or plain and unadorned. (This overarching tone is, confusingly, usually referred to as 'style' in the classical texts. Since this makes it difficult to distinguish from references to the overall canon of Style I prefer to use the term 'tone'.)

The classical texts distinguish between three kinds of tone: Grand, Middle and Simple:

1 The Grand Tone is ornate and smoothly complex. It adores long words, cleverly deployed in complex figures of thought.

2 The Simple Tone is plain and unadorned. It is the ordinary speech of everyday and is comfortable with slang and colloquialisms.

3 In between these two sits the Middle Tone, somewhat less ornate than the Grand but not yet the common speech of the Simple Tone.

Why distinguish between tones?

Rhetoric draws attention to these different tones because, in a particular situation, it is usually appropriate to adopt one tone over another. For example, a Grand Tone may suit a formal occasion – perhaps a funeral speech for a great leader. A Simple Tone is better suited to calming the angry mob. A Middle Tone may suit a declaration of love, where one wants to convey a certain sense of occasion but not appear over-blown.[1] The Tone should match the occasion and the speaker. From the choice of Tone we can, therefore, learn something about both the speaker and the occasion. It is perhaps most revealing when the Tone jars with either the speaker or the occasion.

Bad Tone

The classical texts caution that the three tones sit dangerously close to bad style:

1 Grand Tone easily becomes what the *Rhetorica Ad Herrenium* calls 'Swollen' Tone. Instead of ornate language artfully employed in complex figures we get inflated language that overuses archaic or sesquipedalian[2] words in clumsy metaphors. It is swollen too because the grandness of the tone is inappropriate for the subject matter.

2 Middle Tone strays from its path when it becomes 'Slack'. Here the failing is to wander to and fro, never getting under way with resolution and virility.

3 Finally, the Simple Tone can become 'Meager'. It loses the audience because it is dry and uninteresting.

Shakespeare is alive to these distinctions and gives us examples of characters who fall to the first two of these faults. Don Armado in *Love's Labour's Lost* is a fine example of someone employing Grand Tone when it is not called for and who, by exceeding the boundaries of ornate language, becomes merely comical:

DON ADRIANO DE ARMADO
  How canst thou part sadness and melancholy, my tender juvenal?
MOTH
  By a familiar demonstration of the working, my tough señor.
DON ADRIANO DE ARMADO
  Why tough señor? Why tough señor?
MOTH
  Why tender juvenal? Why tender juvenal?

DON ADRIANO DE ARMADO
  I spoke it, tender juvenal, as a congruent epitheton
  appertaining to thy young days, which we may nominate
  tender.

(LLL 1.2)

In Polonius we find a character searching for the Middle Tone who
cannot bring himself to the point:

LORD POLONIUS
  My liege and madam, to expostulate
  What majesty should be, what duty is,
  Why day is day, night night, and time is time,
  Were nothing but to waste night, day and time.
  Therefore, since brevity is the soul of wit
  And tediousness the limbs and outward flourishes.
  I will be brief: your noble son is mad.
  Mad call I it, for, to define true madness,
  What is't but to be nothing else but mad?
  But let that go.
QUEEN GERTRUDE   More matter, with less art.
LORD POLONIUS
  Madam, I swear I use no art at all.
  That he is mad, 'tis true, 'tis true 'tis pity;
  And pity 'tis 'tis true: a foolish figure!
  But farewell it, for I will use no art.
  Mad let us grant him then, and now remains
  That we find out the cause of this effect –
  Or rather say, the cause of this defect,
  For this effect defective comes by cause.
  Thus it remains, and the remainder thus.
  Perpend,

(Ham 2.2)

In both Polonius and Don Armado, Shakespeare is taking the
recognition of bad Style to say, with humour, something significant
about the characters, namely that they are people without good
judgment. These characters cannot hear their own pomposity, they
lack self-awareness and, also, understanding of others.

Perhaps unsurprisingly, we do not easily find examples of the third failing in the plays – characters whose speech is 'dry and uninteresting' do not make for good drama. Even in the character called Dull in *Love's Labour's Lost*, for all that he speaks plainly, it would not be fair to either the character or the actor that plays him to suggest that his speech is 'Meager'.

General rules for Tone

There are general rules for Tone in Shakespeare's plays: Characters that speak in plain and unadorned speech, which is often, though far from always, prose, are usually themselves 'everyday' people rather than nobles or the dramatic heroines or heroes of the plays. Similarly, as a question of character, the proper use of the Grand Tone is indicative of a 'grand' figure – either by position in society or by significance in the play itself. As with the general rule that prose belongs to the ordinary folk, such characterisations are notable for the many exceptions. One way in which Shakespeare undermines them is, as we have seen in the examples above, by taking the Tone to an extreme at which it becomes satirical.

20

Reverse dictionary

My husband bids me, now I will unmask

MM 5.1

Previously I have categorised techniques by their effect but that does not necessarily help for their identification. Below I have set out certain patterns that you might recognise in the text. There are five broad categories of this kind:

1 Repeated words
2 Unexpected word order
3 Something that pushes the argument onto the listener
4 Some form of exaggeration or transformation or comparison
5 Some unifying pattern in the words or the shape of the sentence.

Repeated words

What is noticeable is the repetition of words

1 The same word or phrase being repeated again, again, again.

- *Epizeuxis*: (1) indicates agitated emotions or (2) urgent commands. See page 131.

2 The same short phrase repeated, again repeated but with something intervening.

- *Diacope*: Creates a rhythm that suggests spontaneity. See page 132.

3 The same short phrase repeated, but now there is a longer break between it and seeing the short phrase repeated.

- *Conduplicatio*: Suggests a certain intensity of thought. See page 133.

4 Beginning words are repeated to make the end the same as the beginning.

- *Epanalepsis*: Used when exhorting others. See page 133.

5 The same word or phrase repeated at the start of sentences can be used to show structure. The same word or phrase repeated shows the sentences are connected.

- *Anaphora*: Used to show structure or theme. See page 167.

6 The repetition of the word or phrase appears at the end of the sentences. Again, we can show structure by using the same word or phrase at the end of the sentences.

- *Epistrophe*: Used to show structure or convey considered thought. See page 168.

7 Words or phrases repeated at the start and then at the end the same words or phrases.

- *Symploce*: Used to show connectedness of examples or to convey a mind in a whirl. See page 169.

The unexpected

What stands out is a word unexpectedly out of place, or missing or added:

1 When we place words in an order unusual.

- *Hyperbaton*: Used to draw attention to thematically important words or to thoughts or themes that are changing for a character or significant to them. See page 136.

2 We add conjunctions or 'joining words' or 'connectors' where none are strictly needed.

- *Polysyndeton*: Used to change the rhythm to convey a sense of power and significance to the words. See page 110 and following.

3 Where conjunctions, 'joining words', 'connectors' should be, they are omitted.

- *Asyndeton*: Used to change the rhythm to convey a sense of spontaneity or urgency. See page 111 and following.

4 We string out a list of strong, powerful, forceful, noticeable adjectives or nouns.

- *Comma*: Used to create a sense of verbal violence. See page 157 and following.

5 We suddenly break off as if overcome by –

- *Aposiopesis*: Used to show the strength of emotion or to show sudden discretion. See page 158 and following.

Active vs passive

We note how the argument is posed in a way that pushes some aspect of it onto the listener.

1 Is the argument posed as a question?

- *Rhetorical question*: Creates engagement in the listener who wants to provide an answer even if none is expected. See page 164.

2 It starts one way and then – but no, that is not the way to explain how a speaker may engage in correction.

- *Metanoia*: Used to suggest spontaneity or to draw attention to the contrast between the first choice and the corrected choice. See page 160.

3 Do you note direct address to absent persons or things? Garrick? Irving? Gielgud? Olivier? Do you see how I have written this book for you? Do you know the time it took me?

- *Apostrophe*: Used to convey grief or indignation by allowing us to picture the object directly addressed. See page 161.

Amplification

We see some form of exaggeration at work.

1   An extreme word creates a shock.

- *Exaggeration*: Used to make things seem greater or lesser than they are. See page 152.

2   We pile up a heap, a mound, a hill, a very mountain of words.

- *Congeries*: Used to indicate spontaneous thought and rising passion. See page 153.

3   The same idea is repeated in identical, synonymous, or similar words.

- *Pleonasm*: Characters are trying to work out what the right word should be. Also used for characters who are idiots and can't work out what to say. See page 153.

4   To make a comparison is to clarify, as the break of a cloud reveals the sun behind it.

- *Comparison*: Allows the speaker to suggest how the listener should view an idea. See page 155.

5   We see something likened to another and understand that this book is like a shot of caffeine to an actor.

- *Simile*: Allows the speaker to suggest how they see the initial idea by its comparison. See page 156.

6   Not by comparison, nor by simile alone, can we make comment. But sometimes by creating a riddle as to what we mean.

- *Litotes*: Used to create a sense of anticipation, a riddle – if not this then what? Or to comment on something discreetly. See page 165.

7   I promised I wouldn't mention the rhetorical technique that
    works by mentioning something you then explain you won't
    talk about. So I won't.

    • *Paralepsis*: Allows you to mention something when you
      know you shouldn't or have no solid grounds to do so.
      See page 159.

Transformation

The main thing talked about has been transformed into something
different.

1   We speak in symbols or images.

    • *Metaphor*: The comparison allows us to say something
      about the object. It allows concise provision of a range of
      information because the image used in the comparison
      carries with it significant information. See page 141.

2   The senses speared by a striking image.

    • *Catechresis*: A particularly striking form of metaphor.
      See page 149.

3   One thing is made to stand as a symbol for others that are
    connected to it.

    • *Metonymy*: A form of metaphor in which the author can
      pull out the most significant aspect of the thing
      discussed. See page 150.

4   One part of a thing is made to stand as a symbol for the
    whole.

    • *Synecdoche*: By the choice of the thing made to stand as
      a whole we see the focus of the character's interest. See
      page 149.

Illusions of logic

By some pattern of similarity or connection in the language we try
to convey some connection of thought.

1   Words are repeated, round and round, revolving on a single consonant or vowel sound.

   * *Alliteration* or *Assonance*: The connectedness that arises from the common sounds suggests a conceptual connectedness. See page 175.

2   Linking by words different ideas, ideas that thus have connections, connections that seem to embody an underlying reason.

   * *Anadiplosis*: The linking of the words suggests the ideas are also linked. See page 181.

3   We hear the same root word changed, and having heard the connection of the root, the hearer thinks there is something deeper at work.

   * *Metabole* and *Polyptoton*: The connectedness of the root word suggests a connection of thought. See page 177.

4   Groups of three things seems stronger, clearer, and better.

   * *Tricolon*: A list of three things appears complete and whole. See pages 179 and 180.

5   We take an idea and muse on it, returning to consider it but in different terms, thus to dwell upon it without dullness.

   * *Refining*: Allows us to consider an idea from many angles and experiences without becoming boring. See page 182.

6   One idea is contrasted with its opposite.

   * *Antithesis*: The use of the contrast suggests an unchallengeable truth. See page 174.

7   Words are used in the first half of the sentence, then the second half reflects back the words.

   * *Antimetabole*: The reflection suggests there is an underlying truth being exposed. See page 172 and following.

8   An idea is set out in the first half of the sentence, but reflected back in the second part of the sentence.

   * *Chiasmus*: the parallel of the ideas suggests that there is an underlying connection being brought out. See page 172 and following.

21

Style in performance

The discussion so far has sought to explain how general concepts of Style were understood by classical rhetoric. How then can the actor and the director take advantage of this guidance to reverse engineer Shakespeare's text for performance? Generally, when first looking at the text:

Note the beginnings and endings

1   Mark the words chosen to begin lines and the words chosen to end lines. Particularly note if there is an unusual word order that means, as a result, a word is placed at the beginning of a line or at the end of a line. Those words are usually important for dramatic theme, for mental or emotional state. After all Shakespeare has had to work to put them in these places of prominence.

Note the unusual

2   Is there a usual form of wording that has been played with, for example a missing conjunction[1] in a list, or an extra word where it is not strictly needed, or an unusual word order, or a contraction?[2] Anything of this kind is capricious, it reflects a choice that Shakespeare made to play with the words and Shakespeare does not play with the words except for good reason.[3]

3   If there is unusual word order – what word has been moved
    out of place? Is there a special significance to that word?
    What thought process means that the character only gets to
    that final word right at the end?

4   If there is unusual grammar, what would it sound like if the
    grammatically unusual aspects were repaired? How would
    that repair change the sound of the speech, the rhythm, or
    the intensity? What thought process leads the character to
    adopt that grammatically unusual structure? (e.g., they drop
    out the conjunctions because the characters is so caught up
    in the idea, new to them, that they just want to get the idea
    out and haven't fully formed it yet.)

Note the metre

5   Mark where you think the stress would fall in a word. If the
    line is verse, is the stress where it would be expected to fall
    in that verse form? If it isn't why is that? Are there are any
    missing beats? Where do they come? What audible effect do
    they create?

6   Observe if there is a particular verse form at work. Most of
    the time it will be blank verse, unrhymed iambic pentameter.
    Has Shakespeare chosen not to use blank verse? If so, why?
    What effect does it create?[4] Has Shakespeare broken from
    the strict expectations of that verse form? If so, where is the
    break? How would the line differ if he had stuck with strict
    iambic pentameter? What would be the audible difference?

7   Are any of the verse lines short (i.e., if the line was in iambic
    pentameter are there all five feet? If so, what does it sound
    like to give silence to the time that would normally be taken
    to fill out the full line? Or does another character share the
    verse line (i.e., the first speaker has, say, two feet of the
    iambic pentameter and the second character has the
    remaining three)? If they share it, how do they share it? Is
    one interrupting the other? Or, like lovers, one finishing the
    sentence for the other?

Note the imagery

8   Identify images (metaphors, comparisons, examples – real or
    fabulous) that are used by the character. What is their
    nature? Do they evoke some particular sense, sight, taste,
    touch? Does the image change during the course of the
    speech? If so, what is the nature of the change? Is it the
    character correcting themselves – saying, 'no, that isn't quite
    right'? If so, what is the point of contrast?

9   Pay particular attention when the image offered by the
    character is an image of themselves. What image have they
    chosen? If they have chosen a part of themselves to stand
    for the whole, what part? What parts have they thereby
    discarded as less important or of no importance?

Having marked these thoughts in rehearsal, how are they reflected
in the performance? Are these thoughts – as to what image to
choose, as to what part is to identify the whole of them, as to where
the stress falls – happening in the moment? What has prompted
them for the character? How is that being acknowledged in the
performance? The asking of the questions that rhetoric prompts is
only the beginning of the process. In the end, the questions are gone
and only the answers remain.

22

Style in rehearsal

And go we, Lords, to put in practice
LLL 1.1

How best to deploy a knowledge of rhetorical techniques in performance?

As a director an awareness of the effects produced by rhetorical techniques and a confidence that Shakespeare's text is deliberately crafted to make use of them is the first benefit of knowledge of Style. It gives the confidence to guide performance, to use text to resolve debate and to insist on deeper, granular[1] readings in which thoughts follow the words and argument.

It is obviously easier, however, if everyone in the rehearsal room has that same understanding. The following is a suggestion for how to achieve that common understanding efficiently and effectively. Your own experience and needs may, of course, suggest their own refinements.[2]

- First, establish a general understanding of the way that rhetorical techniques work and the potential insights they might give to understanding and interpreting a text.

- Second, demonstrate how that insight, once possessed, might be used to unlock character puzzles.

Introducing Style

The following are exercises intended to address both aspects by introducing consideration of rhetorical techniques into the rehearsal room in a structured manner. Ideally, that consideration needs to happen early in the process so that the actors are alert to the contribution that knowledge of the rhetorical techniques gives to the rehearsal process and, in particular, to resolving how a character feels in any particular scene.[3]

What is the difference between a conversation and a speech?

Exercise

The director or teacher poses this question and the group considers its answer and the consequences of those answers.

Discussion

There are two key differences to bring out in the discussion:

- First, a conversation is an inherently two-way mode of communication. The participants know that everyone is expected to contribute and is, therefore, actively involved. The listener is active, not passive.

- Second, as a consequence of its interactive nature, a conversation has built in to it opportunities for clarification and correction, for feedback and review. As a result, the opportunities for misunderstanding are mitigated. In contrast, a speech has a passive audience, who do not expect to contribute and whose interest, because passive, is more easily lost. Moreover, there are no inherent opportunities for feedback and review in a speech. Accordingly, if the speaker is not to risk losing the audience in the course of speaking, such opportunities need to be built in either by repetition of the argument or by deliberately creating feedback moments by inviting question.

These are structural differences. They do not vary as a result of the subject matter under discussion or the words being used. They are built into the nature of the mode of communication. It is that idea, that communication involves structural constraints and is more than simply the words chosen to express the ideas, that we are trying to bring out in this exercise. It is a clear example of how rhetoric asks us to think in detail about how words work.

Sometimes the suggested answers do not pick up on the points addressed in the preceding paragraphs but turn on something about the speaker, for example, that in a speech the speaker is dominant, or that the speaker will have planned what they are going to say in a speech but not so in conversation. If these answers are offered, explore: Are these factors really aspects of the difference between a conversation and a speech? I suggest not. They are about the qualities of the speaker and can be found in either a conversation or a speech, even if they are more commonly found in the latter. Getting the participants to think about the mode of communication and the demands that it creates allows them to begin distinguishing between the different aspects of communication – the occasion of speaking, the character of the speaker and, of course, the words used.

What are the consequences of these two structural differences? Together they make it more difficult for the listener to appreciate and remember the orator's argument. They are passive listeners, not actively engaged. They can become lost in the argument without being given a way to return to understanding of it. As a result, rhetorical theory suggests ways in which these issues can be addressed and countered. That is why we see, for example, the advice in Disposition to begin by stating the focus of the argument and to finish with a brief recap of the arguments, as well as the suggestion that the middle include a moment where the speaker identifies the topics to be covered. In this way we provide a map of our argument that mitigates the chances of the listener becoming lost, or if they do, gives them a way back onto the right route. It is part of why we see the advice in Style to make use of the rhetorical technique of questioning – because by thrusting a question onto the audience (even if it is immediately answered by the speaker) it creates a sense of active communication between speaker and audience.

Introducing rhetorical technique as conveying meaning

Exercise

The participants are shown a copy of a speech that contains rhetorical techniques of repetition or unexpected word order. They are asked to identify the rhetorical technique, not by the name of that technique but by spotting something unusual or unexpected in the sentence structure. They are then asked to alter the passages so that the rhetorical technique is removed and replaced. So, for the techniques of repetition, removing that repetition; for the techniques that use unusual structure, putting the sentence into its more usual order. They are then asked to speak the lines out loud both in their original form and in these rewritten versions in order to hear the difference that the rhetorical technique has made. They are then asked to consider what difference, if any, they consider there is between the two.

I suggest using the passage from the speech by President Obama at the Democrat National Convention in 2004, set out at page 108 and following, that was used to introduce the discussion on Style. It contains examples of the use of repetition[4] to achieve different emotional and mental effects and I have given a helpful discussion of the effects created in that chapter.

Discussion

First consider the sentence, 'Tonight, we gather to affirm the greatness of our Nation – not because of the height of our skyscrapers, *or* the power of our military, *or* the size of our economy' (emphasis added). The participants may be asked – is there anything grammatically unusual about this sentence? Get them to focus on unusual structure rather than on the choice of words. The idea is to draw out the use of *asyndeton* which is shown by the extra conjunction 'or' between 'skyscrapers' and 'the power of our military'. What effect does this additional 'or' have? Does it change the meaning? If not, why is it present? Get the participants to speak out loud that sentence with and without that first 'or' included. What difference do they hear? What emotions does that conjure?

Note, there are a number of other techniques used in that
sentence alone, including asserting something by denying its
opposite, *litotes*, unusual word order, *hyperbaton*, and examples of
increasing significance, *climax*. The focus of the discussion is on one
of the techniques of repetition, *polysyndeton*, not because the other
techniques are unimportant but because consideration of
polysyndeton allows discussion of how word order and rhythm
conveys meaning quite apart from any semantic meaning of the
words used. The use of these additional rhetorical techniques is
relevant, however, because they show how even in the twenty-first
century, techniques so old as to have Latin and Greek names are
deployed by modern politicians. Why? Because they work.

Second consider the first part of the final sentence, 'That is the
true genius of America, a faith – a faith in simple dreams, an
insistence on small miracles.' Again, the participants may be asked
– is there anything grammatically unusual about this sentence? The
focus is still on questions of structure rather than on the images or
the words chosen. It is not that these are rhetorically irrelevant but
rather that the purpose of the exercise is to bring home the idea that
rhetorical technique delves deeper into the relationship between
words and meaning than choice of words alone.

Here the desired outcome is that they notice the use of the
repeated 'a faith – a faith', *diacope*. Why is that phrase repeated? If
the answer given is simply 'emphasis', resist this simplistic answer
– what kind of emphasis? What kind of effect is achieved by
this technique? The answer may be revealed by getting the
participants to speak the words out loud – first without the
repetition and then with it. What difference do they hear? How
does the change of rhythm that it produces alter the impression of
the speaker?

The participants may also note the use of *asyndeton* at the end of
the section. What effect does this produce? Again, the effect may be
demonstrated by repeating the phrase with and without the
asyndeton. Does the use of *asyndeton* compliment the use of
diacope? If so, in what way? An important aspect of the discussion
is that the meaning is being conveyed by something other than the
addition of new words. It is being achieved by altering the way in
which the existing words are perceived. That signals to the actor or
student the potential significance of the author's adoption of a
particular rhetorical technique.

Widening the circle of knowledge

The way that rhetorical techniques work has been introduced by consideration of some specific examples of figures of repetition. Now it is necessary to increase the knowledge of the students of the kinds of rhetorical techniques that are available. The list of techniques is too long to make it practicable or even desirable to try to show them all. Rather, following the scheme of the previous section of the book, it is useful to introduce the simple categorisation of rhetorical techniques given at page 122. The overarching idea being to familiarise the actors or students with the way in which choice and arrangement of words serves the purpose of conveying a particular meaning.

Exercise

Take examples of techniques from each of the categories given in the Reverse Dictionary (repetition, the unexpected, active vs passive, amplification, transformation, false logic) and consider with the participants the way in which they achieve their effects.

Discussion

Most effective is to demonstrate the difference that the presence or absence of the rhetorical technique makes. This can be done by showing the example and then the same information presented in a different, plainer way. The effect of the technique is then isolated from the semantic meaning.

Language best shows the man

From this base of general principles it is possible to move consideration of how Shakespeare uses rhetorical technique to indicate character. For this purpose broad examples are helpful and, in particular, comparisons between characters before and after their minds are disordered. For we see in Shakespeare's text how the disordered nature of the character's thinking is replicated in the rhetorical techniques on display.

Exercise

Two examples are given below and may be used to facilitate a discussion of how character is reflected in rhetorical technique. For the purpose of the exercise, copies of the speeches discussed should be provided to the actors or students. Ideally, they will then hear them spoken out loud at least once before engaging in a discussion that draws out the points raised below. It may then be useful to hear the speeches read again with the further understanding given by the discussion informing their performance.

The Winter's Tale

As a first example, consider Leontes in *The Winter's Tale*. There is a clear moment in the play where Leontes is restored to his senses; whether his previously disordered state is madness or an understandable tumult born of his belief that his wife is having an affair with his best friend matters not. That moment comes in the trial scene and we can compare the speeches before and after to see how they differ.

> Ha' not you seen, Camillo –
> But that's past doubt; you have, or your eye-glass
> Is thicker than a cuckold's horn – or heard –
> For, to a vision so apparent, rumour
> Cannot be mute – or thought – for cogitation
> Resides not in that man that does not think –
> My wife is slippery? If thou wilt confess –
> Or else be impudently negative
> To have nor eyes, nor ears, nor thought – then say
> My wife's a hobby-horse, deserves a name
> As rank as any flax-wench that puts to
> Before her troth-plight. Say't, and justify't.
>
> (*WT* 1.2)

This is part of a conversation that Leontes is having with Camillo. We see that Leontes struggles to maintain a clear line of thought, interrupting himself even as he speaks, expanding from each thought to a further. This is a man who cannot let an idea go, the thought that Hermione may be slippery, becomes the idea she is a hobby-horse, becomes her identification with a flax-wench that has pre-marital sex. He shifts from statement to question but poses a question to which he demands only one answer. Listing things, eyes, ears, thought, he does not do so in a considered way but bounces from one thing to the other connecting each with a conjunction, the first of which is unnecessary but whose presence reflects in its emphasis Leontes own strength of feeling as well as his desire for certainty. That uncertainty reflected in his ever-deepening demands for proof, sight of the adultery, or then rumour of it, or then just the thought of it. This is a mind both disordered and fixated, like a ship caught in the circling waters of a whirlpool.

In the trial scene the words of the oracle do not restore Leontes; only the news of the death of his son does that. The speech that follows is in clear contrast to the pattern of speech that went before even though it is an occasion of great emotional significance. In what follows, there is a the telling of a clear tale, with the high points of it and the necessary consequences addressed in turn.

> Apollo, pardon
> My great profaneness 'gainst thine oracle.
> I'll reconcile me to Polixenes,
> New woo my queen, recall the good Camillo,
> Whom I proclaim a man of truth, of mercy;
> For, being transported by my jealousies
> To bloody thoughts and to revenge, I chose
> Camillo for the minister to poison
> My friend Polixenes, which had been done,
> But that the good mind of Camillo tardied
> My swift command. Though I with death and with
> Reward did threaten and encourage him,
> Not doing it and being done, he, most humane
> And fill'd with honour, to my kingly guest
> Unclasped my practice, quit his fortunes here –
> Which you knew great – and to the certain hazard
> Of all incertainties himself commended,
> No richer than his honour. How he glisters
> Thorough my rust! And how his piety
> Does my deeds make the blacker!

> (*WT* 3.2)

Measure for Measure

As a second example, consider Angelo's speech after having met Isabella for the first time in *Measure for Measure*. This coldly rational lawyer's speech is, of a sudden, thrown into inversions that reflect the tumult that Isabella's presence has generated.

First, we have Angelo at his most rational. Here he argues with Escalus as to the nature of justice. He does so in regular iambic pentameter using sentences that follow regular order, subject, verb, object. The verse is so regular that Angelo is able to state his conclusion to match the metre and to conclude with the crucial edict of death. He has sufficient control of his thoughts to set out arguments by means of techniques that speak to the logic of his debate, such as the *antimetabole* we see in, 'What's open made to justice that justice seizes'. That itself forms part of an extended *tricolon* that ends with the extended image of the hidden jewel that passes on unremarked and unmissed.

> 'Tis one thing to be tempted, Escalus,
> Another thing to fall. I not deny
> The jury passing on the prisoner's life,
> May in the sworn twelve have a thief, or two,
> Guiltier than him they try. What's open made to justice,
> That justice seizes. What know the laws
> That thieves do pass on thieves? 'Tis very pregnant,
> The jewel that we find, we stoop and take't
> Because we see it; but what we do not see,
> We tread upon, and never think of it.
> You may not so extenuate his offence
> For I have had such faults: but rather tell me,
> When I that censure him do so offend,
> Let mine own judgment pattern out my death,
> And nothing come in partial. Sir, he must die.

> (*MM* 2.1)

Then we have Angelo after his first encounter with Isabella. The smooth iambic pentameter of the former speech has left him and been replaced by broken lines and silences. Note now the repetitions as if the thoughts will not depart in orderly fashion but must be dwelt on, stirred up again. The words repeated are no longer in the

pseudo-logical form of *antimetabole* but the stuttered repetition of
diacope and *epizeuxis*. Note the uncertainties reflected in the
repeated use of the question form. Note how the questions
themselves are re-ordered even as they are asked, such is the
uncertainty and turmoil of the formerly clear-thinking man. He no
longer even knows the right question to ask. Moreover the imagery
and the use of antithesis reflects the paradoxes that are the theme of
the speech – the virtue that has tempted him.

> From thee: even from thy virtue!
> What's this? What's this? Is this her fault, or mine?
> The tempter, or the tempted, who sins most, ha?
> Not she; nor doth she tempt; but it is I
> That, lying by the violet in the sun,
> Do as the carrion does, not as the flower,
> Corrupt with virtuous season. Can it be
> That modesty may more betray our sense
> Than woman's lightness? Having waste ground enough,
> Shall we desire to raze the sanctuary
> And pitch our evils there? O fie, fie, fie!
> What dost thou, or what art thou, Angelo?
> Dost thou desire her foully for those things
> That make her good? O, let her brother live!
> Thieves for their robbery have authority
> When judges steal themselves. What, do I love her,
> That I desire to hear her speak again,
> And feast upon her eyes? What is't I dream on?
> O cunning enemy, that, to catch a saint,
> With saints dost bait thy hook! Most dangerous
> Is that temptation that doth goad us on
> To sin in loving virtue. Never could the strumpet
> With all her double vigour, art and nature,
> Once stir my temper: but this virtuous maid
> Subdues me quite. Even till now
> When men were fond, I smil'd, and wonder'd how.

(MM 2.2)

Reverse engineering

By this point the actor or student should appreciate that communication involves consideration of more than simply words, that word order and arrangement can convey meaning and emotion, that Shakespeare makes conscious use of rhetorical technique to convey questions of character. The next exercise attempts to show how we can reason backwards from the choice of rhetorical techniques to learn something of the state of mind of the character using them.

Exercise

The participants are given the extract from *Hamlet* below. The session leader facilitates a discussion of what we can tell about Hamlet's state of mind from the way he expresses himself.

Discussion

In the discussion of rhetorical techniques we have seen that certain of them are associated with heightened emotions and with anger and agitation – figures of repetition such as *diacope* and of omission such as *asyndeton* and of *amplification* such as *congeries*. Others are associated with considered thought, with reasoning and with logic, such as *anadiplosis* and *antimetabole*. We should, therefore, expect that the former techniques are to be found in passages where the character is agitated and the latter absent. If we were uncertain whether, in a particular moment, a character was rational and considered, or excited and passionate, or even playing at being excited, then we might look to see the techniques being deployed and ask whether they suggest an answer.

In *Hamlet* the madness of Hamlet, whether feigned or real, and the degree to which it is active, are key questions for both the production and performance. One particular moment when these tensions are manifest is when Polonius and Claudius put Ophelia before Hamlet to see if she is the cause of his unhappiness. In the following example we can witness the increasing anger and excitement of Hamlet as his confrontation with Ophelia progresses and, consistent with our theory, an increasing shift towards deployment of the former kind of rhetorical techniques. Their presence argues for a real agitation, as opposed to feigned for the observers' benefit, and for strong passions rather than resignation or mutedness in the performance.

At first Hamlet is still enough in control to deploy a sophisticated argument that relies on *antimetabole*, where the words in the first part of the sentence are reflected back in the second, and *parallelism*[5] and *contrast*: beauty sooner corrupts honesty, than honesty purifies beauty:

> HAMLET
> Ay, truly. For the power of Beauty will sooner
> transform Honesty from what it is to a bawd
> than the force of Honesty can translate Beauty into his
> likeness. This was sometime a paradox, but now the time
> gives it proof. I did love you once.
> OPHELIA
> Indeed, my lord, you made me believe so.
>
> (*Ham* 3.1)

As Hamlet's fury builds we see him shift to the questioning form, interrogating Ophelia but not pausing for answers. Now we begin to see, *hyperbaton*, unusual word order – not, 'I did not love you', but 'I loved you not.' He piles a list of adjectives, *congeries*, onto himself without troubling himself with conjunctions, *asyndeton* – 'I am very proud, revengeful, ambitious;' not, 'I am very proud, revengeful and ambitious.' To this list he then tacks on another without pause, not naming the offences but rather listing their effects upon his thoughts, his imagination and his actions. There is yet more unusual word order, *hyperbaton* – not, 'we are all arrant knaves', but, 'we are arrant knaves all'.

Note how in both instances where Hamlet speaks with an unusual word order the change allows Shakespeare to give Hamlet a word of emphasis with which to finish his sentence. In the first case, ending with the negation abruptly changes the meaning of the sentence right at the very end and reflects the sudden change from loving to not loving within Hamlet. In the second case, the 'all' is arguably redundant because the use of 'we' encompasses everyone in the first place. Yet, adding it allows Hamlet to emphasise the universality of his pronouncement. In both cases, the power of the effect can be heard by speaking out loud the lines with their usual word order and then with the unusual word order that Shakespeare has given them. As one would expect, the effect is audible.

HAMLET

You should not have believed me. For virtue
cannot so inoculate our old stock but we shall relish
of it. I loved you not.

OPHELIA

I was the more deceived.

HAMLET

Get thee to a nunnery! Why wouldst thou be a
breeder of sinners? I am myself indifferent honest but
yet I could accuse me of such things that it were better
my mother had not borne me. I am very proud,
revengeful, ambitious, with more offences at my beck
than I have thoughts to put them in, imagination to give
them shape, or time to act them in. What should such
fellows as I do crawling between earth and heaven? We
are arrant knaves all – believe none of us. Go thy ways to
a nunnery. Where's your father?

(*Ham* 3.1)

Now in full spate we see *asyndeton* again because Hamlet's emotional turmoil allows him no time for the usual conjunction between 'chaste as ice [or] as pure as snow'. His speech is clipped and the thoughts spat out without full formation so that he has to return to them and amplify them – no sooner having told her to go, and then repeated the command, than he returns to his theme, the treachery of women driving men to madness, larding it with repetition of words and the key words all starting with the same letter – marry, men, monsters. Again, it is vital to test the analysis by speaking out loud the alternatives. To hear Hamlet's lines with the 'or' replaced and then again with it removed, is to witness the remarkable power of a rhetorical figure to convey emotion by a simple change of rhythm.

OPHELIA

At home, my lord.

HAMLET
> Let the doors be shut upon him, that he may
> play the fool nowhere but in's own house. Farewell.

OPHELIA
> O help him, you sweet heavens!

HAMLET
> If thou dost marry, I'll give thee this plague for
> thy dowry: be thou as chaste as ice, as pure as snow,
> thou shalt not escape calumny. Get thee to a nunnery.
> Farewell. Or, if thou wilt needs marry, marry a fool, for
> wise men know well enough what monsters you make
> of them. To a nunnery, go, and quickly too. Farewell.

> (*Ham* 3.1)

General application

These first exercises have aimed at getting the participants to appreciate the ways in which language may convey meaning and emotion beyond simply the choice of words. Then to show how particular rhetorical techniques lend themselves to particular effects and how this may be used to convey aspects of character. Finally, the potential use of this understanding to reverse engineer a scene has been illustrated. The general application of this understanding to the text applies the reasoning that we saw in the third and fourth exercises more generally. When confronted with a difficulty in the text, particularly one where it isn't immediately clear what emotional state the character is in at that moment, or from moment to moment within the scene, then it can be useful to make particular note of the rhetorical techniques. Asking the questions suggested in Chapter 21 may bring these out.

Appendix: What Shakespeare learned at school

Sir, I am too old to learn

KL 2.2

Did Shakespeare go to school?

From the ages of 7 to 14 William Shakespeare attended the King's Grammar[1] School in Stratford. There is no direct record of his attendance but it can be inferred from his status as the son of a prominent Stratford alderman who was entitled to send his son to the school. The inference is confirmed by his plays. In Act 4, Scene 1 of *The Merry Wives of Windsor*, for example, there is a scene in which a boy called William is taught by a Welsh schoolmaster, Sir Hugh Evans. The lesson is based on a Latin grammar book that was a common text in schools of the time. Had William Shakespeare gone to the King's School in Stratford he too would have had a Welsh schoolmaster, Thomas Jenkins, and surely been taught the same text.

What would he have learned there?

A considerable level of conformity existed in England as to the curriculum, which was based on a programme and drew from a selection of works of classical and renaissance authors recommended by the Humanists of continental Europe, chief among them, the Dutch educational theorist Erasmus. The Humanists were hugely influential in promoting education. Their success can be seen in the increasing numbers going to university in the sixteenth century when, it has been suggested,[2] attendance at university reached levels that would not be seen again until the late nineteenth century.

Would his audience have been educated?

The Elizabethan audience for plays was varied. The cheapest cost of entrance, the penny that made you a groundling, was still a substantial amount,[3] which suggests that theatregoing was the preserve of the lower middle classes and above. That in turn suggests a substantial and significant proportion of theatregoers would have had at least a grammar school education. That proportion would have risen for those plays written for the more expensive indoor performances at Blackfriars or for special commissions at the Inns of Court[4] or the royal court. Certainly, the expectation of a familiarity with schooling can be seen in jokes about teachers in *Love's Labour's Lost* and *The Merry Wives of Windsor* and references to school equipment such as hornbooks[5] and commonplace books.

What was a Humanist education for?

Education was to promote religion, moral virtue, wisdom and eloquence. It was thought that these qualities were linked and that the best way to inculcate them was through the study of classical language and literature.

What did they study and how?

The first years were given over to learning Latin, which was done by memorising and imitating simple texts and dialogues, often with a strong Christian moral message. Later years were devoted to a course of Latin classics: Terence, Cicero, Virgil, Caesar, Sallust, Ovid and Horace. Finally, this knowledge was complimented by a course of creative writing exercises in a range of genres.

More advanced students, in which Shakespeare was perhaps numbered, would in the later years of school learn Ancient Greek the better to understand the New Testament. Both because Latin preceded it in the learning and because at the grammar school level it was lightly touched, it is unlikely that Ancient Greek played much influence on Shakespeare's learning. His encounters with the Greek playwrights and authors would have been indirect, through their Latin and English translations. That can be seen in *Troilus and Cressida*, whose story of Troy draws from versions other than Homer such as those of Chaucer, Lydgate and Henryson.

In their study of the classical authors, imitation and analysis of the classical authors as models was encouraged. This was both to deepen the understanding of those authors but also to enhance the student's own writing. The teacher asked of his pupils not just, *what* is Cicero doing in this passage? But also, *why* is Cicero employing this technique here? It is that same distinction between *what* and *why* that this book seeks to encourage in those approaching Shakespeare's plays.

In approaching a new author Erasmus suggested that pupils read each text four times:[6] First, reading to get the general meaning. Second, going slowly, word by word, observing the language chosen and the grammatical structure. Third, reading with a rhetorical lens, identifying tropes, schemes and figures, elegant expressions, useful maxims, anecdotes, histories, comparisons. Finally, the fourth read should have a focus on the moral message of the piece.

That fourth review is worth noting for the modern audience: schooled in the, perhaps more cynical, view that sometimes drama is simply entertainment, we should note that the sixteenth century did not hold to this attitude. For the Elizabethans there was no genre of work, whether history or legend, prose or poetry, that was not considered to have a moral aspect; indeed, to be primarily of value for its moral lessons. A commentary on Ovid's *Metamorphoses* from 1584 explains the usefulness of fables thus:[7]

> Poetry is naught but philosophy arranged in metre and conveyed in story, through which the doctrines and precepts of the liberal arts and morality are illustrated.

Grammar school education therefore inculcated not only a moral reading of literature but also the use of story. Stories became the examples that supported and illustrated an argument and acted as a model for the pupil's own writing. Again from the commentary on Ovid's *Metamorphoses*:

> Lastly, the poems are of interest for other reasons, not the least of which is that they teach the careful reader all the tools of rhetoric, of the words and figures, of how our ideas should be arranged, and pleasingly and clearly explained using an abundance of rhetorical technique.

This is a point worth appreciating. The Elizabethans read the classics not as remote objects of beauty and examples of a lost time. They read them for the instruction they might give.

That does not mean that their entertainment value was irrelevant. As Thomas Wilson (1560) puts it:

> [Delight and laughter] ... is the reason, that men commonly tarry the end of a merry play, and cannot abide the half hearing of a sour checking sermon.[8]

Ultimately the schoolboy was to learn how to express himself well in both prose and verse. A key part of this process was both translation and imitation. In translation, from Latin to English and vice-versa, the pupil was expected to render the same effect found in one language in the other. It thus required an understanding not only of meaning but of the manner of expression.

Imitation was the rendering of new matter in the style of a well-known author. Ben Jonson, in his *Timber*, considers it, after wit and labour, the third pillar of the successful poet:

> The third requisite in our poet or maker is imitation, *imitatio*, to be able to convert the substance or riches of another poet to his own use. To make choice of one excellent man above the rest, and so to follow him till he grow very he, or so like him as the copy may be mistaken for the principal. Not as a creature that swallows what it takes in, crude, raw, or undigested; but that feeds with an appetite, and hath a stomach to concoct, divide, and turn all into nourishment. Not to imitate servilely, as Horace saith, and catch at vices for virtue, but to draw forth out of the best and choicest flowers, with the bee, and turn all into honey,

work it into one relish and savour; make our imitation sweet; observe how the best writers have imitated, and follow them.

Exercises

For practice, the pupils were given versions of the fourth-century Greek book of writing exercises, Aphthonius' *Progymnasmata*. This set out a progression of fourteen exercises in composition. Among the exercises were ones that expressly foreshadow the task of a playwright: The exercise of *ethopoeia*, personification, was the writing of a speech that expresses the feelings and behaviour of a historical or legendary figure. This was said to be useful in learning how to adapt your expression to the emotional state of the speaker: the calm and prudent man speaks differently to one who is fearful or furious. A particular example given by Aphthonius is to write as Hecuba[9]; it is just such a speech that Hamlet calls on the player to perform and then comments on the success with which the player has managed the task:

> Is it not monstrous that this player here,
> But in a fiction, in a dream of passion,
> Could force his soul so to his own conceit
> That from her working all his visage wann'd,
> – Tears in his eyes, distraction in his aspect,
> A broken voice, and his whole function suiting
> With forms to his conceit – and all for nothing –
> For Hecuba?
>
> (*Ham* 2.2)

Debating

Similarly, exercises in which the student was encouraged to practice arguing for both sides of the case, while intended to prepare them for a career in the law, also served to give experience of putting himself into the position of others and expressing their viewpoint; fine training for a playwright. We even see such exercises, called *quaestio* or 'questions', played out on the stage: 'To be or not to be, that is the question.' Still others of these exercises were in the form of debates or *controversiae*. In *The Orator*, a 1596 debating manual that suggested debate titles and set out sample arguments for both sides, one of the suggested debates is topic 95 of 100 entitled: 'Of a Jew, who would for his debt a pound of flesh of a Christian.' The introduction to the sample arguments in *The Orator* reads as a summary of Portia's argument in *The Merchant of Venice*:

> The Jew refused to take his money, and demanded the pound of flesh: the ordinary Judge of that place appointed him to cut a just pound of the Christian's flesh, and if he cut either more or less, then his own head should be smitten off: the Jew appealed from this sentence.

Verbal richness

The identification and understanding of rhetorical Style was a central part of the grammar school education. Exercises encouraged students to play with stylistic techniques. Another of the standard texts was Erasmus' *De Copia*. This sought to encourage ways of enriching writing through rhetorical Style and encouraged variety of expression. It includes demonstrations of this 'copiousness', for example giving 195 different ways to say, 'your letter pleased me greatly'.[10]

The making of a playwright

Those seven years of grammar school education would have given the young William Shakespeare a sure foundation as a playwright. Not only the techniques of good English prose and verse but also the example of great writers of antiquity, dissected, imitated and remembered, to draw upon. Yet those seven years have their limitations both in terms of the breadth of reading and the youth of the mind that absorbs their lessons. It would be wrong, therefore, to assume that Shakespeare's learning ended at the point that his formal education ceased.

None of the grammar school set texts go into the detail of rhetorical invention although some of them touch upon the topics of invention lightly.[11] That suggests that Shakespeare's interest in rhetoric continued beyond the grammar school gates and that he familiarised himself with other texts later in life. Indeed, this ought to be obvious. After all rare is the person who eschews all further reading the moment the school door closes behind them; and of playwrights, I dare say there are none such. Yet it is not uncommon as a view. T. W. Baldwin in *William Shakespeare's Small Latine and Lesse Greeke* demonstrated how widely Shakespeare had read of Latin literature at school but seems to have assumed that his school reading was the sum of his learning. Yet it is clear that Shakespeare's reading continued long after the grammar school. An obvious example is the impact of North's translation of Plutarch's *Lives*, which gives the plot to several of Shakespeare's later works and yet forms no part of the grammar school reading list.

Thomas Wilson's *Arte of Rhetorique* is another work that Shakespeare demonstrably had reference to and yet formed no part of the standard curriculum. As with many of his other reference works, Shakespeare takes passages from Wilson and lightly adapts them to his purpose. They are identifiable still. Also discernible are the deeper lessons of rhetoric within Wilson. When Wilson (1560: 132) seeks to explain how the rhetorical technique of amplification may be achieved through comparison he gives the example of how, when speaking of two that fought together, we praise the one that lost in order to make the winner seem better:

> Likewise, notable adventures done by a few, are more praiseworthy than such as have been done by a great number. Therefore the battle of Muskelborowe, against the Scots, where so few English were slain and so many Scots dispatched, must needs be more praiseworthy than if the number of Englishmen had been greater.[12]

Who can read that passage and not think immediately of the words that Shakespeare gives to Henry V before Agincourt:

> If we are mark'd to die, we are enow
> To do our country loss; and if to live,
> The fewer men, the greater share of honour.
>
> (*H5* 4.3)

Why did Shakespeare not go to university?

We cannot be certain. The most probable answer is that his family could no longer afford to send him there. The fortunes of his father, John Shakespeare, had taken a significant turn for the worse at some point in the middle of the 1570s when William was at or coming to the end of his grammar school education. Whatever the reason, it had consequences for Shakespeare's social standing.

Shakespeare's lack of a university education was an object of remark in his own time. Robert Greene's *Groate's Worth of Witte* contains the first reference to William Shakespeare as a playwright and it comes in the form of an insulting comparison with the so-called University Wits:

> ... there is an upstart Crow, beautified with our feathers, that with his Tiger's heart wrapped in a Player's hide, supposes he is as well able to bombast out a blank verse as the best of you: and being an absolute Johannes factotum, is in his own conceit the only Shake-scene in a country.

To have gone to university entitled you to call yourself a gentleman and to style yourself a Master of Arts. In the status conscious society of Elizabethan England such gradations mattered.

Colin Burrow (2013) suggests that Shakespeare was conscious of the limits of his formal education and deliberately makes fun in his plays of characters with small Latin, mocking them before Shakespeare is himself mocked. Often those who deploy classical tags or classical allusions in the plays do so in contexts that delight in the pomposity of such allusions, as with the plays within plays in *Love's Labour's Lost* and *Midsummer Night's Dream*. On other occasions and in the context of performance before those who knew their classics, such as the plays performed at the Inns of Court, Shakespeare displays his own classical learning more judiciously – as for example in his conscious reference in the plot elements of *Twelfth Night* to its source in a comedy of Plautus.

Certainly, the case for Shakespeare's classical learning is unassailable. His works are as replete with classical allusions as those of any other author of his age. Nor is he unusual in his lack of university education, either among the population generally, or among the more specific set of playwrights. The author of the most successful tragedy of the times, *The Spanish Tragedy*, was Thomas Kyd who was no courtier and, like Shakespeare, had not gone to university.

Given our knowledge of Shakespeare's schooling and reading it is astonishing, however, to find the charge that Shakespeare was an educational ignoramus still being laid against him in the twenty-first century. That charge is now tied up in the manufactured controversy over his authorship of the plays. It is used to form the basis for an argument that, such is the learning within them, they must have been written by another. Those that make that argument betray only their own considerable ignorance of the time, the depth and focus of the grammar school educational system, and, frankly, their lack of imagination when compared to the greatness of Shakespeare's own. If they wish to persist and persuade others of their argument then they need to equip themselves with better points than those deployed to date.

NOTES

Chapter 1

1 See the example from President Obama on page 111 of this book and that of Constance on page 167.

2 A short appendix at the end of the book delves deeper into the question of what Shakespeare learned at school.

3 That is the third of Aristotle's three kinds of speech: demonstrative, deliberative and judicial. See Chapter 5.

4 Frankly, whatever you paid for this book, it wasn't enough . . .

5 Consistent with his Advice to the Players quoted above.

6 Line 215 in the Arden Third Edition.

7 Interview with the author, 19 January 2018.

Chapter 2

1 Feedback from a workshop in July 2020.

Chapter 3

1 Plato, *Phaedrus*. Rhetoric has often been an object of concern to philosophers. For example, the philosopher Locke in An *Essay concerning Human Understanding* (1690), in a vein similar to Plato, called it, 'that powerful instrument of error and deceit.' The fears of the philosophers reflects rhetoric's extraordinary power.

2 Called in Latin, *exordium*.

3 Called in Latin, *narratio*.

4 Called in Latin, *confirmatio*.

5 Called in Latin, *confutatio*.

6 Called in Latin, *peroratio*. Oddly, out of all the Latin terms for the parts of a speech the Peroration is perhaps the only one that has any claim to be commonly recognized. It is a reminder that audiences have always been most interested in knowing when a speaker is drawing to a close.

7 Called in Latin, *elocutio*.

8 Ignore the patronising tone – he's simply trying to say that techniques work without the hearer knowing why they work. But to apply them requires the speaker knowing why they work.

9 Called in Latin, *memoria*

10 Called in Latin, *pronuntiatio*. (And in Greek, *hypokrisis*, which I have always thought is a great word to describe acting.)

11 Note the clear echo in *Ham* 3.2, 'suit the action to the word, the word to the action.'

Chapter 4

1 The quotes from Thomas Wilson that open the sections on Invention, Disposition, Memory and Style are all from page 7 of *Arte of Rhetorique*, that for Delivery, from page 8.

2 A helpful summary of research on the science of learning is to be found in *The Science of Learning* (Deans for Impact 2015).

3 From 132: 'wee must bee well stored euer with such good sentences [used here in the sense of *sententia*], as are often vsed in this our life, the which thorowe arte beeing increased, helpe much to perswasion.'

   At 220: 'HE that mindeth to perswade, must needes be well stored with examples.'

4 The systematic approach to acting developed by the twentieth-century Russian director Konstantin Stanislavski. Much simplified, it emphasises the idea of the actor 'experiencing' the role; recreating internally the lived experience of the character.

Chapter 6

1 An English language letter-writing manual published in nine editions between 1586 and 1635, that draws on Erasmus' Latin text book, *De conscribendis epistolis* (1522 CE), and summarises many of its lessons.

2 See Mack (2005: 82).

Chapter 7

1 That is, instead of an argument in the form A and B, therefore C, one is simply given the conclusion, C.

Chapter 8

1 Rosenblum, Schroeder and Gino (2019). The authors established that when people speak in politically incorrect language they were perceived as being less strategic, that is to say – more sincere, less calculated. This improved the impression of authenticity with consequences for persuasiveness.

2 'Considering the dulnesse of mans Nature, that neither it can be attentiue to heare, nor yet stirred to like or alow any tale long told, except it be refreashed, or finde some sweete delite: the learned haue by witte and labour, deuised much varietie. Therefore, sometimes in telling a waightie matter, they bring in some heauie tale, and moue them to be right sorie, whereby the hearers are more attentiue. But after when they are wearied, either with tediousnesse of the matter, or heauinesse of the report: some pleasaunt matter is inuented, both to quicken them againe, and also to keepe them from sacietie.'

3 'The occasion of laughter, and the meane that maketh vs mery (which is the second obseruation) is the fondnes, the filthines, the deformitie, and all such euill behauiour, as we see to be in other.'

4 See the editorial introduction to *Julius Caesar* in the Arden Third Series, edited by David Daniell. At page 60 it is observed, 'Cassius' trick of modern speech appears most sharply in his dialogues with Brutus when he is manipulating him.'

Chapter 9

1 Sarkar (2006: 85).

2 McKeon (1942: 32).

3 'Now in mouing pitie, and stirring men to mercie, the wrong done, must first be plainly tolde'

4 'Neither can any good bee done at all, when wee haue sayd all that euer we can, except we bring the same affections in our own harte, the which we would the Iudges should beare towards our owne matter . . . There is no substaunce of it selfe, that wil take fire, except ye put fire to it.'

5   This is a technique called *apostrophe*.

6   As Thomas Wilson (1560: 150) states, 'In moving passions, and
    stirring the Judges to be grieved, the weight of the matter must be set
    forth before their eyes'. ('In mouing affections, and stirring the Iudges
    to be greeued, the waight of the matter must be set forth, as though
    they sawe it plaine before their eyes.')

Chapter 10

1   'A state therefore generally, is the chiefe ground of a matter, and the
    principall point whereunto both he that speaketh should referre his
    whole wit, and they that heare should chiefly marke'

2   That is to say, those concerned with proving or rebutting a charge of
    some kind.

3   'expounde it plainly and in briefe words, setting out the meaning,
    make them harken to their sayings. And by no meanes better shall the
    standers by knowe what we say, and carie awaie that which they heare,
    then if at the first we couch together, the whole course of our tale in as
    small roome as we can,'

4   As we shall see in a moment, Shakespeare has Othello follow this
    advice to the letter when defending himself before the Senate of
    Venice.

5   'Wee shall make the people attentiue, and glad to heare vs, if we wil
    promise them to speake of weightie matters, . . . promise to tell them
    things concerning either their owne profit, or the aduancement of their
    countrie, . . . Or . . . we may promise them strange newes, and
    perswade them we will make them laugh, . . .'

6   'Therfore not onely is it wisedome, to speake so much as is needefull,
    but also it is good reason to leaue vnspoken so much as is needelesse,
    . . .'

7   And, it must be said, the Antony of *Antony and Cleopatra*.

8   This preference is what underlies a number of cognitive biases such as
    confirmation bias, sometimes tellingly referred to as 'my-side thinking'.

9   'Therefore, when the Orator shall touch any place, which may giue
    iust cause to make an exclamation, and stirre the hearers to bee sorie,
    to bee glad, or to bee offended: it is necessarie to vse Art to the
    vttermost . . . to set the Iudge or hearers in a heate: or els to mittigate,
    & asswage displeasure conceiued with much lamenting of the matter,
    and moouing them thereby the rather to shewe mercie.'

Chapter 12

1   For those not familiar with the story: Leontes, the King, is convinced
his wife, Hermione, has had an affair with his best friend, Polixenes.
He plots to kill Polixenes but his agent for the task, Camillo, betrays
the plan and both flee. Hermione is taken prisoner and put on trial.
Leontes, acting as both judge and prosecutor is seemingly impervious
to all argument and evidence for her innocence. Then news is brought
that their son has died and Hermione is overcome, faints and is
reported dead. Leontes seems finally to recognise the tyranny of his
actions. He goes into mourning and penance. The story then turns to
Bohemia where his infant daughter has been transported in disguise
and grown up as a simple country girl. She catches the eye of
Polixenes' son and the two elope. When all gather in Leontes' court,
Paulina reveals that she has a statue of Hermione to show. When they
view it, the statue is revealed to be the living Hermione.

2   See the discussion in Chapter 10: 'Beginning' at page 55 and following.
Compare with the example from Othello, which takes the same
structure.

3   *Quale sit* in Cicero's identification of the three possible options; see
page 55.

4   Over the years many times in workshops I have seen precisely the
danger of a performance based on a single attitude, what I would call
a 'one-note' rendition. I have also seen how applying the rhetorical lens
and breaking down the speech into six parts brought six different
shifts in performance that generated interest, variety and liveliness.
One of the advantages of the rhetorical analysis I am advocating is
that it serves as an auto-director, helping an actor approaching a
speech cold to get the kind of feedback that one might otherwise look
to a director for.

5   It might reasonably be said – well, we know the importance of the
interplay between characters. And, true, any director worth their salt
will help bring this out. The advantage of the rhetorical analysis is the
boost that it gives to bringing this issue into awareness. It does so by
the questions it makes us ask of the text. Asking those questions does
not require a director to be present and so helps at an early stage in
preparation. It also helps the director by sign-posting in the text
moments where, and why, the issue of reaction might need to be
addressed or looked for as an issue.

Chapter 13

1 Do let me know what has worked for you in your rehearsals. You never know, there may be a second edition! You can get in touch with me through the website at www.benetbrandreth.com

2 These are significant questions, not briefly answered. To the first we may say that there are two ways to work out what matters: First, the speaker doesn't guess but explains what *should* matter to the listener and why. This is the most difficult to accomplish successfully although also the most frequently adopted tactic. The second is to frame our argument by drawing on what we know about the particular listener, or on categories into which that listener falls – old or young, parent or not, business owner or not, and so forth. To the second we may say that the key is to provide a multiplicity of arguments and examples knowing that some will work with some listeners and not others. The chief difficulty here is to do so in a way that is subtle, stylish and engaging. We return to it in consideration of Style.

3 I mean by this the moment at the beginning of rehearsals where all gather together to read through the script for the first time and get a feel for the play as a whole.

4 It is, of course, possible to go straight to this second step but it can be revealing to discover the differences between the actor's own response and that of the character.

Chapter 14

1 Referred to as *elocutio* in the Latin texts.

2 This is an example of the rhetorical technique called *tricolon*. Cicero was so famous for using it that they have become known as 'Ciceronian Triads'. We find them everywhere: 'I came, I saw, I conquered'; 'Truth, Justice and the American Way'; 'Love, Honour and Obey'.

3 A central principle of the theory of Style is that merely having an idea for a good argument is nothing until you have the right way to express it. Some rhetorical theorists such as Cicero went further still, contending that if the words differed then the idea itself would be changed. This is the theory of *res in verba*, which is the Latin phrase for 'the subject-matter expressed in words', and identifies the theory that to express an idea in particular words is to frame that idea in a particular way. The necessary consequence is that using different

words results in a different idea being expressed. At a certain level of abstraction this is obviously correct but, in practical terms, not usually an issue for the speaker's purpose or the listener's understanding. For that reason Style is not limited to the question of how to make the words sound beautiful to the ear, or even how we might express things memorably. Rather it is the idea that the argument can only be adequately, accurately, expressed if the right words are chosen and set in the right order.

4 I have deliberately chosen a modern example because I want to emphasize that these points about Style are not solely of historic relevance but apply wherever and whenever language is used and that modern orators are making use of the same techniques for the same purpose as Shakespeare or Cicero.

5 The technique is sometimes called *litotes*.

6 You can test this yourself – next time you are in conversation with someone ask a random question, irrelevant to the conversation, but to which Google offers an answer. Rare is the person who will not reach for their phone then and there to get that answer. Who was number one in the singles chart in the week of your birth? I'll wager you felt an urge to know just reading this question – yet what has that to do with your current task, rhetoric? Back to it.

7 This technique is sometimes called *polysyndeton*.

8 Once again we find that modern psychological research supports classical rhetorical precepts. In 'The Psychology of Curiosity: A review and reinterpretation', George Loewenstein (1994) identifies four ways of involuntarily provoking the curiosity of others: 1. Posing a question or riddle; 2. Exposure to a sequence of events with an anticipated but unknown outcome; 3. The violation of expectations; and 4. Possession of information by someone else. All four factors are being deployed by President Obama here to gather the audience's interest.

9 This is the greatest power of the triad, the way it conveys a sense of completeness. And, for that reason, we find it everywhere: 'beginning, middle and end'; 'gold, silver and bronze'; 'past, present and future'; etc.

10 These examples must be spoken aloud for the difference to be truly apparent.

11 A technique called *diacope*.

12 A technique called *asyndeton*.

13 28 August 1963.

14 This is a technique called *anaphora*.

15 Shakespeare's schooling is discussed in the Appendix at page 211 and following. The educational theorist Erasmus recommended that pupils read each passage four times, the second and third passes were specifically devoted to consideration of the use of language and rhetorical technique.

16 Such as Susenbrotus' *Epitome troporum ac schematum*, or Sherry's *A Treatise of Schemes and Tropes*.

17 First published in 1577; enlarged edition in 1593.

18 Discussed in Mack (2005: 88).

19 A technique called *antimetabole*.

20 Using techniques sometimes called *parallelism* and *contrast*.

21 A technique called *hyperbaton*.

22 As we shall see later, the power of changing the word order is to allow the speaker to draw attention to the word that is out of place – here the unexpected denial of his love. In this passage it also suggests that Hamlet is struggling with the question of whether he truly loved Ophelia ever; as if he begins by stating it was so but even as he says it realises it was not. The disorder and uncertainty of his thoughts begins to show itself through the unusual word order.

23 Sometimes called *congeries*.

24 Sometimes called *asyndeton*.

25 This is sometimes called *hyperbaton*

26 This is a technique called *asyndeton*.

27 Sometimes called *alliteration*.

Chapter 16

1 When we hear spoken English we hear a sequence of syllables spaced in time. The time relationships between syllables make up the rhythm of a language. English is a 'stress-timed' language, which means that there are (usually) regularly timed stressed syllables with, between these, an uneven and changing number of unstressed syllables. Other languages, Mandarin Chinese being an example, are 'syllable-timed', which means that each syllable is (usually) given nearly equal weight and time. As you can imagine, the rhythms produced by each language are very different.

2 The classical rhetorical manuals don't use our terms 'rhythm' and 'metre' but talk instead in terms of 'number'. They mean the same

things we would indicate by the terms 'syllables' and 'stress' but the term used by classical rhetoric is, in my view, helpful because it doesn't use terminology that is usually associated with verse. As a result it reminds us that these are features of words rather than of the particular use of verse form.

3   One of the issues that arises with Shakespeare's plays is that sounds and the placement of stress have changed over the centuries. The difference between the original pronunciation of words and that we use now means that some rhymes have been lost and some rhythm altered. This is apparent from the couplet ending of Sonnet 116: 'If this be falsehood and upon me proved / I never writ nor no man ever loved.' It seems very likely that 'proved' and 'loved' rhymed in Shakespeare's day but no longer. 'Pruh-ved' has become 'proo-ved'. It is of interest to know the original pronunciation and sometimes knowing it reveals a pun that has now been lost – as in the opening to *Romeo and Juliet* where it has been suggested that the lines: 'From forth the fatal loins of these two foes / A pair of star-crossed lovers take their life' contains a pun in the word 'loins' that is now missed: in Shakespeare's day the word 'loins' and the word 'lines' would have been pronounced the same way. In my opinion, however, there is ultimately nothing to be done about this and it doesn't matter. It is perhaps an argument in favour of the idea that sometimes modernising the language of the plays, if done judiciously, can serve to make them closer to Shakespeare's intention than keeping the original wording. The alternative being to treat the text with the kind of reverence that ultimately condemns it to a place in the museum rather than the living canon of plays. To return to original pronunciation also creates a different danger. That pronunciation is now so alien that it contrasts too strongly with modern expectations. It leaves kings and princes sounding like Worzel Gummidge (Google it). It is in that respect a good example of the importance of expectation on the part of the audience. If you are to challenge that expectation, you must have a reason for doing so. This is a problem not just of rhetoric but also more widely. The morality of *The Taming of the Shrew* is now so alien to our expectation as to make it very challenging to present to the modern audience in a way that isn't deeply off-putting; at least in my opinion, but now I begin to stray from the purpose of this book.

4   Sometimes, in words that end '-ed', that second vowel is pronounced in order to create a further syllable and thus ensure that the verse line has the right number of syllables and the stress is put in the right place. Think of Hamlet's line, 'In the rank sweat of an enseamed bed'. It would contain only nine syllables if we do not sound out the '-ed' of

'enseamed', rather than the ten that pentameter calls for. Shakespeare uses the need to spell out each possible syllable of 'enseamed' to allow the actor playing Hamlet to make audible the way Hamlet's disgust curls its way around the idea of the fouled bed. This is deliberate. To add another syllable is no difficulty at all; Shakespeare might as easily have written, 'in the rank sweat of a FOUL enseamed bed'. The needed extra syllable would be there in the word 'foul' but we would have lost something of the horror Hamlet has at the word 'enseamed', horror that is audible when it is pronounced over three rather than two syllables. Thus 'numbers' to use the classical rhetorical term, 'syllables' to use the modern aspect of that idea, serve the dramatists purpose.

5 One of the ways in which pronunciation varies across regions and across time is in the place where we usually put the stress. Stress placed in an unexpected place by the speaker can seriously interfere with the listener's understanding of what was said.

6 'Penta' being a prefix meaning 'five' as in a pentagon, with five sides, or a pentagram, a star with five points.

7 The effect can be made stronger still when the writer 'end-stops'. This term refers to lines of verse that end naturally, in a pause such as we might mark with a comma, a period, a semi-colon or so forth.

> Shall I compare thee to a summer's day?
> Thou art more lovely, and more temperate.'

These lines are both end-stopped. But, where the sentence runs over two (or more lines) then it is not end-stopped – as in this example:

> Whether 'tis nobler in the mind to suffer
> The slings and arrows of outrageous fortune

However, it may still be appropriate to take a breath at the end of the first line. Whether it is or not is something to be tested in rehearsal.

8 Arguably the first two words are a 'trochee' – that is to say the stress is on the first syllable, TA-dum.

9 That is to say, the line has 11 syllables and not the usual 10. This is called a feminine ending.

10 This is a 'trochee'.

11 It is not just me saying that. Shakespeare's contemporary, Ben Jonson, in the *Eulogy* in the First Folio, comments on Shakespeare's careful crafting of verse to fit his ends. There Jonson says that Shakespeare's lines are (with emphasis added) such that, 'nature herself was proud of his designs, And joy'd to wear the dressing of his lines! Which were so richly spun, *and woven so fit*'. Indeed, the guidance that Shakespeare

offers through his verse form apparently caused some Victorian commentators to state, rather fearfully, that it was, 'a form that could control you without your knowledge' (Martin 2012: 20). That being so, performing Shakespeare but not knowing about rhythm and metre puts tremendous pressure on the native, intuitive, understanding of these concepts. Why put yourself under this pressure? Better to read on.

12 The Arden Performance Editions are particularly helpful for bringing out these issues because they clearly identify broken lines, weak endings, short lines and so forth.

13 A technique called *polysyndeton*.

14 A technique called *asyndeton*.

15 He gives the example of Cicero speaking of Catiline, 'The man lives still, lives?'

16 'the oft repeating of one worde, doth much stirre the hearer, and makes the worde seeme greater, as though a sworde were oft digged and thrust twise, or thrise in one place of the body.'

17 Perhaps think of it as the way in which the eye naturally travels up the mountain, or from the base of the tree to the crown. Or, if you doubt the idea of a natural progression, ask yourself when you last looked first at the roof of a house and then down to the door . . .

18 Does not Polonius say (*Ham* 1.3):

> This above all: to thine own self be true,
> And it must follow, as the night the day
> Thou canst not then be false to any man.

19 This rhetorical technique is called *hyperbaton*.

20 The passage of time sometimes makes it difficult to appreciate that the word order is unusual because we think of it as simply dated. That is to say, we think that the word order is only unusual to modern ears but would have been normal to an Elizabethan. Generally, that is not true. Elizabethan word order in ordinary speech was more modern than we appreciate. That is because most of us encounter Elizabethan word order in the plays of Shakespeare or the language of the King James Bible. However, both deliberately used older language forms to lend themselves gravitas. The King James Bible, which dates from the beginning of the seventeenth century, was also in large measure based on Tyndale's translation, and thus had as its source material a text from the beginning of the sixteenth century.

21 As opposed to, 'I am [willing to resign] my crown, but still my griefs are mine' – the familiar form of subject, verb, object. Instead Shakespeare gives us, object, subject, verb.

22 As we have seen from Quintilian's advice about keeping lines short and pausing at the end of each in order to help the audience's understanding of what you are saying, classical rhetoric is alive to the structural problems that exist when you try to convey ideas through speech. Shakespeare would understand that there are no opportunities in his plays for his audience to stop the action and say, hang on, I didn't quite catch that, can you repeat? So important messages are rarely given just once. We are familiar with this idea from the advice we got at school about essays – tell 'em what you're going to tell 'em, tell 'em, tell 'em what you told them. Much of the advice about the ordering of speeches, what rhetoric calls Disposition, is addressing this issue.

23 The fact that there are four opportunities being given calls to mind Erasmus' guidance to Elizabethan students of a text to read it four times through. See page 213 and following.

24 Lucius Licinius Crassus (140 BC–91 BC).

25 See for more, the discussion on Tone and Style that follows at page 184 and following.

26 'Sea-change' used in *The Tempest* is an example of Shakespeare doing just this.

27 See Lai, Howerton and Desai (2019).

28 Literally '. . . or, for its significance . . .'

29 The use of audible correction by the speaker is a technique sometimes called *metanoia*.

30 Vehemencie of words, full often helpe the matter forwardes when more is gathered by cogitation, then if the thing had bene spoken in plaine wordes. . . . when we heare one say, such a woman spittes fire, we gather straight that she is a deuill.

31 Indeed, Thomas Wilson calls it 'abusion' (1560: 201).

32 Among all the figures of *rhetorique*, there is no one that so much helpeth forward an Oration, and beautifieth the same with such delightfull ornaments, as doth amplification. For if either wee purpose to make our tale appeare vehement, to seeme pleasant, or to be well storied with copie: needes must it be that here we seeke helpe, where helpe chiefly is to be had, and not els where.

33 'When I see one sore beaten, to say he is slaine: to call a naughtie fellowe theefe, or hangman, when he is not knowne to be any such.'

34 Wilson gives an example, at page 215, from Cicero's prosecution of Verres, '. . .not a thief, but an extorter, not an adulterer but a ravisher of virgins . . .' He also gives the example, 'Thou has not robbed him of his money, but thou hast taken away his good name, which passeth all worldly goods'. The echo of which is clear in *Oth* 3.3:

Who steals my purse steals trash; 'tis something, nothing;
'Twas mine, 'tis his, and has been slave to thousands;
But he that filches from me my good name
Robs me of that which not enriches him,
And makes me poor indeed.

Chapter 17

1 We discussed the then Senator Obama's use of this technique at
page 108 and following, 'Tonight, we gather to affirm the greatness of
our Nation – not because of the height of our skyscrapers, or the
power of our military, or the size of our economy.'

2 Abraham Lincoln's Gettysburg Address (1863).

Chapter 18

1 See also the discussion at page 112.

2 See the discussion of *logos* in the chapter on Aristotle's Modes of
Persuasion.

3 Cunning because, 'slow and steady wins the race', is true except when
it isn't.

4 Think of the example given at page 34 above, of Justice Shallow – 'as
the Psalmist saith'.

5 That Shakespeare is familiar with argument by contraries appears
from his mocking of the idea in *The Tempest*, where Gonzalo proposes
a new utopian state and finds his argument undermined by the
paradoxes it creates:

> GONZALO
> I' the commonwealth I would by contraries
> Execute all things; for no kind of traffic
> Would I admit; no name of magistrate;
> Letters should not be known; riches, poverty,
> And use of service, none; contract, succession,
> Bourn, bound of land, tilth, vineyard, none;
> No use of metal, corn, or wine, or oil;
> No occupation; all men idle, all;
> And women too, but innocent and pure;
> No sovereignty; –

SEBASTIAN   Yet he would be king on't.

ANTONIO
  The latter end of his commonwealth forgets the
  beginning.

(Tem 2.1)

6 We might have included *alliteration* and *assonance* in one of the earlier
   sections, perhaps repetition or alteration. For both work by the
   repetition of a common element but with alterations in each
   subsequent repetition. Thus we see the difficulty of categorisation of
   technique. There are no clear boundaries and rarely consistent rules.
   The ear is the final judge. Test its judgment by trying the same lines
   shorn of the technique – what difference do you hear?

7 It was the foundation of an Anglo-Saxon and Middle English poetic
   form – accentuate-alliterative – and from the earliest texts on rhetoric
   onwards, there is extensive guidance on its beauty.

8 Why is this so? There are lots of theories but in the present case it is
   probably because it takes the listener two examples to realise that
   there may be a pattern in operation and thus they are alert for the
   example that confirms that pattern and find cognitive satisfaction in
   that confirmation. Of course, as with every expectation, rhetoric can
   play with it. That is why there is a 'rule of threes' in comedy. The first
   two examples set up the pattern and then the third subverts the pattern
   in some way – with luck, amusingly.

9 As *Rhetorica Ad Herrenium* (3.19) explains: 'It is neatest and most
   complete when composed of three [cola]'.

10 In Latin the replication was of the number of syllables.

Chapter 19

1 Your choice of tone depends on the object of your affections, of
   course. But that is the point.

2 A long, cumbersome word that means using long or cumbersome
   words. This is what passes for humour among linguists.

Chapter 21

1 A joining word – 'and' or 'but' or 'or'.

2 For example *'tis* rather than *it is*.

3 It is worth acknowledging here the problem of the editions. By that I mean simply that we do not have a version of the texts that Shakespeare authorised. The difference between the versions that we do have is not always trivial. Therefore, it might legitimately be asked if the change is actually just an accident of transcription or the passage of time. The answer to that is two-fold: first, the occasions on which it arises are relatively rare even if, when it does, the difference can be particularly significant. Second, and more importantly, it doesn't undermine the reason for asking the question in the first place: if your conclusion after asking, 'why are the words in this order?' is that it is an accident, so be it. That is still more fruitful for the performance than ignoring the issue altogether.

4 In 'Shakespeare's Bewitching Line' (Stagg 2018), the author comments, 'The seven-syllable lines in *Macbeth* are a metrical version of the deformity they render, where syllable counting is less important than the gruesome shape made during (and by) the counting.' In *Love's Labour's Lost* the use of the rhyming couplets is to create a sense of a cloistered and controlled world of the character's own creation. Their world is as unnatural as the way of speaking itself.

Chapter 22

1 I discuss what I mean by this at page 6.

2 Again, I am extremely interested to learn about your experiences with rhetoric in performance. Please do get in touch at www. benetbrandreth.com.

3 Similarly, those deploying rhetoric as a tool of literary criticism will benefit from understanding from the outset why rhetorical techniques matter for understanding what the author is trying to convey.

4 *Asyndeton* and *polysyndeton*, as well as examples of *diacope*.

5 Many techniques use parallelism – that is to say, some form of matching (some kind of parallel), between the first part and the second part. Thus *isocolon* uses phrases of the same length and same word order. *Antimetabole* uses the same words but reflected back.

Appendix

1 The name 'Grammar' referred to their original purpose in teaching Latin to future priests and members of religious orders. It is now a

NOTES 235

term applied to selective secondary schools in England. In Shakespeare's day it was used because these schools taught Latin as part of the *Trivium* – the starting point for a liberal arts education consisting of grammar, logic and rhetoric. Students who went on to university would then learn the *Quadrivium* – arithmetic, geometry, music, and astronomy.

2 Mack (2005: 3).

3 Approximately equivalent to half the disposable income of a manual labourer in a week.

4 The institutions responsible for training and regulating barristers (trial advocates). The still standing great hall at Middle Temple in London is where the first performance of *Twelfth Night* is said to have occurred.

5 A board with a sheet with the alphabet and, often, the Lord's Prayer written on it, all protected by a thin layer of bone.

> MOTH
> Yes, yes! He teaches boys the hornbook. What is a, b, spelt backward, with the horn on his head?
>
> (*LLL* 5.1)

6 Mack (2005: 15).

7 Mack (2005: 17).

8 'And that is the reason, that men commonly tarie the ende of a merie Play, and cannot abide the halfe hearing of a sower checking Sermon.'

9 'say on: come to Hecuba' (*Ham* 2.2).

10 Don Armado in *LLL* is full of artificial copiousness of this kind:

> . . .draweth from my snow-white pen the ebon-coloured ink, which here thou viewest, beholdest, surveyest, or seest.

11 Mack (2005: 40).

12 'Likewise, notable aduentures done by a fewe, are more praise worthie, then such as haue bene done by a great number. Therefore, the battaile of Muskelborowe, against the Scottes, where so fewe Englishmen were slaine, and so many Scottes dispatched: must needes be more praise worthie, then if the nomber of Englishmen had bene greater.'

SUGGESTED FURTHER READING

Below I have set out a few books that will take you deeper into rhetoric. I have offered several on Style that address and identify, in far greater detail than this book, rhetorical techniques.

On style

- *The Elements of Eloquence* by Mark Forsyth. A hugely entertaining journey through different rhetorical techniques. It gives both modern and classical examples but, most importantly, explains why the technique works. An ideal starting place.

- *Farnsworth's Classical English Rhetoric* by Ward Farnsworth. A more detailed examination of rhetorical techniques and the purpose to which they may be put. It is less entertaining but more comprehensive than *The Elements of Eloquence*.

- *Shakespeare's Wordcraft* by Scott Kaiser. Designed as a tool for actors it has the merit of explaining and identifying rhetorical technique without reference to jargon and is focused on Shakespeare's works. It doesn't go as far as the previous two books in explaining why the technique is being used as opposed to helping one to identify that there is a technique in use.

- *Shakespeare's Use of the Arts of Language* by Sister Miriam Joseph. A substantial and hugely detailed academic examination of rhetoric in Shakespeare and how he used rhetorical technique to create character and inform dramatic theme.

On rhetorical criticism

- *Rhetoric* by Peter Dixon. A short and fascinating account of rhetoric as a tool for literary criticism.

On Shakespeare and rhetoric

- *Forensic Shakespeare* by Quentin Skinner. An examination of the influence of rhetoric on Shakespeare's work and, in particular, the idea that Shakespeare was using the plays as a forum for debate.

PARTIAL BIBLIOGRAPHY

Primary sources

- Anonymous (circa 80 BCE), *Rhetorica ad Herennium.*
- Aristotle (n.d.), *The Art of Rhetoric*, freely adapted from the translation by John Henry Freese.
- Cicero, Marcus Tullius (46 BCE), *The Orator*, freely adapted from the translation by Moor, E. N. P. (Metheun & Co 1904).
- Cicero, Marcus Tullius (44 BCE), *Treatise on the Topics.*
- Jonson, Ben (1641), *Timber, or, Discoveries.*
- Quintilian (circa 95 CE), *Institutes of Oratory*, freely adapted from the translation by Rev. John Selby Watson.
- Wilson, Thomas (1560), *Arte of Rhetorique*, freely adapted from the version ed. Mair, G. H. (Benediction Classics), from which the page references are taken.

Secondary sources

- Barton, John (1984), *Playing Shakespeare: An Actor's Guide* (Methuen).
- Burrow, Colin (2013), *Shakespeare and Classical Antiquity* (1st edn., Oxford University Press).
- Deans for Impact (2015), *The Science of Learning* (Deans for Impact).
- Dixon, Peter (1971), *Rhetoric* (Methuen).
- Farnsworth, Ward (2010), *Farnsworth's Classical English Rhetoric* (David R Godine).
- Forsyth, Mark (2013), *The Elements of Eloquence* (Icon Books Ltd).
- Habinek, Thomas (2017), *Ancient Rhetoric from Aristotle to Philostratus* (Penguin Classics).

- Joseph, Sister Miriam (1947), *Shakespeare's Use of the Arts of Language* (Columbia University Press).
- Keith, William M. and Lundberg, Christian O. (2008), *The Essential Guide to Rhetoric* (Bedford St Martin's).
- Kennedy, Milton Boone (1942), *The Oration in Shakespeare* (University of North Carolina Press).
- Lai, Vicky T., Howerton, Olivia, and Desai, Rutvik H. (2019), 'Concrete processing of action metaphors: Evidence from ERP', *Brain Research*, 1714, 202–209.
- Lanham, Richard (1991), *A Handlist of Rhetorical Terms* (University of California Press).
- Loewenstein, George (1994), 'The psychology of curiosity: A review and reinterpretation', *Psychological Bulletin*, 116 (1), 75–98.
- Mack, Peter (2005), *Elizabethan Rhetoric* (2nd edn, Cambridge University Press).
- Martin, Meredith (2012), *The Rise and Fall of Meter: Poetry and English National Culture, 1860–1930* (Princeton University Press).
- McDonald, Russ (2001), *Shakespeare and the Arts of Language* (Oxford Shakespeare Topics, Oxford University Press).
- McDonald, Russ (2017), 'Rhetoric and Theater' in Michael J. MacDonald ed., *The Oxford Handbook of Rhetorical Studies* (Oxford University Press).
- McKeon, Richard (1942), 'Rhetoric in the Middle Ages', *Speculum*, XVII.
- Rosenblum, M., Schroeder, J., and Gino, F. (2020), 'Tell it like it is: When politically incorrect language promotes authenticity', *Journal of Personality and Social Psychology*, 119(1), 75–103.
- Sarkar, Subhas (2006), *TS Eliot: The Dramatist* (Atlantic Publishers).
- Skinner, Quentin (2014), *Forensic Shakespeare* (Oxford University Press).
- Stagg, Robert (2018), 'Shakespeare's Bewitching Line', in Peter Holland ed., *Shakespeare Survey* (Vol. 71, Cambridge Univeristy Press).

GLOSSARY

Alliteration   Rhetorical Technique: Repeated consonant sounds. The
connectedness of the sounds suggests a connectedness in the idea –
conveying a sense of rightness.

Amplification   Rhetorical Technique: Any rhetorical technique that seeks
to make the idea or statement more significant in the mind of the
listener by exaggeration of some kind. To make things seem greater
or lesser than they are.

Anadiplosis   Rhetorical Technique: Each phrase begins with the words
that ended the previous phrase. The link between the phrases suggests
there is an underlying logic at work.

Anaphora   Rhetorical Technique: The same word or phrase repeated at
the start of each sentence or phrase. Indicator of argument structure
and theme.

Antimetabole   Rhetorical Technique: The words in the first half of the
sentence are reflected back in the second half. Gives the impression of
an underlying rational structure to the idea.

Antithesis   Rhetorical Technique: The pairing of opposites. The presence
of the contrast suggests that there is some deeper truth being identified.

Aposiopesis   Rhetorical Technique: A sudden breaking off of speech.
Indicator of emotion: usually overcome by that emotion or suddenly
aware of the need for discretion.

Apostrophe   Rhetorical Technique: The speaker directly addresses the
idea or the scene described. Intended to create an emotional response
in the listener – particularly of grief or horror or indignation.

Argumentum in utramque partem   To argue both sides of the case – a
rhetorical exercise in which one practices arguing both for and against
a position. Much used in Elizabethan schooling on rhetoric and, it has
been argued, the underlying dramatic idea of several of Shakespeare's
plays.

Aristotle   (384 to 322 BCE) Greek philosopher who, among many other
contributions, wrote a manual on the theory of rhetoric, *The Art of
Rhetoric*.

Arte of Rhetorique   A manual of rhetoric by Thomas Wilson first
published in around January 1553. It is the first English-language

textbook on rhetoric and style. There are clear indications in Shakespeare's plays that he had read this book.

Assonance Rhetorical Technique: Repeated vowel sounds. The connectedness of the sounds suggests a connectedness in the idea – conveying a sense of rightness.

Asyndeton Rhetorical Technique: Conjunctions (joining words like 'but', 'and', 'or') missing where they would be expected. Indicator of emotion: spontaneity, excitement, urgency, immediacy.

Ben Jonson Elizabethan Playwright. He wrote a series of notes, referred to as his *Timber or Discoveries*, that discussed, among others things, the playwright's process. In it he wrote, 'Language most shows a man: Speak, that I may see thee.' It is this idea, that the choice of language reveals the character, that encapsulates the value of rhetoric for performance.

Canons of rhetoric The study of rhetoric was traditionally divided into five areas, or canons, of study: Invention, Disposition, Memory, Style and Delivery.

Catechresis Rhetorical Technique: A shocking and unusual comparison. A memorable form of metaphor.

Chiasmus Rhetorical Technique: A form of antimetabole where one idea is related to another in the first part, then in the second part the relationship is reversed: As A is to B, so B is to A.

Cicero Marcus Tullius Cicero (3 January 106 BCE to 7 December 43 BCE). Roman politician and lawyer. Considered to be one of the finest orators in history. He wrote extensively on rhetoric, its history, theory and practice. His works were hugely influential on questions of style both for the way they were written and for his theorising within them about what constituted good style.

Comma Rhetorical Technique: Single words strung together in a list. Indicator of emotion: creates a sense of verbal violence.

Comparison Rhetorical Technique: The relation of one idea to another. Intended to show how the speaker views an idea and wants the listener to view it.

Conduplicatio Rhetorical Technique: The same word or phrase repeated but with a substantial amount of words in-between. An indicator of emotional state: usually to convey the intensity of the thought process.

Confirmation The part of the speech where we set out the arguments for why we are right. The advice is to begin with the strongest argument in our arsenal.

Congeries Rhetorical Technique: A list of adjectives or nouns. Intended to convey rising emotion or spontaneous thought on the subject.

Contraries Rhetorical Technique: Another word for antithesis.

Corax   The possibly legendary Greek figure from the fifth century BCE who is said to have first set out a system of persuasive speaking.

Declamation   A dramatic set piece oration.

Deliberative   One of the three types of occasion on which rhetoric is called for; the others being Demonstrative and Judicial. Deliberative rhetoric is where we seek to determine the correct course of action. It is the domain of politics.

Delivery   One of the five canons of rhetoric. The part of rhetoric that is concerned with how to deliver a speech. The advice given is familiar to any actor – don't swallow your words and suit the action to the words, the words to the action. For more see Chapter 4.

Demonstrative   One of the three types of occasion on which rhetoric is called for; the others being Deliberative and Judicial. Demonstrative rhetoric is where we seek to praise or damn some person or thing.

Diacope   Rhetorical Technique: The same word or phrase repeated but with something briefly in-between. An indicator of emotional state: usually spontaneous thought.

Disposition   One of the five canons of rhetoric. The part of rhetoric that is concerned with how to order the arguments that Invention has suggested to us. For more see Chapter 10

Division   The part of the speech where we set out our road-map for the argument that is to follow. For example, 'I shall first address the legal argument, next the political and finally the economic.'

Elocutio   The Latin term for 'Style'.

Epideictic   Another name for Demonstrative Rhetoric

Epistrophe   Rhetorical Technique: The same word or phrase repeated at the end of each sentence or phrase. Indicator of argument structure and to convey considered thought.

Epizeuxis   Rhetorical Technique: The same word or phrase repeated again and again. An indicator of emotional state: usually agitated emotions or urgent command.

Erasmus   Desiderius Erasmus Roterodamus (28 October 1469 to 12 July 1536). Dutch Humanist whose educational theories and textbooks were hugely influential in Elizabethan times. Emphasised the study and imitation of classical authors.

Ethos   One of the Modes of Persuasion. The argument from authority. The answer to the question – why should I be heard on this topic?

Exordium   The opening part of a speech. In it we should aim to win the favour and attention of the listener, identify the focus of our argument and set out our right to be heard, our *ethos*.

Figures   The category of rhetorical techniques where we take a word or phrase, keep its ordinary significance, but give it new life by artistry. The rhetorical question is a figure because it keeps the ordinary meaning of the words but by using the question form we give them an importance or emotional effect they would otherwise not have.

Hyperbaton Rhetorical Technique: A word out of place, or missing or added where it should not be. Draws attention to thematically or emotionally important words.

Hypotaxis Words ornately ordered. See 'Tone'.

Iamb The name for a metrical foot consisting of two syllables where the second syllable carries the stress, e.g. 'to BE'.

Institutes of Oratory A manual on rhetoric by the Roman rhetor, Quintilian. Its twelve books provide a manual for educating Roman youth in rhetoric and contain an explanation of the theory and practice of rhetoric. It was an influential source for Elizabethan manuals and training on rhetoric

Invention One of the five canons of rhetoric. The part of rhetoric that is concerned with devising arguments and studying what kinds of argument work and what don't. Considered to be the most difficult but also the most important part of rhetoric. For more see Chapters 5 to 9.

Isocolon Rhetorical Technique: Phrases of equal length, often presented in threes as 'Tricolon': I came, I saw, I conquered.

Isocrates A native Athenian teacher of rhetoric and the founder of the first school of rhetoric, promoted the power of reason and moral integrity as essential parts of rhetorical training. Sound speech, in Isocrates' view, could only reflect sound reasoning, which led ineluctably to the good.

Judicial One of the three types of occasion on which rhetoric is called for; the others being Deliberative and Demonstrative. Judicial rhetoric is called for when we seek to prosecute or defend against some charge. Arguably, it is the kind of rhetorical occasion that most interest Shakespeare.

Litotes Rhetorical Technique: Saying something by denying something else. Intended to allow the speaker to say something discreetly. Or used to generate a sense of anticipation in the listener.

Logos One of the Modes of Persuasion. The argument from reason. The answer to the questions – why am I right on this topic? And, why are they wrong on this topic?

Memory One of the five canons of rhetoric. The part of rhetoric that is concerned with how to memorise a speech but also with how to build up a stock of material that can be deployed to invent arguments. For more see Chapter 4.

Metabole Rhetorical Technique: The same root word is repeated but in different form. The link between the words suggests there is an underlying connection to the idea being expressed.

Metanoia   Rhetorical Technique: Correction by the speaker. Used to suggest spontaneity of thought or to draw attention to the distinction between the first suggested idea and the corrected idea.

Metaphor   Rhetorical Technique: To speak in symbolic terms. Allows the abstract to be made concrete, generates emotion, allows multiple messages to be conveyed concisely by making comparisons.

Metonymy   Rhetorical Technique: One object stands as representing another. A form of metaphor in which the aspect most important, emotionally or thematically, is highlighted.

Metre   The basic rhythmic pattern of a line of verse. As an example, iambic pentameter is the pattern of ten syllable lines where each of the five pairs of syllables is in the form unstressed–STRESSED, e.g. 'to BE or NOT to BE'.

Modes of Persuasion   Aristotle suggested that we can divide ways of persuading into three groups: First, arguments that persuade because of who the speaker is. This category is called *ethos*. Second, arguments that persuade by appeal to the emotions. This category is called *pathos*. Finally, arguments that persuade by appeal to reason. This category is called *logos*. As Aristotle explains in *The Art of Rhetoric*, Bk 2.1:

> Since rhetoric exists to influence decisions the speaker must not only try to make the argument of his speech worthy of belief [*logos*] but he must also make his own character look right [*ethos*] and put those who are to decide into the right frame of mind [*pathos*].

The Modes of Persuasion are a useful division because, by simplifying and categorising arguments, they allow us to think more easily about the shape of an argument. The analogy is with a map: a stylised depiction of major features of terrain cannot hope to capture all the beauty or interest of the actual land, but by simplifying matters and showing how they relate to each other, navigating becomes easier. For more see Chapters 6 to 9.

Narration   The part of an argument where we identify the essential facts that the listener will need to know. It usually follows the opening, called the *exordium*, and is then followed by the substance of the argument.

Paralepsis   Rhetorical Technique: Stating something by denying you will talk about it. Allowing the unmentionable to be mentioned.

Parallelism   Rhetorical Technique: Phrases or sentences of matched length and/or structure. The parallels convey considered thought and can suggest the existence of an underlying truth that the parallels reflect.

Parataxis   Simple ordering of language. See 'Tone'.

Pathos One of the Modes of Persuasion. The argument from emotion. The answer to the question – why does it matter that I am right on this topic?

Peroration The closing part of a speech. In it we should attempt to summarise the argument that has gone before and include a final emotional appeal.

Petrus Ramus Sixteenth-century educational theorist who split the five areas, or canons, of rhetorical study into two parts: Invention and Disposition were left to be studied in the university and Memory, Style, and Delivery were retained for study at the grammar school. The obvious consequence is that many people only ever encountered rhetoric as style and not substance. The intellectual heart of rhetoric was shorn away to be encountered only by the few who had a tertiary education.

Pleonasm Rhetorical Technique: The same idea repeated rapidly in different words. Intended to convey the idea of characters trying to work through their own thoughts: either because they aren't certain of those thoughts or, sometimes, because they are idiots.

Polysyndeton Rhetorical Technique: Extra conjunctions (joining words like 'but', 'and', 'or'). Changes the rhythm and conveys a sense of power or significance to the phrases joined by the conjunctions. Also serves to suggest that a list is never ending.

Proofs Things that we might deploy in support of our argument. Aristotle thinks there are two kinds of proofs – natural and invented. Natural proofs are matters of evidence – documents, witness testimony and so forth. Invented proofs are matters of argument – logical deductions, inferences, analogies, metaphors, images and so forth.

Proposition In the division of a speech, this is the brief, one-sentence, summary of our argument. It is supposed to come before we get into the detail in the Confirmation.

Quintilian Marcus Fabius Quintilianus (c. 35 to c. 100 CE). Roman rhetor, tutor to the Emperor Domitian's family and author of *Institutio Oratoria*, or the *Institutes of Oratory*.

Refutation or Confutation The part of the speech where we address the arguments of our opponent and say why they are wrong. In some arguments this will be more important than putting the positive case.

Rhetor Someone who teaches rhetoric.

Rhetoric *The art of discerning in any particular situation the available means of persuasion* – Aristotle.
The golden art of enchanting the soul – Plato.
That powerful instrument of error and deceit – Locke.
The use of language as a symbolic means of inducing cooperation in a being that by nature respond to symbols – Burke.

Rhetorica ad Herennium   A Latin textbook on rhetoric dating from
sometime around 80 BCE. It was incorrectly thought to have been
written Cicero, although by the Elizabethan period this was known to
be a false attribution. It was an influential source for Elizabethan
books and training on rhetoric.

Rhetorical Questions   Rhetorical Technique: The formulation of an issue
in question form. There are numerous sub-categories of rhetorical
question but the key purpose is to create an active state in the listener
by posing a riddle that the listener wants the answer to.

Status of the case   It is important to focus the listener on the point where
you intend to make your argument – this is called identifying the status
of the case. Cicero explains there are three options: you can argue over
whether the thing happened, *an sit* in the Latin, or over how to define
it (for example whether it meets the legal test of murder), *quit sit* in the
Latin, finally one can argue over the value of the event, its quality or
quale sit in the Latin. Almost invariably in Shakespeare the characters
chose to argue over the third issue, not whether the event happened
but what is the value of those actions? Are they good or bad?

Style   One of the five canons of rhetoric. The part of rhetoric that is
concerned with finding the right words and the right way of ordering
those words to express the idea, convey or invoke the emotion. The
identification of patterns of words, 'rhetorical techniques', that achieve
particular effects on the listener. Sometimes also used as term to
describe 'Tone'; see 'Tone'. For further references within the book see
Chapters 14 to 20.

Symploce   Rhetorical Technique: The same word or phrase repeated at
the beginning and the end of each sentence or phrase. Indicator of
argument structure or emotional state: usually to show a mind in a
whirl.

Synecdoche   Rhetorical Technique: A part stands for the whole. A form
of metaphor that allows the author to highlight the important features.

The Art of Rhetoric   Aristotle's foundational work on the theory of
rhetoric. Hugely influential, many of the basic elements of rhetorical
theory originate from *The Art of Rhetoric*. It is divided into three
books: The first defines rhetoric as, 'the art of discerning in any
particular situation the available means of persuasion.' The second
introduces the Modes of Persuasion, the division of types of persuasion
into three categories, *ethos, pathos* and *logos*. The third looks at
aspects of Style. It can sometimes be difficult to read because it does
not appear to have been drafted as a work for publication but as notes
either for or from lectures given at Aristotle's school in Athens.

Thomas Wilson   (1524 to 1581) English judge, diplomat and politician.
He was the author of works on logic and rhetoric in English. He wrote

The Arte of Rhetorique, an influential English-language text book on rhetoric to which Shakespeare almost certainly had reference.

Tone The feel of a speech – is it grand with long words and complicated sentences? Or is it simple, plain and unadorned? The tone of a speech should be suited to the occasion and to the speaker. When it is not, it jars. There are traditionally three tones: Grand, Simple and that which falls between these two extremes, Middle. Grand Tone is associated with 'Hypotaxis', ornate word order with multiple clauses, and Simple Tone is associated with 'Parataxis', simple word order with simple sentence construction. For further references within the book see Chapter 19.

Tricolon Three parallel words, phrases, sentences, presented in succession. Perhaps the most famous example is *veni, vidi, vici* – I came, I saw, I conquered.

Trochee The name for a metrical foot consisting of two syllables where the first syllable carries the stress, e.g. 'WHETHer'.

Trope The category of rhetorical techniques where we take a word or phrase and change its significance. Metaphors are examples of tropes because they take an image and relate it to something different.

ABOUT THE AUTHOR

Benet Brandreth is a barrister specialising in intellectual property rights and was appointed Queen's Counsel in 2018. He is fascinated by the power of language. That interest is reflected in a range of activities from the law to performance. He has written two critically acclaimed novels based on William Shakespeare's life, *The Spy of Venice* and *The Assassin of Verona*, as well as a number of scripts for television and radio. He is also an award-winning comedian. His interest in public speaking developed early and he was twice winner of the World Student Public Speaking Competition. Since 2005 he has given workshops on classical rhetoric to institutions as diverse as the Royal Shakespeare Company, the Donmar Warehouse, the London Library and the US Naval Academy. He lives in London with his two sons and an extremely patient wife.

You can find more information and videos about rhetoric as well as details of forthcoming workshops at www.benetbrandreth.com.